Walking with God in the 21st Century

Martin Kaonga

Produced by Softwood Books, Suffolk, UK
Text © Martin Kaonga, 2024
All rights reserved.
Without limiting the rights under copyright reserved above, no part of this publication may be reproduced, stored, or introduced into a retrieval system, or transmitted, in any form or by any means (electronic, mechanical, photocopying, recording or otherwise) without the prior written permission of both the copyright owners and the publisher of this book.
Second Edition
Paperback ISBN: 978-1-0686502-7-7
Hardback ISBN: 978-1-0686502-8-4
www.softwoodbooks.com

Dedicated to my wife, Susan Kaonga, and my children - Taonga Kaonga, Bupe Kaonga and Lumbani Kaonga - for their support when I was burning the midnight oil to write this book.

CONTENTS

Preface — 7

PART 1: Am I not a child of God?

Lamentations of a Christian in the 21st century — 11

Cursed but not forsaken — 21

The concept of walking with God — 43

PART 2: How can we walk with God?

Walking with God involves doing some activities with Him — 55

What should I do in my walk with God? — 91

What is God's commitment as we walk with Him? — 135

Noah preserves human and wildlife as he walks with God — 143

PART 3: What are the challenges facing Christians in the 21st century?

Science, technology, and multimedia: a challenge to the Christian faith — 157

Socio-cultural challenges facing Christians in the 21st century — 173

Wolves in sheep's skin — 193

PART 4: Is walking with God in the 21st century an illusion?

Unmasking the god of this world — 237

Can I walk with God in the 21st century? — 291

How can I walk with God in the 21st Century? — 325

Conclusion — 357

PREFACE

While the advancements in science, technology and media, and the significant changes in socioeconomic and cultural settings are laudable developments of the 21st century, they have also created a hostile environment for the Christian practice. Antagonistic government laws and regulations, the relationship between science and religion, and the media, coupled with internal problems in the Church and shifts in sociocultural norms, are exerting enormous pressure on Christians to compromise their faith, abandon the faith, or face persecution.

In several countries, Christians are seen as soft targets. Have you ever found yourself in a situation where the sceptics have criticized the Christian faith to the extent that you momentarily questioned your beliefs? Have you met people who have described your core Christian beliefs and practices as intolerant, archaic and discriminatory? Have you ever felt despised because of your faith in Jesus Christ? Amid all these challenges, how realistic is the expectation that Christians should live a holy and blameless life in the 21st century?

In my 28 years of ministry, I have met many Christians who have faced serious challenges in ministry, work environments, marriage, Church, education, and family life, to the extent that they have either backslidden or relapsed to paganism. They found their challenges so unbearable that they chose to opt out of faith rather than bear the pain. Is there a threshold of challenges beyond which we can't contend for the faith?

Some people have entertained a narrative that trying to live a holy and blameless life in our generation is not possible. They argue that the 21st century is probably the most hostile environment for anyone who seeks to practice Christianity. Even governments and other institutions that have traditionally practised or supported the Christian faith have passed laws and regulations that antagonize the Christian values.

This book examines the feasibility of a believer faithfully walking with God in the 21st century. It is divided into four major parts. The first part reviews the frustrations devout Christians face in this age, which have forced some to question their identity in Christ. It further introduces the concept of walking with God.

Part two will equip the reader with relational features of walking with God, which fall into three categories: what we do in partnership with God; what God does unilaterally as we walk with Him; and what we must do as we walk with God. This section also uses Noah's work of preservation of humans, livestock, and wildlife as a case study for teasing out practical aspects of walking with God.

Part three summarizes key scientific, technological, media development, sociocultural, environmental, and ecclesiastical challenges facing a Christian in the 21st century. The last part evaluates whether walking with God in this century is an illusion or a practical reality. The section specifically unmasks the god of this world, analyses the potency of God's resources for Christian living against the Devil's strategy.

Apart from embedding the discussion in the Bible, the author also draws from a wealth of extra Biblical materials, several years of in-depth Bible studies, 28 years of pastoral care, PhD research into models describing the relationship between science and religion, and a 35-year career integrating faith and science. The book is written for the persecuted Church, Church leaders, students and Christians who seek to walk with Christ amid the storms of the 21st century.

PART 1
Am I not a child of God?

Christians are facing many challenges on their paths of righteousness. In the 21st century, they are encountering fierce opposition from different sectors of society for their courage to practice and defend their faith. Anti-Christian hostility has reached unprecedented levels, leaving others to wonder whether living a godly life in this era is achievable. This section of the book summarises some of the lamentations of persecuted believers, explores whether the cursed human race is forsaken, and it introduces the concept of 'walking with God.'

PART

An Introduction to the Grid

CHAPTER 1

Lamentations of a Christian in the 21st century

Every Christian in the 21st century is facing three types of challenges, occurring at unprecedented levels: battles with self, battles within the Church and those originating from outside of the body of Christ. Have you ever encountered systematic hostility or ill-treatment in your family, in your place of work, in the Church or in the marketplace because of your Christian faith? Has your faith been challenged by science, the aggressive media, antagonistic laws and regulations, natural and human-made disasters, anti-Christian educational practices, unpleasant family feuds and practices, hostile work environments, and strange worldwide views? Are you mocked, persecuted, and lied about because you are a Christian? How do you feel when your plan to do good during the day is shredded by a single sinful act or even a series of wrongdoings? Christians throughout Church history have faced similar challenges, but those of this century are unprecedented.

While some challenges originate from outside the Church, those from within are equally destructive. The risk of being led astray because of wolves in sheep's skins, who teach heresy and prophesy falsely within the Church, is real. This is compounded by the on-going internal battles between the soul and the flesh within a saint's life. Have you ever purposed in your heart to do good and ended up doing something bad? Walking with God requires obedience to His commandments amid these challenges of the 21st century. There is intense pressure on the saint to compromise or give up the faith. Are you weary, discouraged or struggling to keep the faith? You are not alone.

This Chapter briefly introduces the battle between the Spirit and the flesh in our age of advancements in science, technology, multimedia, and theological and philosophical scholarship within a dynamic and complex socioeconomic, cultural, and political environment.

Persecution of Christians in a dynamic and complex world system

Humans have faced diverse and complex challenges in their walk with God from the moment they disobeyed God in the Garden of Eden. Satan has used different strategies to drive a wedge between people and their God. In the Garden of Eden, he incited Adam and Eve to disobey the commandment of God regarding the tree of knowledge of good and evil. Since then, generations of God's people have been subjected to progressively complex and dreadful challenges to keep them away from the LORD. Cain, one of the sons of Adam and Eve, killed his brother, Abel, who offered an acceptable sacrifice to the LORD. Similarly, the persecution of Christians is historical: *from the days of John the Baptist until now, the kingdom of God suffers violence, and the violent take it by force* (Mark 11:12). Persecution in the Church age has progressively increased: the herald of the Kingdom God, John the Baptist, was beheaded; Jesus Christ was killed; the apostles were martyred and Christians in subsequent generations have suffered from unprecedented persecution in many countries. You may also be experiencing some form of persecution, but you are not alone.

In 2019, the Inconvenient Truth reported that the overwhelming majority (80%) of persecuted religious believers are Christians. Many Christians living in the 21st century are bleeding in their hearts because they are facing fierce persecution. Organizations monitoring religious persecution have estimated that three-quarters of the Christian population have suffered low to medium persecution, while a quarter has experienced high to very high levels of persecution. Recent statistics have shown that more than seventy million Christians have been killed for their faith since the crucifixion of Christ. The 2023 Open Doors World Watch List estimates that more than 360 million Christians suffer high levels of persecution and discrimination for their faith. The World Evangelical Alliance also estimates that over 200 million Christians in at least sixty countries are denied fundamental human rights solely because of their faith. But the cost of following Jesus for believers from the Moslem background is high, and even more so for women. The persecution of Christians is predicted to significantly increase in the 21st century.

Christian persecution manifests in different ways: governments may pass laws that discriminate against Christians, resulting in this minority group facing stiffer punishments for breaching the law. The national laws that regulate marriage, divorce, inheritance, sexuality, child upbringing and work may also be used to discriminate against Christians. In most severe cases, persecution may be violent, with Christians facing physical attacks and threats from the governments or wider community. The International Christian Concern reported that Boko Haram and the Fulani militants turned Nigeria into the 'the biggest killing ground of Christians in the world.' It estimates that between 50,000 and 70, 000 Christians have been killed in the last 14 years in this West African nation. In some countries, Christians are socially excluded from communities and forced to worship in secret for fear of public criticism.

Article 18 of the Universal Declaration of Human rights enshrines freedom of religion, belief, and conscience as a right for all peoples. It includes freedom to change your religion or belief, and freedom to manifest one's religion or belief in teaching, fellowship, practice, and observance. However, legal and social restrictions placed on Christian worship is evident in several countries. For example, Christians in the Middle East and Northern Africa have been persecuted and their population has almost halved in the last 100 years. Christians in the region, especially in Iraq and Syria, have encountered shocking levels of persecution. They have become targets for those exhibiting anger against the West.

In some countries, persecution takes the form of state control, regulation, and restriction of Christian activities. This may be necessitated by social pressures from competing faiths, social movements, and institutions. At times Christianity is considered as a threat to national and cultural identity. Countries which have dominant non-Christian faiths and those that identify with secularism or are nurturing political ideologies that are anti-Christian are suppressing Christians.

There are countries where Christian gatherings and sharing of the gospel are forbidden. In 2016, Russia passed a law that forbids people from preaching the Gospel in the open air. The shocking levels of persecution have stretched the faith of many believers and not everyone has stood firm in the faith. Some believers have backslidden, others are struggling to keep the faith, while many have relapsed to paganism. Many hearts are bleeding, and some believers are wondering why they should face such atrocities.

As the Church age advances, knowledge is increasing, and the environment (education, science, media, and the culture) in which Christians practice their faith is very dynamic and increasingly hostile. We are experiencing scientific and technological advancements, increasing theological scholarship, an increase in false prophecies and teachings, higher frequency of natural disasters, strong anti-Christian campaigns, increased moral decay, and other events limiting our faith. These issues interactively create an environment where practising the Christian faith is restricted.

Christians in the postmodern and 'post-church' era face serious challenges in practising their faith leading some people to nurture a belief that the nature and magnitude of problems we face in the 21st century are beyond what we can handle. They dismiss Christianity as an illusion or an escape route for people who are not brave enough to face the realities of life today.

As our young and energetic people are exposed to the teachings of existential philosophies in universities and other institutions of higher learning, Christianity is being forced out of the public space and relegated to the confines of Churches. What makes the situation complex is the limited capacity of the Church to provide intellectual responses to philosophical and theological arguments, which scholars are propagating in lectures, journals, and public debates. Statistics suggest that almost 40% of Christian students registered at universities, especially in Western countries, never enter a Church building again after completing their education; and 50 - 80 percent of Christian students walk away from their faith or stop attending Church during their college years.

In our world where secular humanism, pluralism, and relativism have permeated the fabric of life, Christianity is viewed by some people as a backward worldview that flourishes in the minds of the simple, illiterate, and oppressed people who are deprived of opportunities to exercise their rights and realise their potential. Removal of God from the public sphere and secularization of the Church have increasingly challenged Christian living.

The philosophy of secular humanists teaches that the universe, human beings and all other things that exist consist only of matter and energy that present themselves in the shapes we see; humans were not created by a personal God but are products of a chance process of evolution; God does not exist and the Bible is not the authoritative Word of God as Christians claim; the only source of knowledge is human discovery and human reason shapes the ethics; human behaviour must be modified through education, economic redistribution, and scientific advancements; moral standards are not absolute, but relative often determined by individual preferences based on what makes them happy; self-fulfilment is the apex of good life; and humankind does not need God to cope with death and other difficulties in life. This belief system dismisses Christian beliefs, values, principles, and practices as naive. The false philosophies and teachings are corrupting the Christian doctrines when heretics integrate them in their teachings and prophecies.

As our world becomes intellectually empowered, Christians are facing many difficult questions about abortion, homosexuality, artificial intelligence, pain and suffering, evolution, unanswered prayers, competing worldviews, miracles, suffering and evil, and dissenting human philosophies. The core doctrines of creation, salvation, the Trinity, the humanity and deity of Christ, incarnation, authority of the Bible, among others, are challenged. These diverse pressures militate against Christianity and its values, and ultimately determine how we live our lives. Satan leverages these difficult questions to sow seeds of doubt and to lure us into questioning the reality of our faith in God. How do we address these issues while walking with God?

The battle between the Spirit and the flesh

Many Christians and some non-Christians genuinely believe that God has called believers to be holy and blameless in their walk with Christ. In Antioch, people who observed the lifestyles of the disciples of Jesus Christ concluded that their character was like that of their Master. It is not surprising therefore that society keenly watches how Christians live their lives. To many people, who may not have an opportunity to read the Bible, the life of a Christian is a standard against which they measure their moral and spiritual state. Sadly, many unbelievers and young Christians have been put off by ungodly lifestyles of some believers. One could argue that this is an unrealistic expectation because Christians are forgiven sinners who are undergoing sanctification. Does this imply that looking out for the character of Christ in Christians is totally misplaced? Is exhibiting the character of Jesus Christ an unrealistic expectation in the life of a Christian?

Many believers have earnestly desired to live godly lives, but they have struggled with sin, which the enemy has used to imprison and torment them. Paul, in his letter to the Romans, expressed the frustration of such believers. He said, *I have discovered this principle of life – that when I want to do what is right, I inevitably do what is wrong. I love God's law with all my heart. But there is another power within me that is at war within my mind. This power makes me a slave to sin that is within me* (Rom. 7:21-23 NLT). This is not the cry of an unbeliever. Paul was writing to the body of Christ to deal with a problem they were grappling with. We may be tempted to think that this problem was endemic to believers in those days. However, there are believers today who rightly identify with this struggle. If we carefully examine our lives, we will soon realise that this is a daily occurrence in the lives of many Christians.

From a very tender age, my seniors taught me the importance of reflecting on the previous year, wiping out my memory of shortcomings, and starting a new year with fresh and robust resolutions. I was assured that if I fully implemented this act, I would easily achieve all my life goals. Unfortunately, I quickly learned that most of such well-celebrated resolutions are breached within the first week of the year, leaving the individuals utterly disappointed. This breeds so much discontentment that some people have concluded that Christianity is a myth. They have wondered whether living a godly life is really for people on planet earth. Whenever you find yourself in such a predicament, remember that you are not alone.

Paul helps us to understand that doing things that are wrong when we want to do what is right is the principle of life of a fallen man or woman. Since a principle is a rule, law, belief, or chain of reasoning that governs the behaviour of an object or human being, doing what is wrong when we want to do what is right is normal human behaviour. But this behaviour is associated with a part of an individual or self. Our inner being defines what we want to do but what we end up doing depends on our choice. We can choose to either access and exercise God's power to achieve His purpose for our lives or submit to Satan's power which prevents us from doing God's will. Our success owes more to our intimate fellowship with God than hard work.

When Satan suppresses our ability to do God's will, our flesh submits to his authority. He highjacks it to accomplish his own plans, which are always contrary to God's plan for our lives. The Bible unmasks the being that dominates our flesh and battles with our soul as the Devil whose agenda is to steal, kill and destroy what God gives to His children. Imagine how much damage he causes to unsuspecting billions of humans who have no access to God's power which resists him. Anytime we depend on self to do what is right, we are destined to fail.

We may be inclined to feel pity for unbelievers, but Paul unveils another shocking truth. He asserts that our inner being loves God's law and yet we cannot do the right things we want to do. There are two powers at work in our lives: the power to do right and the power to do wrong. Paul describes this as the struggle between the power of the law of God and the power of the law of sin.

Despite our love for God's law, the law of sin and death wages war in our mind to enslave us to sin. Paul helps us to understand how vulnerable we are to the law of sin, and he detests the spiritual prison and consequences of this battle. The Bible provides many examples of God's people who struggled with sin.

Samson, born a Nazirite, was an Israelite who was consecrated to the service of God, under vows to abstain from alcohol, let the hair grow, and avoid defilement by contact with dead bodies (Num. 6). He was dedicated to God from the moment of his conception to the day of his death. His assignment was to begin the rescue of Israel from the Philistines (Judges 13:5-8), but he never did it because of his involvement with Delilah. Although God set Samson aside and provided his parents with strict guidelines for his upbringing, his love for Delilah blinded him to the extent that he compromised his calling and could not use God's power to rescue Israel. The consequences were dreadful. Solomon, Saul, and Judas Iscariot are other vivid examples of people who struggled with sin.

David provides a unique example of an individual who succumbed to sin but repented and returned to the Lord. He walked with the Lord and was singled out from among his brothers, later becoming a king in the House of Israel. However, he stumbled when the power of sin triumphed over his desire to do what was right. David committed adultery with Bathsheba, Uriah's wife, and arranged for her husband to be killed at the battlefront with the sword of the Ammonites. As David schemed to sleep with Uriah's wife, a gentle voice must have whispered in his ear to refrain from adultery, but he went ahead. After discovering that she was pregnant, he tried to implicate the husband with the pregnancy. Realising that his efforts were unfruitful, he brutally eliminated his soldier, Uriah. These events demonstrate that the battle between David's soul and his flesh was ferocious.

In a separate incident, Ananias and Sapphira sold their piece of land to give money to the Church, but they retained part of it (Acts 5:1-11, KJV). Imagine, Ananias confiding in his wife that they had realised a fortune from the sale of their land and the couple agreeing to withhold part of the pledge. The Holy

Spirit reminded them that they were under oath to hand in all the money they had realised from the sale of their land. However, they succumbed to sin and disregarded the law of God to honour their vow. This act of disobedience tested and grieved the Holy Spirit and it cost them their lives. Is God's power not superior to the lustful desires of the flesh? Were these people God's children? I believe they were. In our walk with the Lord, as we carry out an inventory of our lives, we will soon realise that we may have struggled or are still struggling with sin to the extent that we begin to doubt whether we are saved.

Children of God throughout the Church age have succumbed to the lust of the flesh. Paul laments, *Oh, what a miserable person I am! Who will free me from this life, which is dominated by sin and death?* (Rom. 7:24, NLT). Have you ever experienced such a state of helplessness as Paul expressed in this letter to the Roman Church? Have you ever felt miserable after lying, gossiping, committing adultery or fornication, abusing company resources, being involved in a road rage, or abusing your partner or your child? Have you ever asked God not to lead you into temptation but to deliver you from the evil one? And yet, the works of the flesh began to manifest shortly after your prayer. The frustration that accompanies these manifest failings is overwhelming.

Paul expresses the helplessness of humanity imprisoned by the law of sin and death when he yearns for freedom from a life dominated by sin and death (Rom. 7:24 NLT). This sounds like the distress call of a person trapped in a dreadful and life-threatening situation, requiring urgent help. Such a cry of a person, who desperately needs help, reveals our vulnerability to sin and worldly pressures when we depend on self. Many people, who find themselves in this state, have become depressed, committed suicide, developed mental problems, or even resorted to searching for evil powers to try and liberate themselves. What makes the situation even more depressing is the realisation that we are not able to free themselves from such spiritual bondage. When we are trapped in this spiritual state, we need assistance to regain our spiritual freedom. Who will free me from this life, which is dominated by sin and death?

The 21ˢᵗ century challenge

Christians in the 21st century are facing unique challenges arising from advances in science, technology, multimedia, and theological and philosophical scholarship within a dynamic and complex suite of socioeconomic, cultural, and political conditions. Apart from persecution, disputes within the Church, false teachings, and spiritual battles between the Spirit and flesh are exerting intense pressure on Christians. Many of these overburdened Christians are getting weary of the struggle to keep their faith. Some have lost their way and are uncertain as to where to turn. Faced with such enormous challenges, is it possible for a 21st century Christian to confidently walk with God? Or is the commitment to obey the commandments of Jesus Christ mere wishful thinking? These questions are addressed in the following chapters.

CHAPTER 2

Cursed but not forsaken

Many people who do not know the Lord believe that their sins are unforgivable, and God has already condemned them. The strong feeling of guilt drives them away from His presence. When we resign ourselves to damnation because of our guilty conscience, we usually feel helpless and hopeless, and some people have committed suicide. Judas Iscariot felt guilty and helpless after betraying innocent blood. *When Judas, who had betrayed him, saw that Jesus was condemned, he was seized with remorse and returned the thirty pieces of silver to the chief priests and the elders* (Matt. 27:3 NIV). Then, he hanged himself. Judas Iscariot became a vessel of wrath fitted with destruction. Similarly, after eating the fruit of the tree of knowledge of good and evil, Adam and Eve realised they were naked (Gen. 3:6-9). They were gripped with fear, shame, and a deep sense of guilt. Their intimate relationship with their Father ended abruptly. These beautiful creatures of God hid themselves among the trees because they could no longer enjoy His presence. They covered their nakedness with tree leaves to deal with the consequences of their fall. God cursed them for their disobedience (Gen. 3:16-17), but did He forsake them? What were the implications of their fall for God's purpose and plan for humanity and the wider creation?

God curses His creation

The tragic rebellion of humanity against God in the Garden of Eden triggered divine curses (Gen. 3:14-19), which altered the status of humanity and his interactions with God and other earthly creatures. After Adam and Eve ate the forbidden fruit, God cursed them, the serpent, and the ground. The web of relationships between God, humans, and non-human creation was destroyed. God cursed the serpent above all domesticated and wild animals; it would crawl on its belly and eat dust all the days of its life; the seed of the woman would bruise the head of the serpent's seed, which would also bruise the heel of seed of the woman. The cursed serpent was a loose cannon in the world seeking to destroy the seed of a woman. The ground (the means of human livelihood) became hostile, and humanity would struggle to scratch a living from it. For the woman, the pain in childbearing would increase, while the husband would rule over her. The quest for knowledge of good and evil estranged them from their God. The friendly and loving Father suddenly became their most feared being. Worse still, access to the tree of life was denied. This is not what Adam and Eve bargained for when they were lured into eating the fruit from the tree of knowledge of good and evil.

A single act of disobedience in the Garden attracted curses with effects beyond the generation of Adam and Eve. After abusing their freedom of choice, they forfeited access to fruit trees, the tree of life, the beauty of the Garden's wildlife, rivers, and other provisions. Tragically, humans compromised their mandate to rule over God's earthly creation. Their assignment to expand the original model of care for creation in the Garden of Eden to the vast expanse of the earth was severely compromised. They were no longer capable of performing their primary function of managing the earth with accountability to God. This had negative repercussions on the welfare of God's creation. It could not function according to the will of its creator. Life in the Garden became untenable for Adam and Eve, and they were evicted from their home. This marked the beginning of neglect, abuse, and mismanagement of God's creation, and hence the environmental issues we face today.

Curses inherited by descendants of Adam

After God evicted our ancestors from their beautiful original home and workplace, they started a new life outside the Garden. As they began to build a family, it soon became clear that the curses they attracted for their disobedience had caught up with their descendants and they experienced the first death in their family when Cain killed his brother, Abel. Although Moses did not record the emotional stress Abel's death caused in the family, this strange occurrence must have traumatized Adam and Eve.

Cain committed a heinous act despite God warning him not to yield to sin crouching at his door, seeking to control him. God cursed Cain (Gen. 4:1-15) and banished him from the ground, which swallowed the blood of his brother. No longer would the ground produce good crop yields for him, no matter how hard he worked. God also made Cain a homeless wanderer on earth. Realising the gravity of being banished from the land and from the presence of God, Cain told Him that the punishment was too great for him to bear. He feared that anyone who found him on the way would kill him. But God placed a mark on him and assured him that no one would take his life. God still loved Cain despite his despicable act. He also loves you despite what you have done.

Cain and his descendants never knew God and murder streamed in their bloodline. Lamech, a fifth generation Cainite, boasted to his two wives that he had killed a young man. This revealed the gulf between humanity and God. The hearts of Cainites were so desperately wicked that they could not call on the name of God. Rebellion against God is recorded in subsequent generations throughout human history. God told Noah that every inclination of human heart is evil from childhood. Individuals, families, kings, cities and nations, employees and believers in the Church have committed evil and attracted the wrath of God. Evil has also permeated institutions, which have committed crimes that have confounded human reason. We are living in a world where people and organizations are committing evil with impunity. The cursed humanity has been enslaved by the curse of decay and death.

What are the effects of God's curses on creation?

Genesis 3 describes the fall of humanity and God's pronouncements of curses on man and all other earthly creatures. These curses completely changed how earthly creatures functioned and related to their God. The eternal life-sustaining support for God's creation was compromised. Understanding the curses and how they play out in our Christian lives helps us to understand how we must totally depend on God to redeem and preserve us in Christ. When we read the curses, God placed on Adam and Eve, the serpent, all cattle and all the beasts of land, and the ground, we sometimes easily gloss over them.

After Adam and Eve ate the fruit of the tree of knowledge of good and evil, their status and the world around them suddenly changed. God cursed man and all other earthly creatures. The entire animal kingdom was cursed. All the domesticated animals and all beasts of land could no longer access the eternal life-sustaining support. But the serpent was cursed more than all other earthly creatures in the animal world. The mobility and diet of the serpent suddenly changed; it was condemned to crawling on its belly and to eating dust throughout its life. The habitat of the wild animals and their food supply were compromised because God cursed the ground which became infested with thistles and thorns. The emergence of these plants probably altered the composition of plants making it difficult for cattle and other animals to graze and browse easily. This implicitly altered the soil conditions. The status of the animals, plants and their environment changed. We are still struggling with different invasive plant species and hostile conditions in our environment.

The discussion Eve had with the serpent disrupted life in the Garden and attracted severe curses. This conversation was the origin of the disorder in the Garden, which God had entrusted to man for stewardship. God therefore put enmity between the serpent and the woman, and between her Seed (Jesus Christ) and the seed of the serpent; *He shall bruise your head, and you shall bruise His heel* (Gen. 3:15). The redemption of the fallen humanity and other earthly creatures would be accomplished when Jesus Christ bruises the head of serpent. A key manifestation of this curse is elaborated in Revelation 12:4-5: *the dragon stood before the woman who was ready to give birth, to devour the Child as soon as it was born. She bore a male Child who was to rule all nations with the rod of iron.* While cursing the woman, God provided a solution to the fall of humanity. But

Satan tried to prematurely kill the Son of God to eternally destroy God's plan for man and other earthly creatures.

The fall of man had serious consequences on the first marriage. As God pronounced judgment on Eve for her transgression in the Garden, He said, *I will greatly multiply your sorrow and your conception; In pain you shall bring forth children; Your desire shall be for the husband; and he shall rule over you* (Gen. 316 NKJV). The man and woman God created to enjoy and display the pure love of God suddenly had a dysfunctional marital relationship. The marriage first shakes when Adam blames God for giving him a wife who lured him into eating the forbidden fruit. The woman he passionately described as the bone of his bones and flesh of his flesh suddenly became a thorn in his flesh. The fall introduced frustration in this marriage relationship. It undermined Adam's authority and wife's submission, which were part of the created order. The fall introduced strife between husband and wife because the couple failed to uphold God's intended pattern of spiritual leadership, and it caused the greatest disaster in history. We continue to witness marital disharmony in homes where the husbands and wives disregard God's model of marriage.

Eve would no longer enjoy the gift of procreation and the harmonious relationship with her husband. Having children may bring her great joy, but childbearing would be stressful and painful. The marriage relationship would now be strained instead of being a source of love, comfort, and belonging the woman would desire. The *woman's desire shall be for the husband, and he shall rule over her* (Gen. 316 NKJV). This judgment only states what will take place, it is not a biblical command for men to dominate women. The curse implies that man and woman would live in conflict and their relationship would become problematic. It means the woman would tend to scratch the curse-fuelled itch to seize control over her husband, but he should rule over her. The curse may also imply that the woman's desire for her husband would be frustrated by his role as an authority in her life. Whatever the case, the harmony that characterised the pre-fall marriage suddenly disappeared.

Acknowledging that Adam heeded to the voice of the wife and ate the forbidden fruit, God says, *cursed is the ground for your sake; In toil you shall eat of it all the days of your life. Both thorns and thistles it shall bring for you* (Gen. 3:17-18). This curse signalled the onset of an ecological disaster and a shift in Adam's means of livelihood. God cursed the ground, which should provide a habitat and food for humans, cattle, and wildlife, as well as providing minerals, water, and other resources. The ground would bring forth thistles and thorns which would afflict people and wildlife, change the composition of plants and the ability to provide grazing and browses for cattle and wildlife. The innocent ground was cursed for Adam's sake. *Against its will, everything on earth was subjected to God's curse* (Rom. 8:20 NLT). Creation never committed sin but was cursed because Adam's disobedience. It is like a pet suffering the consequences of its master's wrongdoing.

The cursed ground probably presents difficulties in growing crops and feeding livestock, and will require more inputs (manure/fertilizers, pesticides, herbicides, seeds) than a curse-free land. Man would toil to eke out a living from the ground. Adam would also have to endure the stress of changing his diet from eating fruits from multiple trees in the Garden to eating the herb of the field. This judgment requires excessive work and sweat of the face for every unit of bread man secures from the land until he returns to dust. God said, *In the sweat of your face, you shall eat bread, till you return to the ground, for out of the ground you were taken; for dust you are, and to dust you shall return* (Gen. 3:19 NKJV). This curse introduces physical death and drastically changes the lifespan of humanity.

The days of Adam and Eve and their descendants on earth were suddenly numbered. They would no longer eat of the tree of life and live forever. *The LORD God said, "Behold the man has become like one of Us, to know good and evil, and now, lest he put out his hand and take also of the tree of life, and eat, and leave forever"* (Gen. 3:22 NKJV). The LORD God evicted Adam and Eve from the Garden because they betrayed His trust by doing the very thing they were commanded not to do. Their status changed, and they would henceforth have no access to the tree of life. The finite lifespan of humanity stems from denied access to eternal life-sustaining substances from the tree of life. Consequently, the rate of replacement of aging and dying cells in the body decreases with advancing age until it can no longer sustain the body organs resulting in death. This also applies to other lifeforms on earth. Denied access to the tree of life condemns man and other living things to gradual death as the body progressively changes from a complex and efficient functioning system to a disorderly, random, and chaotic mass which returns to dust.

When our ancestors disobeyed God in the Garden, the intricate web of relationships in God's community were seriously impaired. The relationships between God and man, between God and non-human creation, between man and other earthly creatures, among humans, and between and within plant and animal kingdoms, were compromised. Depending on the entities involved, these relationships are described as enmity, parasitism, cannibalism, predation, overgrazing, overharvesting, pollution, adultery, fornication, murder, idolatry, infection, oppression, slavery, and racism, to mention but a few. Humanity became sinful and fell short of the glory of God. Other earthly creatures became corrupted because of human sin. All relationships within God's ecosystem were ruined. Unfortunately, the corrupted creation could not redeem itself from its dysfunctional new nature.

The curse of decay and death

Having become slaves to sin, creation has been subjected to vanity through the curse of decay and death. There is a fundamental vanity to life on earth because of the curse of entropy, the curse of decay. A Professor of Physical Chemistry at Oxford University, P.W. Atkins, concluded in his book, *The Second Law*, that …. the deep structure of change is decay. At root, there is only corruption, and the unstemmable tide of chaos" (1, 200). Philosophers, scientists, theologians, and Christians have recognized this fundamental futility. Scientists understand the universal law of decay, the Second Law of Thermodynamics, which states that all natural change proceeds towards natural disorder, randomness, and chaos. The disorder and randomness are scientifically known as 'entropy'. It means that complex systems naturally become less complex without external inputs. Ordered systems, without an external design and energy input, disperse or spread to increased disorder. The principle of the Second Law of Thermodynamics can therefore be restated as "entropy always increases" for any closed system. Disorder naturally increases because the quantity of available or usable energy in the universe is decreasing as the energy powering the universe is being degraded, becoming less available. Even without human interference, nature increasingly becomes disordered and chaotic with time. This environmental decay confirms the Biblical model of original creation followed by a fallen world under the curse of death. This model, equivalent to the scientific law of entropy, is a confirmation of what we observe taking place in the environment today.

The Bible describes "entropy" as "a curse that devours the earth (Isa. 24:6) because its inhabitants have transgressed the laws, changed the ordinances and broken the everlasting covenant (Isa. 24:5). The Psalmist, King David, said, *In ages past you laid the foundation of the earth, and the heavens are the work of your hands. Even they will perish but you remain forever, they will wear out like old clothing. You will change them like a garment, and they will fade away* (Psa.102:25-26 NLT). The Prophet Isaiah also prophesied that ... *the earth will wear out like a garment, And Its Inhabitants will die in like manner, But My salvation shall be forever, And My righteousness shall not wane* (Isa. 51:6). Mark W. Cadwallader helps us to understand how a new garment loses its "newness" as it degrades according to the Second Law of Thermodynamics. The fibres of the cloth lose their strength and resiliency as the chemical bonds in their structure – how they are knitted together - break apart, unwinding and losing their organization. Eventually, the cloth reaches its state of maximum disorder when it disintegrates into dust particles. Mark concludes that these "fundamental principles of textile decay represent both the increasing micro- and macro-molecular disorganization which governs all types of decay according to the Second Law of Thermodynamics. The Bible shows its hold on truth because it revealed long before thermodynamics became a word, that the whole of creation is in bondage to decay.

The holy Scripture tells us that creation is condemned to death because of sin. When our ancestors first sinned in the Garden of Eden, God cursed His creation: *cursed is the ground because of you, ... for you are dust and to dust you shall return* (Gen. 3:17, 19). This was the curse of death which is fundamentally the curse of decay. Decay in living things means gradual death. Living things age as more body cells die than are replaced. They eventually die when their organs are no longer able to sustain the body because they lack sufficient new cells. Death occurs when the body decays beyond repair. The natural process of decay can be accelerated, and death could occur when the body is subjected to hostile conditions, including sin and demonic attacks, injury, diseases, harmful chemicals, excessive heat, pollutants, smoke, and fire. Our lives end when the original complexity of our interdependent body parts disintegrates beyond repair. Similarly, decay in the environment is the disintegration of the original complexity of the earth's interdependent ecology. We can therefore safely conclude that the curse of death pronounced on humanity and his environment is a curse of decay affecting all created things and the whole world in general. This implies that environmental problems have both spiritual and physical undertones.

We are taught that fundamental decay and corruption are basic to Biblical doctrines. Traditional Christianity and Judaism have always taught that we live in a fallen world because of sin. The world is under a case of death and decay because it is separated from God's eternal life-sustaining support. The whole creation is therefore heading toward a complete change. The gospels declare that heaven and earth shall pass away (Matt. 24:35; Mark 13:31; Luke 21:33). The Word of God also tells us that the world is withering and passing away.

Mark W. Cadwallader concludes that creation presses toward increasing disorder because human beings are fundamentally disordered in their motivations. God who has perfect integrity and therefore requires justice, has had to curse the physical creation and subject it to futility (Rom 8:20) because of sin. An incorruptible Creator of life cannot eternally give life support to a corrupted creation. If He did, He would not be incorruptible."

Is sin linked to sociocultural and environmental crises in our society today?

How often have we linked environmental decay to sin? Yet, they are connected. Corruption of the environment is a symptom of the curse of death pronounced on creation because of sin. Hosea lamented that *there is swearing, deception, murder, stealing, and adultery. They employ violence so that bloodshed follows bloodshed. Therefore, the land mourns, and everyone who lives in it languishes along with the beasts of the field and the birds of the sky; and the fish of the sea also disappear* (Hos. 4:2-3). When we sin, the order and beauty of human society becomes twisted and contaminated. Without the restraint of the government, the grace and truth of God, society naturally degenerates toward disorder and chaos. The Bible connects these three things (sin, curse on the world, and environmental decay) quite specifically. It states that *the earth is also polluted by its inhabitants, for they transgressed law, violated the statues, broke the everlasting covenant. Therefore, a curse devours the earth, and those who live in it are held guilty* (Isa. 24:5,6). The environment is in bondage to decay because of sin, just as the whole world and the people in it are under the curse of death.

The Devil tries to deceive humanity to dissociate 'natural' and 'human-induced' disasters from the curse pronounced upon creation. He portrays God as a villain who afflicts His people with terrible curses causing unnecessary suffering. If He was such a terrible God, He could have destroyed all creation, but the curse resulted in hardship in doing the necessary work and fulfilling the life's processes. The fallen humans also corrupted the non-human creation resulting in a dysfunctional creation. *Against its will, everything on earth was subject to God's curse* (Rom. 8:20 NLT) and decay. But the Devil does not tell us the righteous and just God must judge sin but with love. He downplays the full story about the nature and impact of curses God put on it because of sin.

We seem unable to halt ecological deterioration. It seems almost as if *a curse devours the earth* (Isa. 24:6). Over three decades after the first earth day, environmental problems have become more widespread and complicated. Despite passing several environmental laws and regulations, environmental problems are extensive, complex, and urgent. Several environmental issues including climate change, biodiversity loss, land degradation, freshwater change and soil nutrient depletion have exceeded the safe planetary boundaries. Other environmental problems corrupting the order and diversity in the creation include chemical waste, radioactive waste, deforestation, non-point source water pollution, ground water pollution, infectious waste, and extinctions of many plants and animal species throughout the world. The curse of our creative productivity which results from overextraction, and use of natural resources produces large quantities of waste materials that cannot be recycled by the earth. Most governments of the world have invested huge sums of money to address environmental crises, but there has been limited progress.

Today, we are experiencing some of the worst effects of environmental, energy, economic, financial, social, and cultural crises. The World Meteorological Office (WMO) reported that 2023 was the warmest year in the 174-year observational record, surpassing the previous joint warmest years (2016 and 2020) which were 1.27-1.29 °C above the 1850–1900 average. The global mean sea level reached a record high in the satellite record (since 1993), reflecting continued ocean warming as well as the melting of glaciers and ice sheets. The effects of such climate change were observed across the globe. The 2023 fire season in Canada, USA, Greece, Canary Islands, Spain, Portugal, and Algeria took a heavy toll on human life, the environment, livelihoods, and infrastructure. In the same year, a fire devastated a town on Maui, the second largest island of Hawaii, killing 99 people. Ethiopia, Somalia, and Kenya experienced the worst drought in four decades. The unrelenting drought that has devastated the Horn of Africa has left more than 20 million people facing acute food insecurity.

Most world's soil resources are in fair, poor or very poor conditions, with the main threat coming from soil erosion. Human disturbances on landscapes (e.g. clearing the forest, land levelling, mining, and unsuitable agricultural practices (bare soil conditions, abuse of chemicals, terraces dismantling, lack of buffer strips) often accelerates soil erosion processes. It has been reported that the average erosion rates in cultivated lands is near the average tolerable soil loss rate.

Nature is in crisis. Up to one million species are threatened with extinction, many within decades. In 2023, joint Stanford University and the National Autonomous University of Mexico studies showed that the passenger pigeon, the Tasmanian tiger, the Baiji, or Yangtze River dolphin rank among the best-known recent victims of what many scientists have declared as the sixth mass extinction. In agricultural lands, erosion, compaction, nutrient imbalance, pollution, acidification, water logging, loss of soil biodiversity and increasing salinity have affected land quality across the globe, reducing its ability to support plant life and to grow crops. Torrential downpours sent muddy water racing through streets in Libya, Greece, and Spain and flooded parts of Hong Kong, New York City, and areas in Scotland in 2023. Thousands of people died in the Libyan city of Derna when a heavy downpour resulted in floods that breached a dam. It destroyed infrastructure and swept people and properties to the sea. The WHO estimates that at least 3.4 million people died from COVID 19. The curse of death has not spared human and environmental health.

Social and cultural challenges are also linked to the curse of decay which permeates human institutions and the environment. Have you encountered financial, economic, energy, and other sociocultural crises? Have you ever considered if there are spiritual undertones behind these unprecedented societal challenges? The 2021–2023 global energy crisis began in the aftermath of the COVID-19 pandemic in 2021, with much of the globe facing shortages and increased prices in oil, gas, and electricity markets. This was exacerbated by the Russia-Ukraine war. The world is also experiencing other challenges including low economic growth, high cost of living, and ideological and religious challenges. All these are happening in a world where traditional cultural practices and values are disintegrating due to globalization and modernization resulting in disconnection and destruction of the social and cultural worlds of individuals and societies. In some cases, this has resulted in loss of identity, social cohesion, and a sense of belonging for affected communities.

Attempts to hedge ourselves against environmental and sociocultural crises don't seem to be working. Insurance companies are tightening their conditions and increasing the premiums. The force majeure, a clause that is included in contracts to remove liability for unforeseeable and unavoidable natural disasters and catastrophes created by humans, appeals to a greater force or the concept of an 'act of God'. But these disasters are happening with higher frequency and intensity, and insurance companies are incurring huge costs to compensate victims of these disasters. Futility and despair are the consequences of living in a world relentlessly decaying, and thoroughly infected by sin and pain.

Every part of creation is suffering from the consequences of the curse of decay and death. All earthly goals and ambitions when pursued as ends in themselves are leading to frustration. Cadwallader explains that the ability of the earth to sustain life is arguably wearing out 'like a garment'. Paul concludes that *the earnest expectation of the creation eagerly waits for the revealing of the sons of God. For the creation was subjected to futility, not willingly, but because of Him who subjected it in hope; because the creation itself also will be delivered from the bondage of corruption into the glorious liberty of the children of God. For we know that the whole creation groans and labours with birth pangs together until now. ... but we also who have the firstfruits of the Spirit, even we ourselves groan within ourselves, eagerly waiting for the adoption, the redemption of our body.* Humans try to dodge their accountability to God, making nature the standard, and justify doing whatever is "natural" to mitigate the curse of death through science. But all earthly goals and ambitions when pursued as ends in themselves lead to frustration. Meanwhile, the whole creation groans and labours with birth pangs together to be freed from the curse of death and decay. Man's fundamental rebellion against God is brought to light, hidden as it may be behind a facade of science and sophistication. All these events paint a world in free fall, but is it?

Has God forsaken the decaying creation?

God did not forsake His creation after cursing it. From the day God cursed man and other creatures on earth, He activated the redemption plan which He developed before creating the world. He is always ready to redeem us at any cost. David acknowledged this when he said, *the Lord looks down from heaven on all mankind to see if there are any who understand, any who seek God* (Rom. 5:8 NIV).

When Adam and Eve disobeyed God, His priority was how to redeem them from sin while maintaining His integrity as a just and righteous judge. My story illustrates God's mercy in His judgment of sin. At the age of eight, I learned a bitter lesson. My cousin, who was 10 years older than I had warned me against tampering with his possessions. However, I was curious to find out what he had tucked away in the rear portion of our kitchen's grass roof. While everyone was away from home, I started sifting through a low hanging grass roof of our kitchen where my cousin normally hid items, which he considered hazardous to children. It wasn't long before I detected a nylon thread, and I knew it had an object still buried in the grass. It was a medium-sized fishing hook. Before I could settle down to examine it properly, disaster struck. The hook pierced my left index finger. As an eight-year-old, I didn't know what to do. However, my father rescued me from my ordeal, but he disciplined me for my mischief. Despite my disobedience, his real focus was on relieving me from the pain I was in. God cursed Adam and Eve for their disobedience, but He also demonstrated His love for them by providing for humanity and other earthly creatures to be reconciled to Him. *God demonstrates His own love toward us, in that while we were still sinners, Christ died for us* (Rom. 5:8 KJV). Even in a battered and bruised world, God's original plan and purpose for humanity and other earthly creatures has never changed.

God demonstrated mercy through the curses he pronounced on humanity and other earthly creatures. The sovereign LORD was not obligated to keep and care for humans and other earthly creatures after the fall. After all, creation was corrupted, and the eyes of LORD God are too pure to behold evil. He could have considered the corrupted creation not fit for purpose and could have disposed of it. But He went to the Garden of Eden to look for Adam and Eve. You and I were also lost in sin and yet His eyes consistently looked out for us. Do you remember the story of the prodigal son (Luke 15:11-31)? While he was away, the father always thought about him and looked forward to a day when he would return home. From the day man sinned against God and left the Garden, God kick-started His redemption plan for humanity. James affirmed this when he said, *God jealously longs for the spirit He has caused to dwell in man* (Jam. 4:5 NIV). The human spirit is a source of unusual attraction, which keeps God looking in the direction of a sinner. Adam and Eve judged themselves and hid from God because of their guilt and shame but God's original love for them never died.

God cursed Adam and Eve for their disobedience, but they were still able to reproduce and have descendants. Despite the fall, Adam *called his wife's name Eve because she was the mother of all living* (Gen. 3:20 NKJV). God was still so concerned about the dignity of this first couple that *He made tunics of skin and clothed them* (Gen. 3:21 NKJV) to cover their nakedness. He slaughtered animals, flayed their skins, and made tunics for Adam and his wife. While the LORD denied the couple access to the fruit trees in the Garden, He still gave them the herbs of the land for their food.

God put enmity between the serpent and the woman, and between her Seed (Jesus Christ) and the seed of the serpent. The Seed of the woman would bruise the head of the serpent and it would bruise His heel. Wrapped in this brutal tussle is the prophetic revelation of God's mystery of redeeming the fallen humanity through the suffering, crucifixion, death, and resurrection of Jesus Christ. The curse bred enmity between the woman and the serpent, but it prophesied redemption of humanity from the sin and death. When God denied the first family access to the tree of life, human life became trapped between conception and death. But the Seed of the woman would restore eternal life and would eventually restore our access to the tree of life beyond death. While we, as descendants of Adam, were enemies with God through Adamic sin, we would be reconciled to God through the death and resurrection of the second Adam, the Seed of the woman.

Despite the fall of humanity and the curse placed on him, God made a provision for salvation of all the descendants of Adam through Jesus Christ provided they returned to Him. Notwithstanding the curse of death upon Adam and Eve, they still gave birth to children who feared God. Within the first generation from Adam, Abel offered an acceptable sacrifice to God. He worshipped God although his wicked brother, Cain, prematurely ended his life. Eve gave birth to another son, Seth, whom she said was God-given to replace Abel. According to Josephus, Seth was virtuous and of excellent character, and was endowed with heavenly wisdom. He is seen as the ancestor of all generations of "tzaddikims", the Hebrew word for righteous ones. His descendants feared the Lord. Two Sethites, the seventh generation Sethite, Enoch, and his great grandson, Noah, walked with God. This attribute is unique and through these people God's promise of a messiah would be fulfilled. Human history provides many examples of individuals, kings, and nations of Sethite descent that feared God. Despite the fall, there are descendants of Adam that were cursed, but God has redeemed them.

God still looked out for the rebellious descendants of Adam to protect them against the destructive cancer of sin. When God disrespected Cain and his unacceptable sacrifice, He warned him to overcome sin which was eager to control him (Gen. 4:7). God told Cain that His sacrifice would be accepted if he offered it correctly. But Cain still killed Abel and God cursed him for committing premeditated murder. His attitude and emotions showed that he drifted further away from God. Cain did not allow God to talk him out of his intention to murder his brother. When God confronted him after the murder, he refused to accept responsibility for killing him. God consequently pronounced a more severe curse on Cain than on his parents: the ground would not produce crops for Cain no matter how much he worked it; and he would be a restless wonderer on earth. In mitigation he told God that the punishment was beyond what he could bear. Therefore, God put a mark on Cain so that no one who found him would kill him. He also pledged that, anyone who killed him would suffer vengeance seven times over (Gen. 4:15). How was such a murderer assured of God's protection?

God's judgment of David's sin is another example of His tendency to temper justice with mercy. After committing adultery with Bathsheba, David also killed her husband. God punished him and cursed his family, but David is said to be a man after God's heart. There are several other individuals, families, and nations that disobeyed God and suffered the wrath of God but were not destroyed. While God punishes sin, He tempers justice with mercy, leaving room for redemption of sinners. God will discipline you but will not forsake you.

The LORD does not pride in the death of a sinner. *As I live,' says the LORD God, 'I have no pleasure in the death of the wicked, but that the wicked turn from his way and live. Turn, turn from your evil ways! For why should you die, O house of Israel?* (Ez. 33:11 NKJV). The Apostle Peter also writes, *The Lord is not slack concerning His promise, as some count slackness, but is longsuffering toward us, not willing that any should perish but that all should come to repentance* (2 Pet. 3:9 NKJV). God's default position is to have an eternal intimate relationship with humanity and all other earthly creatures at any cost. Hence, God was not to give up on fallen and cursed humanity and non-human creation because He is the embodiment of true love. If at all any soul should perish, it should not be on His account.

God's plan for humanity and all other creatures, embedded in His love, stretches from eternity past to eternity future. He sticks to the letter of His plan worked out before the creation of the world. Rooted in love within and between the Godhead, the omniscient LORD God foresaw the creation of the earth and all its inhabitants, the fall of humanity, the corruption of all earthly creatures, a dysfunctional creation under the curse of death and decay, and the groaning of humans and all other earthly creatures under the curse. God's love by its very nature did not seek its own. It was willing to bear all things, to believe all things, and to endure all things for the sake of humanity and non-human creation.

The love within and between the Godhead was also thinking of the earth and its inhabitants, not yet created, that it would be willing to bear all things and endure all things, including rebellion against the Godhead. Because of this love, Jesus Christ was chosen before the foundation of the earth to save the fallen and cursed humanity (1 Pet. 1:18-20). J. Vernon McGee writes, 'I realize now that the important thing is that Christ was "foreknown before the foundation of the world but was manifest in these last times for you." To put it very simply, the Cross of Christ was not an ambulance sent to a wreck. Christ was the Lamb who was slain before the foundation of the world because God knew all the time that Vernon McGee would need a Saviour, and He loved him enough to provide that Saviour.' In the perfect unadulterated love, Jesus was willing to be the Lamb of God that would offer himself so that we could go free. The Apostle John speaks of Him being *the lamb slain from the foundation of the earth* (Rev 13:8). Equally humbling is the realisation that *the LORD chose us in him before the creation of the world to be holy and blameless in his sight. In love he predestined us to be adopted as his sons through Jesus Christ, in accordance with his pleasure and will* (Eph. 1:3-5). Even before anything came into being God, through His pleasure, will and love for us, chose us to be holy and blameless sons in His sight.

If we were chosen before the creation of the world to be holy and blameless, and Jesus Christ was chosen before the foundation of the earth to redeem humanity, the fall of man and the resultant curse of death and decay did not surprise God. God provided an antidote before the serpent struck. *Christ redeemed us from the curse of the law by becoming a curse for us - for it is written, "Cursed is everyone who is hanged on a tree* (Gala. 3:13). The death of Jesus Christ was the sacrifice that accomplished the salvation of God's elect. God has called us, sanctified, and preserved us in Jesus Christ (Jude 1:1). When we believe in Jesus Christ, we are marked in him with a seal, the promised Holy Spirit, who is a deposit guaranteeing our inheritance until the redemption of those who are God's possession – to the praise of his glory (Eph. 13-14). While our souls have been redeemed, our bodies are dead because of sin.

Paul said, *if Christ be in you, the body is dead because of sin; but the Spirit is life because of righteousness* (Rom. 8:10). Although our spirit has been made alive and we have a new Christ-like nature by faith in Him, our body remains subject to death due to sin and our imputed sin nature. Our human, physical, temporary body is dying and will eventually die as the result of sin in us and in the world. The Christian is here reminded that the penal results of sin still affect the body so that it must die. Being in Christ, or having Christ in us, does not exempt the body from undergoing the sentence of death passed on all mankind.

Notwithstanding of the indwelling of the Spirit, the body must die, and indeed it is dead because a believer is not delivered from temporal death. However, although the "mortal body" dies now, it is not destined to remain forever under the dominion of death, but shall be raised again incorruptible and glorious, by the power of the same Spirit that raised up Jesus from the dead. But the regenerate spirit is rescued from the spirit's death. The righteousness of Christ imputed, secures the soul, the better part, from death. Not only shall such souls live after the death of the body in felicity and glory, but their bodies shall also rise to share therein.

The curse of death and decay will continue to afflict creation until the sons of God are revealed and creation is delivered from the death and decay. Until our full salvation is revealed when Jesus returns and we receive glorified bodies, humanity will continue to suffer. But we are not alone in this condition. For all creation is waiting eagerly for the manifestation of the sons of God (Rom. 8:19).

Our sin also corrupted the non-human creation which shares in our suffering. *Against its will, it* (creation) *was subjected to God's curse. So, all creation eagerly anticipates the day when it will join God's children in glorious freedom from death and decay* (Rom. 8:20-21). But what comfort do we have in the meantime? Paul teaches us that *what we suffer now is nothing compared with the glory he will give us later* (Rom. 8:18 NLT) after the redemption of our body when salvation is revealed in the end times. What is even more reassuring is that the Apostle Peter tells us that *we are kept by the power of God through faith for salvation ready to be revealed in the last time* (1 Pet. 1:5). Paul concludes that God has given us the Spirit as a deposit guaranteeing what is to come. He has preserved us in Jesus Christ.

Throughout human history, God has always extended an olive branch to His cursed creation through Jesus Christ. His desire is to restore original relationships between Him, humanity, and non-human creation. The LORD God, speaking through Prophet Isaiah, says, *Come now, and let us reason together, says the LORD: though your sins be as scarlet, they shall be as white as snow; though they be red like crimson, they shall be as wool.* (Isa. 1:13 NKJV). When we desert God, He searches for us and invites us to return to Him. He always wants us to reason with Him and to be reconciled to Him. For a sinner is just like a pilot flying a plane that has lost its navigation system and has no link with any radar on the ground. God knows that any descendant of Adam can never work his or her way back to Him without His intervention. He must initiate a rescue mission for incapacitated humans. Paul reminds us that, *God demonstrates His own love toward us, in that while we were still sinners, Christ died for us* (Rom. 5:8 NKJV). While sinners cannot discern and experience the presence of God, He unconditionally loves us and seeks to serve us. God's action to redeem us through the death and resurrection of Christ was not in response to who we are, what we have done or any human effort to return to Him. But God, by His very nature does not want any soul to perish.

In our sinful nature, our tendency is to drift away from God. It is purely

God's grace and love, which sent Christ to the cross to reconcile every sinner to Him. Believers are not perfect. At times we sin. However, if we confess and repent of our sins, God forgives us (1 John 1:9); *a righteous man may fall seven times and rise again, but the wicked shall fall by calamity* (Prov. 24:16 NKJV). This grace is not a permit to continue living in sin or to deliberately sin. Every genuine believer eschews evil.

Everyone created in the image of God is inherently sinful and cursed because of Adamic sin, but we are not forsaken. The plan of God for humanity and other earthly creatures stretches from eternity past to eternity future. Before the creation of the world, the Lamb of God was slain as a sacrifice of atonement for sin to be committed by humanity, yet to be created and judged. The LORD also chose us before the creation of the world and predestined us to be conformed to the likeness of Jesus Christ. After the fall, God pronounced curses on the serpent, Adam and Eve, and the ground. As a just and righteous judge, God must judge sin and curse the sinful humanity. But Jesus Christ redeemed us from the curse of the law by becoming a curse for us. He defeated Satan on the cross and destroyed the power of sin and death.

The curses were founded on mercy and love with the aim of reconciling humanity and all earthly creatures to Himself. They were pronounced and are carried out along with the redemption of all of God's creation. But both humanity and other earthily creatures await salvation ready to be revealed in the last time. Despite the curse of death and decay, God's plan, throughout human history, has always focused on reconciliation of man and other earthly creation to himself. Therefore, we were cursed through Adam, but we were not forsaken. Whatever your sin, and the curse it attracted, God is ready and willing to forgive you. We can walk with Him in this century because Jesus has become a curse for us, if only we can choose to return to Him.

CHAPTER 3

The concept of walking with God

And Enoch walked with God; and he was not, for God took him (Gen. 5:24, KJV)
Noah was a just man and perfect in his generation, and Noah walked with God
(Gen. 6:9 KJV)

'Walking with God' is one of the most abused phrases in Christendom. Christians and non-Christians have attached different meanings to this phrase. It sounds very Christian to describe one's relationship as a walk with the LORD even when such a person is deeply embedded in sin. Before describing the Christian practice of walking with God, it important that we have a common understanding of the phrase. This Chapter introduces the concept of 'walking with God', summarises misconceptions about the phrase, explores its meaning, and examines its use in Christian life.

Walking with God goes far beyond salvation

Becoming a disciple of Christ requires a deeper commitment to obey His commandments. When we accept the lordship of Christ, we are babies in the Kingdom of God. We are expected to grow and develop into mature citizens. In the Bible, I have come across phrases like, 'the Spirit of the Lord was upon him', 'David walked before God', and 'the Lord was with Joseph'. In the New Testament, the true vine-branch relationship, the indwelling of the Holy Spirit in man, and the indwelling of the Godhead in man, are all indicators of the intimacy of an individual's relationship with God. The moment I stumbled across two verses about Enoch and Noah (Gen. 5:24; 6:9), the phrase, "walked with God", jumped into my mind and I earnestly desired to work out how these patriarchs did it in a world dominated by evil.

Many people walked before God, but the description "walked with God" is only ascribed to Enoch and Noah. These two patriarchs discovered the secret of nurturing an intimate fellowship with God. They pressed into the presence of

God and discovered attributes that drew them into an extraordinary relationship with Him. Enoch and Noah knitted their hearts with God's heart. For anyone who has taken this bold step of accepting the lordship of Christ, walking with God must be the lifestyle.

Walking with God goes far beyond salvation. A person may be saved but not fully committed to a very intimate relationship with God for several reasons. These may include shallow faith, lack of understanding of the nature of relationship God desires because of spiritual immaturity, spiritual slothfulness, and other things that weigh us down, preventing us from fully committing ourselves to developing and maintaining a very intimate relationship with God. Once, we are saved we need to grow in our faith from being occasional visitors to becoming permanent residents in God's presence.

God is fully committed to walk with us

God's desire to be with us is never met with an equal human desire to reciprocate His love. When I have an opportunity to meet or dine with prominent people in society, I prepare for the event and cannot wait for that precious moment. I arrange for photographs to be taken and I am ready to do almost anything to ensure I capture such rare moments. I have also seen people quickly pull-out smartphones for selfies with their heroes whenever an opportunity arises.

Zacchaeus, a senior taxman, disadvantaged by his height and negative reputation, climbed a sycamore tree to see Jesus as He passed by. But how do all these efforts to associate with celebrities compare with 'walking with God'? If people work very hard to meet with prominent personalities, how much more should Christians desire to walk with God? I can't quite grasp how Enoch and Noah felt as they walked with the Almighty God. If I had an opportunity to see our patriarchs, I would have one question for them: 'What did you do to walk with God?'

God desires total commitment to our relationship with Him. It is not enough to be saved, attend Church and to even participate in several Church events.

There is something you and I need to do for God's heart and ours to permanently bond. Unless we understand what Enoch and Noah did in their walk with God, our efforts to walk with Him are likely to remain mere illusions. This is particularly important as we strive to ascertain whether Christians in the 21st century can walk with God in a generation that seems to be drifting away from God. As we explore what it means to 'walk with God' we will address a few misconceptions that could distort our understanding of the phrase.

The relationship between God and our patriarchs (Enoch and Noah) does not suggest that walking with God is an activity reserved for a select few. God's desire is to walk with each of His children. We can tell from the way God treated Adam and Eve, and their descendants, that He always reached out for the prodigal sons and daughters and still does. Within an atmosphere of human rejection of God, these men still walked with Him.

There are some people who believe that God physically walked with Enoch and Noah. Don Stewart, a Bible explorer, helps us to understand the complexity of God communicating to humankind in human language. He asserts that for God to reveal Himself to humanity, He used human language, human forms, human feelings, and human concepts so we can understand something about His character and deeds. Steward concludes that God expressed His character and deeds in human terms so that the finite humanity can have a reference point for understanding Him. This implies that 'walked with God' is a metaphor depicting a kind of spiritual relationship that existed between God and the patriarchs.

Were these patriarchs, Enoch and Noah, normal humans like any of us? They were created in God's image with potential to walk with God, just like anyone of us, except they chose to do it. God did not create them with supernatural traits, while denying every other descendant of Adam the opportunity to commune with Him. You and I have the same potential. What does it mean to 'walk' in this context?

In my analysis of God's walk with Enoch and Noah, I have assumed that God revealed several characteristic features of this walk through: what is written in Scripture about these two patriarchs; how God related to other people (including Abraham, David, Joseph, Job, Daniel) who walked before him; how Jesus Christ related to the Father, His disciples and the Church; and through records and observations of human relationships that organically reflect intimate God – human relationships. This approach pulls together attributes that draw the heart of a person and the heart of God together and will help us to model our behaviour to suit God's expectation. With assumptions defined we can now explore 'walking with God'.

Walking before God or walking with God

In the Old Testament, many people were drawn to God and called on His Name. They were called children of God, servants of God, people filled with the Spirit of God, sons of God, and the list goes on, but only Enoch and Noah are explicitly reported to have walked with God. Other servants of God including Abraham, Moses, Joseph, Daniel, Meshack, Shadreck, Abednego, Nehemiah, Elijah, Elisha, Job, and others were righteous and had an intimate relationship with God. Some scholars have claimed that these individuals also walked with God although there is no such explicit declaration in Scripture. Similarly, from the time of John the Baptist billions of people have followed Jesus Christ but how many can be said to have walked with God?

Adoption as a child of God does not automatically translate into walking with God

Believers are declared righteous in the sight of God on account of the righteousness of Jesus. However, this does not mean that such believers automatically qualify to walk with God although they have potential to do so. Every believer is a child of God, an 'adopted son' of God, sealed by the Holy Spirit, part of the body of Christ, and justified by faith in Christ, but not every believer walks with God. Even someone saved by grace and indwelt by the Holy

Spirit may still not be walking with God, there must be a process that lifts a believer to a level where he or she begins to walk with God.

When a prince is born in the royal family, he is a royal, but until he has been fully inducted to the drill of royalty, he cannot be entrusted with secrets of the kingdom, and let alone to associate with certain dignitaries. If for any reason the prince is assigned a role he has not been prepared for, it could easily overwhelm him and even compromise his royalty. God loves His children so much that He takes them through a process of building a relationship to a level where He can confidently walk with them, knowing that the demands of such an intimate fellowship will not crush or burden them.

The Holy Spirit indwells and is always with a believer, but the believer may not even hear the Holy Spirit when He is speaking and may ignore the Holy Spirit, or even spend time without having fellowship with Him. In some cases, the believer may even be involved in sin, ignoring the counsel of the Holy Spirit. These and other conditions illustrate some of the issues that the Lord must help us to deal with before we can claim to walk with God. God does not pull, push, or forcibly lift a believer to walk with Him.

Walking with God stems from a process of disciplined outworking of faith

Admonishing believers, Paul said, *continue to work out your salvation with fear and trembling for it is God who works in you to will and to act to fulfil His good purpose* (Phil. 2:12-13 NIV). Paul stresses four important points.

1. Our course of Christian life should fulfil the good purpose of God and we are usually far from it at the time of salvation.

2. God opens our spiritual eyes to see His good purpose and works in us to develop a desire to achieve it.

3. From the day of salvation, the Holy Spirit helps us to begin to see where we are and where we ought to be.

4. Every Christian should personally work on his or her salvation, but God provides all the resources and tools. This creates spiritual hunger and thirst for God and His word, which drive us closer to Him.

Christians must consistently work out or develop their salvation with an attitude of fear (reverence or respect) and trembling (healthy fear of disobeying God). We are to pursue the process of sanctification continually and obediently to completion so that God's good purpose is fulfilled.

Working out one's salvation is achieved through a partnership between God (who has the plan, process, and resources for sanctification) and the individual who must carry out all the activities of sanctification as God instructs. This demands obedience, diligence, consistency, sensitivity, integrity, faith, and love on the part of a believer. God, our Creator, Redeemer, and Sanctifier is the unchangeable moral and spiritual being defining the ultimate good purpose of our course of life, which must be aligned with the purpose of His will. Dr Arnold said, "God always walks on high levels and those who walk with Him must leave the low valleys with their fogs and mists to go up to mountain tops." The Apostle John, encouraging believers, said, *God is light: in Him there is no darkness at all. If we claim to have fellowship with Him and yet walk in darkness, we lie and do not live out the truth. But if we walk in the light, we have fellowship with one another, and the blood of Jesus, His son purifies us from all sin* (1 John 1:5 – 7 NIV). Light is the nature and operational domain of God, while darkness is the nature of fallen humankind and his medium of operation. Darkness and light can never co-exist because they are mutually exclusive. There is only one way in which God and humans can meet and walk together. The believers must abandon darkness and walk in the light of God where the blood of Jesus Christ is consistently available to purify us from sin. For, it is impossible for God to become or embrace darkness. If we diligently seek God, He will pick us up, and cleanse us and train us to walk with Him. If this provision exists, why do we find it difficult to walk with God?

When God decides to walk with His child, He gives His heart to that believer, who must also give his to Him. Think of a man who approaches a woman with the intention to marry. Can you imagine how a woman who does not know the man will respond? Most serious-minded women will cautiously examine the proposal to ensure the man really means what he says. She is likely to ask several questions. Is he ready for marriage? Does he fully understand what he is committing to? Do we have common interests, values, and beliefs to commit ourselves to a life-long relationship? Is the proposal portraying the will of God for us? God is ready to walk with anyone who understands, and is ready to commit to that level of relationship. David helps us to understand that *the* L*ORD looks down from heaven on all mankind to see if there are any who understand, any who seek God* (Psa. 14:2 NIV). God delights in a person who is dedicated to understanding His nature and will, and someone who diligently seeks Him.

George Washington once said, "*Be cautious to all, but intimate to few; and let those few be well tried before you give them your confidence. True friendship is a plant of slow growth and must undergo and withstand the shocks of adversity before it is entitled to appellation.*" God desires everyone to walk with Him, but not everyone is committed to walk with Him although He has openly declared what we need to do. The good news is that God does not expect us to work our way into His presence. He has all the resources for tutoring and training us to attain the quality of life befitting a companion of God, but He expects us to obey His instructions willingly and voluntarily. Although we are beloved children of God and sealed with the Holy Spirit, we need to grow in our relationship with Him to a level where we can claim to walk with Him. When we draw near to God, we need to go through a process of sanctification to the level where we can walk with God.

The meaning of walking with God

A life devoted to God is usually described as a 'walk'. The metaphor of 'walk' is used many times in the Bible for a 'course of life'. As a social being, a human being cannot lead a self-contained solitary life. God has designed a person to be refreshed by companionship, sympathy, and advice of like-minded people. Keeping anyone in solitary confinement goes against the very social nature of his being.

The tri-personality of God – God the Father, God the Son, and God the Holy Spirit - models the community and intimate relationship that God desires for Christians to have with Him and fellow human beings. The Godhead provides a perfect model of walking together. God's perfect will is to walk with people who display His image of nature and being. God-centred lives that Enoch and Noah lived defined their walk, which was a life of devotion to God. The relationship we have with God defines our Christ-centred life.

While we know that God did not physically walk with Enoch for 300 years, our understanding of a physical walk can help us to analyse the key features of 'walking with God'. Imagine what happens when a husband and wife, or two close friends go for a walk on a beach, on a forest track, or along a country lane. Maintaining proximity, they engage in a close and interesting conversation, laughing, listening to each other, and sharing their hearts. As they walk, they become so engrossed in their discussion and stay focused on each other to the exclusion of almost everything around them. Despite a variety of beautiful things and attractions along their path, they ignore them, except in as far as they enrich their discussion. They are in harmony, enjoying an extremely friendly atmosphere that compels them to consistently want to be together. This is an attractive and special relationship between two committed friends. But this resembles the nature of relationship that Enoch had with God for three hundred years. How did Enoch and Noah "walk with God"?

Walking with God means living in close, constant, and intimate relationship with Him each day of our lives. It refers to a consistent communion with the LORD, always moving toward becoming like Him. Walking with God means dying to self and living your life in and through God. *I have been crucified with Christ. It is no longer I who live, but Christ who lives in me* (Gal. 2:20 ESV).

When Christ saves us, we become so intimately attached to Him that we die with Him and He begins to live in us. Everything a believer is, everything he strives to be, and everything he aspires to become must have its origin in Christ. Paul said, *"For to me, to live is Christ"* (Phil. 1:21). Christ becomes a perfect reference figure of who we must be as we live our lives; He becomes our focus, our goal, and our chief desire. It means giving up everything that prevents us from living the life of Christ. We must live our lives with the filters of Christ. To achieve this, we must consistently seek the knowledge of Christ and live it out.

Walking with God means living by the Spirit and keeping in step with Him. When we yield ourselves to Him, His desires oppose the desires of our flesh, and we cease to gratify them. As children of God, we are led by the Spirit who enables us to bear His fruit and to fear God and obey His commandments. A believer who is filled with the Holy Spirit and is consistently being transformed by the renewal of his mind is strengthened with His power. Such a person can discern the will of God, what is good, and what is acceptable and perfect.

Walking with God means living a life by faith in the Son of God. *And the life I now live in the flesh I live by faith in the Son of God, who loved me and gave himself for me* (Gal. 2:20 ESV). By faith, we believe that we were crucified with Christ and died with Him on the cross, He shed His blood for the remission of our sins, we were buried with Him, and we have been raised with Him. Our sinful nature was crucified and replaced by the nature of the risen Christ. Our faith in Christ is the foundation of our life in Christ. We need faith to please God.

Our understanding of the concept of walking with God is key to building a healthy relationship with God by living a Christ-centred life. It helps us to dispel misconceptions about what it means to walk with God. This relationship demands total devotion to God and dying to self but to live in Christ.

PART 2
How can we walk with God?

In our walk with God, we engage in different activities to sustain our intimate relationship. There are three categories of activities partners in this relation are expected to do. They include things that God does alone, 'things that a Christian does alone', and those that God and a Christian do together. This broad categorisation of activities still assumes that God still empowers Christians as they do their assignments. Understanding what it means to walk with God in practice will help us to know how to keep in step with Him. Can we learn from Noah and Enoch what it means to walk with God?

PART 2

How can we walk with God?

CHAPTER 4

Walking with God involves doing some activities with Him

God and Christians walk together as true friends

Christians who walk with God understand that He only walks with true friends. We must embrace Him as the true friend if we are to walk in step with Him. Before people can engage in any serious business, they need to know each other and build a healthy relationship. Friends are drawn together by a bond of mutual affection, personal regard, mutual respect, trust, and similar interests. Friendship is a mutual and agreeable relationship between two individuals. The Jewish tradition considered friendship so important that prospective friends were required to establish a 'covenant of friendship', which bound them to protect each other at any risk and all their possessions were at each other's disposal. The covenant was a sacred pledge of loyalty between two people or parties, which usually spelled out obligations of each party and was binding on their descendants. To seal the 'covenant of friendship', the two people ate together or shared a meal. When David said, *even my close friend, someone I trusted, one who shared my bread with, has turned against me* (Psa. 41:9, NIV), he referred to his friend who breached their 'covenant of friendship'.

Jonathan, the son of King Saul, formed an unbreakable bond with David through a blood covenant. The Bible says Jonathan's soul *was knit to the soul of David* (1 Sam. 18:1). In their blood covenant, Jonathan and David vowed to be forever loyal to each other and their children. (1 Sam. 18:1-3). As Christians, we need to understand the blood covenant God made with us when we received our gift of salvation. When Jesus held the Last Supper with His disciples, He said, *This cup is the new covenant in My blood, which is shed for you* (Luke 22:20). Each time we have the Lord's Supper, we celebrate the blood covenant. Through His blood, each of us can be forgiven, redeemed, and accepted by the Father. A true friend of God walks with Him because of the covenant of the blood of Jesus

Christ. The following popular statements which communicate some of the salient features of friendship.

The bird a nest, the spider a web, man friendship (Heather Prior).

The strongest marriage is between two who seek the same God, the strongest marriage is between two who flee from the same devil (Robert Brault).

A true friend reaches for your hand and touches the heart (William Blake).

We usually experience three different levels of friendship: acquaintances, friends, and true friends. Someone helpfully distinguished between these levels based on how someone responds to a friend in a difficult situation. He said, *Anyone who has been in a major medical condition will tell you acquaintances sign a card, friends visit you in the hospital and best friends sit with you while you sleep.* An anonymous author also said, *"A friend will bail you out of jail, but a true friend will sit with you in a jail cell.* This communicates the depth of commitment that does not ordinarily feature in our usual acquaintances. True friendship is costly.

Aristotle defined true friendship as a single soul dwelling in two bodies. Two people are friends when they become one in spirit (1 Sam. 18:1, NIV). This is also expressed in God's model of marriage (Gen. 2:24, NIV). God designed marriage between man and woman as the strongest friendship between humans.

There is an essential group of traits, values and beliefs, which a person needs to have to qualify as a true friend. Such a person must be (1) dependable – reliable, trustworthy, supportive and loyal to do what is needed or is right, or to be entrusted with deep secrets or important things, (2) empathetic and a good listener who is non-judgemental, (3) honest, speaking the truth no matter what the consequences may be, (4) a self-confident listener and advisor who listens with interest to both good and boring stories and has the ability to confidently advise on personal and professional matters, (5) a selfless, passionate but humorous individual capable of helping and cheering up someone in difficult times without expecting anything in return, (6) keen to know the other person inside out and to love God and the person unconditionally, (7) able to forgive and give, showing generosity in personality and character, and (8) wise, straightforward in his approach to life, intelligent, and sensitive. These traits can be grouped into traits of integrity, traits of congeniality and traits of caring. These qualities are a good proportion of what is needed to nurture a true friendship with God.

Traits are not often fully expressed in relationships between people we describe as true friends. Relationships usually combine different measures of qualities on a continuum from mere acquaintances through friends to true friends. They range from two friends who share little to those who unreservedly share everything including achievements, failures, weaknesses, and even embarrassing situations. Do such friendships exist? Is this your understanding of your friendship with God?

God walks with true friends who have nothing to hide from Him. Such friends lead lives that are deeply rooted and hidden in Christ. They exhibit a retired habit of devotion, separation from the world, and daily, intimate, secret communion with God. These traits accurately depict the scenario of two intimate friends walking together. Such friends are deeply engrossed with each other and resigned from all the world's attractions, whether willfully or compulsively. As we strive to understand the nature of friendship God desires, Abraham is a good example.

Among the Jews, Abraham was spoken of as 'the friend of God' (Isa. 41:8). God called Abraham and commanded him to leave his country, his people, and his kindred for the land He would show him (Gen. 12:1). The Lord sought friendship with His own creature and love of man through His true friendship with Abraham. God gave his heart to Abraham and Abraham gave his to Him. They mutually loved and delighted in each other, shared deep secrets from the heart, and maintained a constant friendship.

The Lord visited Abraham and confided in him regarding future events, made covenants with him, trusted Abraham that he would command his children and household to keep the way of the Lord. He bestowed upon Abraham immeasurable benefits, accepted his pleas for saints in Sodom and was moved by his influence, and He favored the seed of Abraham. In contrast, Abraham: walked before God and was perfect in his generation; laid bare his heart before God; stood up early in the morning at the point where he worshipped God; trusted God from his heart; obeyed God unquestionably to the extent that he agreed to sacrifice his only son; prioritized his desire for God's glory at all times; and his communion with God was constant. The friendship between God and Abraham shows that the bond between them was not something one simply stumbled into.

God's walk with Enoch and Noah was founded on true friendship that was constantly nurtured, developed, refreshed, and guarded against the error of lawlessness to consistently secure their position in God. Enoch faithfully walked with God for 300 years and the friendship continued to flourish until God took him away without tasting death. God is the source of all perfect qualities of true friendship, and He fully expresses them in His walk with a believer.

However, at our best, we cannot match the qualities God brings to this relationship, but He lifts us to a level where we are able to commune with Him. When we desire to live in God, He provides for us to be nurtured to walk with Him as friends. John alludes to this when he says, "*But if we walk in the light as He is in the light, we have fellowship with one another, and the blood of Jesus Christ His Son cleanses us from all sin.* (1 John 1:7, NKJV). When we choose to walk in the light, we have fellowship with God and have access to the blood of Jesus, which purifies us from sin and presents us in a state worthy of communing with God.

Walking with God involves sharing hearts

Walking with God requires an intimate relationship with Him in which sharing our true nature and personality is normal. When two friends walk together, they trust each other to the extent that they share their hearts or secrets. This is one of the foundational features of true friendship – the ability of two people to freely share their lives. I deliberately emphasized sharing of hearts because I have learned how important the heart is in one's life.

For a Christian: the heart is a repository of wisdom (Prov. 14:33); a sound heart is life to the body (Prov. 14:30); a happy heart makes the face cheerful (Prov. 15:13), makes the mouth prudent, and it makes the lips to promote instructions (Prov. 16:23); the heart weighs its answers (Prov. 15:28); the discerning heart seeks knowledge (Prov. 15:14); the heart receives and hides the Word of God so that man does not sin (Psa. 119:11); the heart plans the course of life (Prov. 16:9); the heart accepts commands (Prov. 10:8); God deposits messages in the heart (Psa. 36:1) and man eats to his heart's content (Prov. 13:25). With a heart a man believes that God raised Jesus from the dead (Rom. 10:9). When a Christian shares this treasure chest with God, he reveals His identity – his strengths, weaknesses and secrets hidden to other people.

A heart that has the above traits is pleasant and attractive, supports life and is a 'tree of life'. It does not only value and serve God and his creatures, but also grows and develops to fulfill the course of human life. Whatever a man or woman does or says while drawing from such a pure heart is effective and productive. But a poisonous heart is destructive. A wicked heart is deceitful above all things and desperately wicked (Jer. 17:9), knows its bitterness (Prov. 14:10), crushes the spirit (Prov. 15:13); turns away from God (Heb. 3:12); is evil from childhood (Gen. 8:21); makes the mouth to say evil for out of the abundance of the heart his mouth speaks (Luke 6:45); is worth little (Prov. 10:20); harbors evil and needs to be circumcised (Jer. 4:14, NIV); and produces sin (Prov. 21:4).

The sinful heart uses fervent lips to cover itself like a silver coating on earthenware (Psa. 26:23), is proud and God hates it (Prov. 16:5) and it is far from God (Psa. 101:4). Such a heart displays characteristics that breed destruction, distrust, suffering, dishonesty, and robs others of their peace and joy. It is also self-destructive and fails to fulfill the purpose for its existence. Such a wicked heart cannot nurture friendship and neither can it commune with God.

The two contrasting conditions of the heart (pure or wicked) define the relational behavior of people on earth. The condition of the heart matters as it determines the nature and character of a person. King Solomon said, *As the water reflects the face, so one's life reflects the heart* (Prov. 27:19). Have you ever wondered why God always looks at the heart when choosing someone for His work?

God assesses our spiritual state based on the condition of the heart. He considers a pure heart as a major precondition for ascending His Mountain and for standing in His holy place. God looked at the hearts of the sons of Jesse when choosing a king for Israel. Jesus said, *Love the Lord your God with all your heart, with all your soul, and with all your mind* (Matt. 22:37 NIV). When David sinned, he went before God with a broken and contrite heart (Psa. 51:17, NIV) and asked God to create in him a clean heart (Psa. 51:10, NIV). David also asked God to search him and know his heart. Solomon therefore advises children of God to guard their hearts.

The heart can be either pure or wicked, can hold very sensitive spiritual assets or evil things, and can spew out good or bad things. Imagine how ugly some of the things the heart stores are and yet we are expected to pour this out to our closest friend. The relationship between man and wife does not only refer to sexual intimacy, but also stresses how two true friends should share explicitly their secrets without feeling ashamed. Such friends share their successes, failures, and embarrassing situations without withholding anything. These friends are each other's confidants and hold a wealth of exclusive information about each other. Sharing your heart is laying bare your real self and renders you vulnerable if the person is not a true friend. A Christian who walks with God pours into the Father's ear all desires, concerns, and complaints.

You may be saying to yourself, this is impossible. How can I tell a friend everything about myself? If you are not comfortable to share your deep secrets with someone you consider to be your true friend, then you need to re-examine your friendship. Perhaps, you still question your friend's qualities, among others, trustworthiness, loyalty, honesty, and dependability. This explains why people need to be cautious when considering people for friendship. Solomon advises the righteous to choose their friends carefully (Prov. 12:26). Even the Lord delights in people who are trustworthy (Prov. 12:22) because He shares His secrets with them. Are there references in the Bible on sharing secrets with friends? Yes, there are.

Have you ever considered a model of friendship between David and Jonathan? The Bible records that, *After David had finished talking with Saul, Jonathan became one in spirit with David, and he loved him as himself. Jonathan made a covenant with David because he loved him as himself. Jonathan took off the robe he was wearing and gave it to David, along with his tunic, and even his sword, his bow and his belt* (1 Sam. 18:1-4, NIV). This Scripture bears the hallmarks of true friendship. Jonathan, King Saul's son and a royal prince, shared his spirit with David and unconditionally loved him, made a covenant with David and gave him his royal robe and armory – instruments of his identity.

As the heir to the throne, Jonathan befriended David, a competitor, who was anointed to ascend to the same throne. What followed was even more dazzling as Jonathan shared deep royal secrets about his father's schemes to kill David. Jonathan protected David at the expense of his own prospects of becoming a king. He shared his deep secrets regardless of the consequences. Jonathan demonstrated a loving, sacrificial and selfless heart toward David. This was possible because David symbolically shared instruments of His identity with Jonathan and he was able to see himself in Jonathan. The shared spirit creates a base for a shared identity. This sounds strange, but this is true friendship that God desires for us.

Jesus Christ told His disciples, "*I no longer call you servants, because a servant does not know his master's business. Instead, I call you friends, for everything I have learned from my Father I have made known to you*" (John 15:15, NIV). Jesus Christ shared with His disciples whatever He learned from the Father. He told the disciples what He was about to encounter – conspiracy between Judas Iscariot and the Jewish leaders to arrest Him, and His suffering, death, and resurrection. In closed-door discussions, Jesus Christ shared His secrets with the disciples. He laid bare all that he would encounter to his closest earthly friends. What about God the Father? Have you forgotten what He revealed to Abraham about His plan to destroy Sodom and Gomorrah (Gen. 18:17-20, NIV)?

After God re-assured Abraham that Sarah would bear him a child within a year, He was about to leave for Sodom and Gomorrah to assess the outcry against the two cities and the extent of their sin. But He decided to share His mission with him. Why did God find it necessary to share what He was planning to do in Sodom and Gomorrah with Abraham? The answer is simple. Abraham was God's true friend. After choosing him as a potential father of many nations He could not carry out such a major assignment in his area without sharing it with him. If you are God's friend, He finds it necessary to share with you the things that relate to your calling and the course of your life.

Are there any parallels in God's walk with Enoch and Noah? Yes, there are. Before the great flood God shared with Noah His deep frustration about the wickedness of humanity and His intention to destroy all creation. After seeing that the wickedness of man and his violence were great in the earth, God regretted having made human beings and His heart was deeply troubled; He decided to wipe out the human and animal species from the face of the earth. God shared with Noah his emotions, His plan to wipe out human and animal life on earth, and His strategy for preservation of Noah's family and breeding pairs representing each bird and animal species on earth as seed for repopulating the earth after the flood. This was the largest human and animal genetic resource conservation project ever undertaken and Noah did it under God's guidance.

Although very little is written about Enoch, Jude reveals aspects of his relationship with God, which suggest that sharing of secrets was an important component of His walk. As Jude warned believers about ungodly men who had slipped in among them, he refers to Enoch's prophecy, *See, the Lord is coming with thousands of His holy ones to judge everyone and to convict them of all ungodly acts they have committed in their ungodliness, and of all defiant words ungodly sinners have spoken against them.* (Jude 14-15, NIV). Who are these men this prophecy is referring to? Jude describes them as ungodly men who: pervert grace as a license for immorality and deny Jesus Christ as the only sovereign and Lord; they pollute their bodies, reject authority, and heap abuse on celestial beings; slander what they don't understand; they have taken the way of Cain, rushed into profits of Balaam's error (using their gifts and calling for selfish gain), and have been destroyed in Korah's rebellion; and they are shepherds who only feed themselves. Enoch prophesied what the Lord shared with him, that Jesus and the saints would judge the world. As a true friend of God, he knew about the final judgment.

In the illustrations above, God shared His heart with man, but children of God also shared their hearts with Him. Abram asked God what He could give him since he had no child to inherit his estate (Gen 15:2). He also asked God whether Eliezer of Damascus, his servant, would be his heir. As an elderly man, he could not discuss this problem openly, but Abram shared it with God, his true friend.

When God told Moses to leave Him alone so He could destroy Israel and blot out their name from under heaven (Deut. 9:13), he asked why His anger was burning against the people He had brought out of Egypt (Exod. 32:11). God relented and did not bring disaster upon the Israelites (Exod. 32:14. The gravity of this discussion is diluted by time. This discussion must have been very difficult. God and Abraham were very open and transparent in sharing their hearts. Believers who are friends of God discuss with Him and even influence His decision at His discretion.

Sharing of deep secrets or hearts is a virtue of true friendship between two people, and between God and man. True friends share their secrets out of necessity and love for each other, and express their emotional state about issues which vary in their gravity and emotive nature, and hence they can only be shared between true friends.

When God and man walk together, their communion is secret

Walking with God requires communion that is secret, unless He chooses to disclose it to other people to glorify Himself or encourage them. God demonstrates this in his instruction to Moses when he said, *"I am going to come to you in a dense cloud, so that the people will hear me speaking with you and will always put their trust in you"* (Exod. 19:9, NIV). He shared this information with Moses in secret before speaking to him in the presence of the house of Israel.

Enoch walked with God for 300 years, but very little is disclosed about their communion other than very broad statements about their relationships. Very little is written about this godly man. For the period he walked with God, what exactly did he discuss with Him? What activities occupied him? We know that he pleased God, he was a righteous man, and he prophesied about ungodly men, but little else. The tendency to keep the communion between God and His true friends secret is a common feature in the Bible.

God invited Moses to join Him on Mount Sinai to give him the law and commandments written for the instruction of the Israelites (Exod. 24:12-18). They stayed together for forty days and forty nights. We know that Moses fasted and spoke with God before receiving the law and commandments (Exod. 31:18) but we don't know the details of their conversation. Most of the things He shares with His true friends are not for public consumption. If a greater proportion of our communion with God happens in secret, we must learn to spend a lot of quality time communing with God to know and love Him as we should.

Apart from praying and fasting for forty days in the wilderness, Jesus prayed all night before choosing the twelve disciples (Luke 6:12-13). During His ministry, He got up very early in the morning and went to a solitary place to pray (Luke

5:16). He also withdrew from the busy world in the evening to be with the Father, discussing His ministry and seeking the Father's will for the day. However, details of what happened during His private time with the Father are not provided.

Jesus understood that the success of what He did during the day very much depended on the quality time He spent with the Father in the morning and in the evening. His prayers and planning meetings with the Father happened at the expense of sleep in early morning hours. Jesus Christ discussed everything He would do in the day with the Father. I believe there was nothing that He did in His ministry that caught the Father by surprise. There are three important lessons I have learned from Jesus' prayer life. First, evening prayers allow me to share my joys, concerns, and failures, and to correct any mishaps in the day's assignments. Second, early morning prayers help me to reflectively look at the day ahead and ask God for His plan and purpose for it. When we listen intently, God speaks into our lives, and counsels, teaches, and guides us to meet the demands of the day. This implies that Jesus had a preview of what would happen in the day.

With the Father, Jesus worked out what needed to be done, the resources needed, and when and how they would do it. Jesus did what He saw His Father do. During the day Jesus also prayed depending on the occasion. This approach ensured that Jesus' will and plan were deeply embedded in those of the Father.

Whatever Jesus Christ did during the day perfectly matched what He agreed with the Father in the morning's prayer. Anytime we pray according to the will of the Father, our request is granted because it reflects what He wants to do at that moment. What would happen if we regularly withdrew to solitary places to have quality time with our Father?

The Jewish tradition valued private prayer so much that houses were built with prayer rooms where individuals would spend time alone with God. Jesus also stressed the importance of praying in a secret place (Matt. 6:6). Jesus started the day fully resourced for every good work He was scheduled to do. He went out with the full backing of the Father.

Corporate prayer has its place in our walk with the Lord, but it must never replace private time with God. There are things God will not tell you anywhere except in your closet. A Christian can never walk with God without spending quality time in solitude. Pressing into God's presence to commune with Him in secret is a foundational attribute of saints. How is your private prayer life?

When God and a believer walk together, their wills and governing feelings are the same

The will of God and His feelings about things are absolute and never change. Whatever He creates must conform to His will and feelings. Before God created the universe, He had a will and everything flowed out of it. Paul captures this when He says, *just as He chose us in Him before the foundation of the world, that we should be holy and without blame before Him in love* (Ephes. 1:4, NKJV). Whatever He created reflected His will and feelings until humans breached the law governing their lives in the in the Garden of Eden. Humans abandoned their identity and habitat in God.

The first family drifted away from the will of God but His will remained intact. Unfortunately, the human will and feelings, polluted by the counsel of the Devil and his world (lust of the eye, lust of the flesh, and pride of life) contradicted the will and hurt the feelings of God. In this state, we were destined for eternal damnation and the wheels of destruction were rolling down the hill like a run-away train with nothing to avert a catastrophic crash. But thank God for His unshakeable will, which still recognizes us as His creatures and yearns for our restoration.

The will of God provides for the restoration of humanity. Anticipating the fall of humanity, God has a plan for redeeming sinful people through the death and resurrection of Jesus. Before the foundation of the world, our Father predestined us to be adopted as His sons through Jesus Christ, according to the good pleasure of His will. God's gracious and merciful hand rescues people from the grip of the vicious and ruthless prince of this world. This act starts and maintains the sanctifying work of the Holy Spirit in the life of a believer. However, God does not impose Himself on us. We must accept the invitation to believe in Him.

As we are reconciled to God, the Holy Spirit realigns our will and feelings. The pleasure and purpose of God's will never change and desires nothing less than a holy and blameless believer who can cooperate with Him. Since God provides a standard for our will and purpose, the Holy Spirit works according to God's plan: *In Him also we have received an inheritance, being predestined according to the purpose of Him who works all things according to the counsel of His will, that we who first trusted in Christ should be the praise of His glory* (Ephes. 1:11-12, NIV). God gave humans a destiny and a compass according to His purpose and will. He works out everything to agree with it. God expects His children to be holy and blameless, and to submit to His sovereign will.

If any acquaintance with God is conditional upon aligning a believer's will and pleasures with those of God, any true friend of God must be holy and blameless. This becomes clear from the way God interacts with Moses, Joshua, and the elders of Israel in the wilderness. When God decided to descend in the cloud to speak to Moses so the Israelites could listen in, He gave Moses strict instructions for the Israelites to consecrate themselves for two days. Why was Moses able to walk up the mountain of God when other Israelites couldn't? The Bible doesn't tell us that Moses consecrated himself each time he went before God. He frequently had discussions with God without elaborate protocols because his lifestyle was consistent with the pleasure of God's will. Can two walk together except they agree? For submissive believers like Enoch and Noah, wills and feelings overlapped with those of God like two cyclists riding a tandem bike.

When God and man/woman walk together, their conversation is sweet

When we walk with God, our conversation is sweet. This does not imply that whatever friends say to each other is always literally sweet. Think of a friend who corrects or rebukes you for doing something wrong. What happens when God rebukes, corrects, or disciplines His child? What about your training in righteousness? Surprisingly, these seemingly difficult conversations can still be part of a sweet conservation.

Let us consider the case of David, the man after God's heart. In Psalm 119:103 (KJV), He exclaimed, *How sweet are Your words to my taste, Sweeter than honey to my mouth!* Reflecting on the life of David, one might wonder whether he really meant what he said for several reasons. First, in David's time, there were few more than the five books of Moses, which contained statutes, ordinances, commandments, promises and doctrine. Some parts of the Law were hard to understand and practice. Second, when David committed adultery with Beersheba and killed her husband, the Prophet Nathan delivered God's verdict to David detailing terrible consequences of his disobedience (2 Sam. 12:1-12, KJV). Third, when David offered to build the temple of God, he was told that he couldn't because his hands were stained with blood.

Intrigued by David's utterance, C.H. Spurgeon asked, "*Did he so love to hear His heavenly Father speak that it did not much matter to him what He said as long as He did but speak, for the music of His voice was gladdening in its every tone to him?*" So long as it was God's Word, it was sweet to him, whatever form it might have taken. This is an attitude that every child of God should have.

David understood that the whole Law of Moses was God's Word and he valued it regardless of its implications for his life. There is a temptation to avoid certain parts of the Bible (e.g. genealogies, difficult ceremonial law) but every portion of Scripture has its place in building a mature and complete Christian. However, we are living in an era where preachers, prophets, apostles, and pastors ignore certain portions of the Word of God. Sometimes we delight only in doctrines of Grace and God's promises.

Sometimes we may be tempted to assess the quality of preaching based on the extent to which our favorite portions of the Bible are taught. With an unwise partiality, we find some of God's Words very sweet, but other portions of God's truth rather sour and unsavory to our palates. If men wrote the Word of God under the inspiration of the Holy Spirit, it must be sweeter than honey regardless of the topic, demands, implications or consequences.

Have you ever witnessed cases where people value a celebrity to the extent that whatever he/she does or says is taken to be the absolute and good thing to say or do? Even when a celebrity commits an evil act, some followers find ways of exonerating their idol. Similarly, within the body of Christ, some Church leaders are revered so much that whatever they say or do is treated as the gospel truth. Just as the Word of God was sweet to David's taste, some people find the words of their idols sweeter than honey to their taste. But there is nothing sweeter than honey except God's Word.

While every Word from God to a believer is meant to be sweet, it important to understand why David appreciated those words that could potentially have left a bitter taste. What factors could determine the taste of the words in one's mouth? The source of the word and how it is communicated, the spirit of utterance, the packaging and the background are key factors. Viewed against eternity, the product of the word is always sweet.

When God speaks, His words are sweet because He is the author of sweetness. Whatever flows out of God is intrinsically sweet. Since love, kindness, goodness, peace, gentleness, joy, longsuffering, and faith constitute the fruit of the Spirit, every Word that God utters embodies these attributes of God, which taken together are honey in the mouth of His child.

As we walks with God, the blood of Jesus is there to cleanse us, the fruit of the Spirit is formed, the image of God takes shape, God creates a pure heart, and facilitates maturity and completeness in character. God's words are based on His nature and character, and those who walk with Him learn to speak sweet words. Enoch and Noah enjoyed the sweet and kind words of God every day and they said sweet and kind words to God as they walked with Him. How would you feel if you exchanged good words with God?

When God and His children walk together, they love each other unconditionally

God is love and it is His nature to love unconditionally. God the Father, God the Son and God the Holy Spirit absolutely love each other unconditionally. Anything that flows out of God is conceived and sustained in love. We are designed to love and be loved. When a child of God is indwelt by the Godhead and willingly submits to Him, s(he) becomes porous to the love of God, which oozes from His being. The Holy Spirit pours the love of God into our hearts. It also permeates the human system and becomes his habitat. This is what enables a child of God to unconditionally love God, his neighbor, and the rest of His creation.

As the image of God is restored in a believer, the image of God's love takes shape in him or her through the work of the Holy Spirit. The only nature that perfectly blends with His love is divine love radiated by a believer walking with Him. Christ commands His followers to love Him and their neighbors.

An expert in the Law asked Jesus (Luke 10:25-27, NIV), *Teacher, what must I do to inherit eternal life?* and the Lord said, *Love the Lord your God with all your heart and with all your soul and with all your strength and with all your mind'; and 'Love your neighbor as yourself.* The Lord's assumes that a follower of Christ has a pure heart set at rest in him, a soul produced by His breath (Gen. 2:7, NIV); strength from the Holy Spirit; and the mind of Christ (1 Cor. 2:16, NIV). God desires that His love, reproduced in a believer, is radiated back to Him. Filled with His love, we should love others as we love ourselves unconditionally.

We can never love God unless we abide in Christ and the seed of God abides in us (John 15:4, NKJV). Believers love one another because the God in us is love. Our spiritual birth and knowledge of God creates unconditional love in us, which we radiate to God, our neighbors and non-human creation. When we abide in Christ, we live in, and share His love. When the Godhead lives in us lives in and through us, the fruit of the Spirit which forms in us contains love that is expressed in our fellowship with God.

When God and children walk together, God's model of marriage and family is valued

In a society where objective and absolute truth, and moral and metaphysical values, are dismissed as spurious, oppressive, illusionary, and misguided, the biblical model of marriage between one man and one woman is demeaned. Truth, values, and beliefs are redefined to suit individual perceptions and preferences.

Postmodernists argue that governments, families, or religious institutions should not impose their concepts of objective and universal truth about marriage on them. Rather, an individual has a sovereign right to define his or her own truth and moral values. Christian truth claims about marriage are dismissed as retrogressive and redundant as critics argue that religion is not true and the Church is an archaic institution based on a collection of human-made rules and belief systems.

The concepts of moral and metaphysical realities are rejected as people embrace relativism. Changing societal values have exerted enormous pressure on the institution of heterosexual marriage. Before considering God's model of marriage, it is necessary to briefly review a few key features of marriage. There is no universally accepted definition of marriage but there are several based on religious, legal, and cultural settings. This institution has attracted a lot of attention recently and generated polarized debates. Some definitions of marriage are listed below.

> Marriage is depicted by *the complexes of social norms that define and control the relations of a mated pair to each other, their kinsmen, their offspring, and their society at large*
> (Hebbel)

> *Marriage is a stable relationship in which a man and a woman are socially permitted, without loss of standing in community, to have children* (H.M. Johnson)

Marriage is a relatively permanent bond between permissible mates (Lowie)

Marriage is the approved social pattern whereby two or more persons establish a family (Horton and Hunt)

Justin Marinchick, a cultural anthropologist, also provided the following definitions:
Marriage is *the state of being united to a person of the opposite sex as husband and wife in a consensual and contractual relationship recognized by law* (Webster Dictionary)

Marriage is *being united to a person of the same sex in a relation* (Webster Dictionary)

Marriage "*is the process in which two people make their relationship public, official, and permanent.*

Marriage is the *formal union of a man and a woman, typically recognized by law by which they became husband and wife, or a combination or mixture of two or more elements* (Google)

Marriage is "*the joining of a male and female in matrimony by a person qualified by law to perform the ceremony, after having obtained a valid marriage license*" (The United States of America)

Marriage is a physical, legal and moral union between man and woman in complete community life for the establishment of a family" (Encyclopedia Britannica)

Marriage is a contract for the production and maintenance of children (Malinowski)

Marriage is a relation of one or more men to one or more women which is recognized by customs or law and involves certain rights and duties both in case of parties entering the union and in the case of children born of it (Edward Westermark)

The sample of definitions above reflects a great diversity of parameters that are considered by different sections of society as key in defining marriage, including legal, functional, gender, cultural, religious, and opt-out features. Although broadly categorized as either civil or religious, several models of marriage now exist.

While God's model of heterosexual marriage was originally considered as the only legally and morally accepted model of marriage, many countries, especially in the West are legalizing same-sex marriages and some human rights groups are campaigning for heterosexual and homosexual marriages to be treated equally. Other types of marriage include: open marriage in which committed partners agree to have sexual relationships with other people; polygamy, including group marriage where spouses have sexual relationships with different members of their group (including two or more husbands with one wife, one husband with two or more wives).

Models of marriage vary from one society to another based on their customs, values, systems of thought and religious beliefs. This institution has been abused and manipulated through application of different belief systems. For example, *Pythagoreans taught that marriage is unfavorable to high intellectual development. On the other hand, the Pharisees taught that it is sinful for a man to live unmarried beyond his twentieth year* (The Woman's Bible, Elizabeth Cady Stanton (1898). The Old Testament provides a variety of models, but God's original model of marriage is between one man and one woman (Gen. 2:24; Ephes. 5:31) and Christians are expected to practice this form of marriage. The key tenets of this marriage include its basis on Biblical teachings, permanency of the relationship between a man and woman, a religious ceremony of consummation and use of a symbol (i.e. ring) to depict the union, social/legal approval, and mutual obligations of husband and wife based on the Word of God.

Believers who enter into marriage depend on God as its architect for guidance, sustenance, and provision. This holy institution is part of a Christian lifestyle and hence the quality of family life it yields is a major attribute of devout Christianity for those who choose to marry.

A family is the basic structural unit of the Church and how it is constructed and managed determines the health of the body of Christ. God values the family so much that anyone who abuses it could be treated as an unbeliever (1 Tim. 5:8). God cannot answer prayers of a husband who is either inconsiderate as he lives with his wife or dishonors her as a co-heir of the gracious gift of life (1 Pet. 3:7). God's model of marriage enhances a believer's walk with God.

In the New Testament, Paul instructs believers on how to raise a godly family by providing guidelines on relationships between husband and wife, and between parents and children (Ephes. 5:22 – 6:1-4). Endowed with the mind of Christ, the Word of God and the Holy Spirit, a believer's godly marriage and family enhance his/her walk with God.

Walking with God demands righteousness

Righteousness is God's nature and is richly engrained in the fabric of His character. God's will, thoughts, actions, motives, desires, attitudes, and decisions are upright. The community of Godhead is righteous. His righteousness defines His nature and environment. It is an indispensable and foundational divine attribute that both God and humans need to interact.

When God redeems a person's soul, He declares the believer righteous and able to access and interact with Him. A believer is justified by faith. This marks the beginning of a believer's relationship with God. David said, *He restores my soul; He leads me in paths of righteousness For His name's sake* (Psa. 23:3, NKJV). Although we can never earn the righteousness of God, it is fundamental to a believer's life and relationship with Him. Without righteousness, life is full of disasters as humans repeatedly tread on landmines and booby-traps that the enemy has planted on their paths.

God guides His children on paths of righteousness. A believer's life is a journey, which involves walking on different paths until the person dies or is taken home. The paths may be viewed as different 'courses of action' that people follow as they walk with God. Every sphere of life including, education, marriage, career, faith, family, business, and vocations believers pursue, with the guidance of the Holy Spirit, are paths. When the righteousness of God permeates them, they become paths of righteousness. Options in any sphere of life are paths, but not every option is a path of righteousness.

David metaphorically depicts life as consisting of several paths, but not all paths will lead a believer to the right destiny. David, a king, a priest, and a prophet, realized that he needed God to guide him on paths of righteousness. He made some wrong choices and ended up on wrong paths and the consequences were dreadful. Believers can also pick some wrong paths in life and they can be costly. David teaches us that God is the only guaranteed navigation system on earth if anyone desires to walk on the right paths and He never condones unrighteousness.

God declares us righteous when He reconciles us to Himself through Christ. When we accept the gift of salvation by believing in Jesus Christ, a divine exchange takes place. He forgives and washes away our sins, and immediately declares us righteous. God then places us on a trajectory of paths of righteousness. This does not mean that we can then take off on our own. I have tried it and failed lamentably. So, what can stop me from walking on these paths on my own?

God's righteousness in us holds only in union with Christ. Although I am righteous, the flesh still struggles to break free and embrace the world. David understood what it means to be anointed and yet tumbled under the influence of the lust of the eye and lust of the flesh. Battered and broken, David retraces his way to God and chooses to submit to His leadership. He had every reason to believe that God restores the soul, renews our strength, and leads us in paths of righteousness. If you are battered and bruised in your walk of faith, there is a redeemer who is ready to deliver or walk with us through that situation.

God leads us on paths of righteousness for His Name's sake. When we are saved, God becomes our Father. We become joint heirs with Christ, children of God bearing His Name. God seals us with the Holy Spirit, the mark of sonship in His family. He imputes righteousness to us through Christ to enter and live in Him while he guides our lives. God defends His name because whatever we do reflects on His character and integrity. He also knows how dangerous it is for His children to walk unaccompanied on these paths.

Believers need God's guidance on their paths of righteousness because the devil has designed different temptations to lure them off these paths. The devil is always lurking in the background, but God guarantees our safety. However, if we wander off, the devil leads us into paths of unrighteousness laden with booby-traps. No one treading these paths remains intact. A documentary on wildlife in a national park in Africa illustrates this tragedy.

A leopard, on a hunting spree, unknowingly strayed into a territory of lions. Before it could figure out its escape route, a pride of vicious lions emerged and before long, it lay on the ground lifeless, turned into meat for the superior hunters. Straying into the enemy's camp spells tragedy. God detests such disasters and His desire is that none of His children strays into the enemy's camp. But God's offer to guide believers is optional - He never coerces anyone to follow Him.

Christians must cultivate and express righteousness at any cost. Those who pursue righteousness: find life, prosperity, and honor (Prov. 21:21); enjoy revelation of the intimate counsel of God (Prov. 3:32) and success God holds for them (Prov. 2:7); and they have blessed homes (Prov. 3:33). The LORD tests and loves the righteous and His countenance shines upon them (Prov. 11:7). We can never live a godly life without the righteousness, which is a gift from God.

God provides every resource to keep His children on the paths of righteousness. Walking with God means our paths and His paths overlap and He can guide us. Solomon had an insight into God's feelings about believers who walk on paths of righteousness. God places an immeasurable value on righteousness. Apostle John said, *If you know that He is righteous, you know that everyone who practices righteousness is born of Him* (1 John 2:29, NKJV). God's children receive the gift of righteousness from their Father. His righteousness gives birth to the righteousness in a believer. It is a mark that you are a child of God.

Solomon provides insights into God's resources available to His children on their paths of righteousness. God guarantees adequate food supply (Prov. 10:3; 12:26); security (Prov. 2:7; 10:9); wisdom accompanied with justice, wealth and treasures (Prov. 8:20-21); answered prayer (Prov. 15:8; 15:29); God's love (Prov. 15:9); a heart that gives measured responses to life's questions (Prov. 15:28); integrity (Prov. 13:2); life (Prov. 10:16); the desires of His child's heart (Prov. 10:24); stability in the midst of a storm (Prov. 10:25); sound wisdom to keep a believer on paths of righteousness (Prov. 2:7; 2:20); life in this land (Prov. 2:21-2); ability to learn (Prov. 9: 9b); and a productive and life-giving mouth (Prov. 10:11). We have everything we need for life and godliness in Jesus Christ.

Despite the resources that God provides for us, we still fail Him. Will God still guide us on paths of righteousness? Imagine yourself holding a toddler as you walk along. Suddenly she stumbles and goes down. As a loving father or mother, you will help her to rise up again. Solomon had this advice for the adversary of God's children: *Do not lie in wait, O wicked man, against the dwelling of the righteous; Do not plunder his dwelling place; For a righteous man may fall seven times, And rise again, but the wicked shall fall by calamity* (Prov. 24:15-16, NKJV). While Solomon is not encouraging believers to habitually sin, he stresses the fact that there is provision for a righteous person to be restored whenever s(he) falls. However, God's desire is that we remain steadfast in our walk with Him. Are we walking in paths of righteousness?

Walking with God requires valuing godly wisdom

King Solomon is a good example of a man who truly valued heavenly wisdom. After experiencing the power of divine wisdom and the earthly challenges, Solomon said, *Wisdom is the principal thing; Therefore, get wisdom* (Prov. 4:7, NKJV). King Solomon, a respected King endowed with much wisdom, a consultant in divine wisdom, and a man who also succumbed to some worldly pleasures, concluded that life without divine wisdom is vanity. But what is this wisdom, which Solomon claims is more valuable than silver and gold?

Many definitions of wisdom exist, including these:

Wisdom is the capacity of judging rightly in matters relating to life and conduct (Oxford Dictionary)

Wisdom is soundness of judgment in the choice of means and ends (ibid)

Wisdom is a habit or disposition to perform the action with highest degree of adequacy under any given circumstance, and avoid wrongdoing (Anon.)

Wisdom is a disposition to find the truth coupled with optimum judgment as to what action to be taken (Anon.)

Wisdom is having knowledge and understanding to recognize the right course of action and having the will and courage to follow it (Anon.)

Wisdom is the ability to discern or judge what is true, right, or lasting (Anon.)

Wisdom is the ability to think and act using knowledge, experience, understanding, common sense, and insight (Dictionary.com)

Wisdom is the fitting application of knowledge (Anon.)

Wisdom is the right use of knowledge (Charles Hardon Spurgeon)

Wisdom is the ability to judge correctly and to follow the best course of action, based on knowledge and understanding (Lockyer, p.1103).

These definitions suggest that there are at least four qualifiers of wisdom: (i) a situation demanding wisdom (circumstance, life, conduct); (ii) action (judge, think and act, use); (iii) quality of action (choice, soundness, fitting, correctly); and (iv) basis of action (knowledge, understanding, experience). In this context, *wisdom is defined as the ability to judge correctly and to follow the best course of action, based on knowledge and understanding* (Lockyer, p.1103). Wisdom requires a person to have adequate knowledge about a given circumstance, and an understanding of people, wildlife, and their habitats, among others. The person should also be able to apply the knowledge and understanding befitting a given circumstance. The qualifiers strongly indicate that wisdom does not come naturally and it demands exceptional qualities. But God has given us freedom to request for it anytime we need it.

Believers exercise wisdom to deal with situations in different situations including business, academic, family, marriage, career, traditional, political, government, and religious settings. However, if we were to assess the conformity of human wisdom against above criteria, would wisdom genuinely satisfy the criteria or assumptions? Due to our sinful nature, our judgment is often woefully inadequate.

Human wisdom falls short of the requirements for adequately dealing with the realities of life. Consider a breakthrough in medicine. After extensive research into ways of reducing miscarriages, scientists developed a synthetic hormone, Diethylstilbetrol (DES), which was prescribed for pregnant women to ensure they did not lose their babies. Alas, the purported remedy turned out to be the cause of a rare vaginal cancer and so the hormone was banned.

In agriculture, some of the pesticides (e.g. DDT, Atrazine, etc) applied in crop fields to control pests have been found to harm human beings and wildlife. There are many other technical and biological innovations introduced on the market, which have come with unintentional harmful effects, demonstrating our inability to adequately understand human beings and other creatures, and to develop products that appropriately address our human and wildlife issues. Several environmental, technical, and biological disasters show that humans are not in full control of their lives and the wider environment. Is there a way out?

Solomon discovered that he needed wisdom to rule God's people because his own wisdom could not measure up to the task. As a king who loved God and walked in the statutes of his father, David, he went to Gibeon to offer a sacrifice to God. After offering a thousand burnt offerings on the alter, God appeared to him in a dream by night and said, *Ask! What shall I give you? In response, Solomon said, …… give your servant an understanding heart to judge your people, that I may discern between good and evil. For who is able to judge this great people of Yours?* (2 Chron. 1:7-12), NKJV). Solomon's request for an understanding and discerning heart reveals his desire to provide quality service to God and His people. His primary concern was how he would lead God's chosen people given his inexperience. Solomon prioritizes ability to judge God's people over long life, wealth, and honor.

We need God's wisdom to conduct our business rightly in God's kingdom and to fulfill God's plan (Prov. 4:7, KJV). Wisdom compensates for our inadequacies. God is the source of true wisdom and He gives it liberally to those who ask for it (Jam. 1:5, KJV). He is wise and expresses this virtue through His words and works. God made wisdom before creating the universe and everything in it (Prov. 3:19, KJV). He set it up to operate from eternity. As a master craftsman, wisdom was beside the Lord, helping to plan and build the universe and everything in it (Prov. 8:30, KJV).

Solomon stresses that wisdom is an indispensable resource in God's creative work of the universe (Prov. 3: 19, NKJV). Jesus needed wisdom to fulfill His earthly ministry. Sustenance of the universe and everything in it rests on God's wisdom, knowledge, and understanding. St Luke records that as Jesus Christ grew, He was filled with wisdom (Luke 2:40, KJV) to the extent that His parents could not understand His response when He said, *Why did you seek me? Did you not know that I must be about My Father's business?* (Luke 2:50, NKJV). During His ministry in Jerusalem, Jesus startled people with His teaching in the synagogue, which was rich in wisdom and the reaction of the people sums it all: *And when the Sabbath had come, He began to teach in the synagogue. And many hearing him were astonished, saying, 'Where did this Man get these things? And what wisdom is this given to Him, that such mighty works are performed by His hands! Is this not the carpenter, Son of Mary, and brother of James Joses, Judas, and Simon? And are His sisters not with us?'* (Mark 6:2, NKJV). The synagogues had Jewish scholars, scribes, and other eminent custodians of the law. However, Jesus defied their theology and reasoning because of wisdom.

Jesus demonstrated a kind of wisdom unknown to the current believers. Religious leaders and people gathered in the synagogue witnessed a rare brand of teaching and miracles that made them struggle with his identity, enquire about the source of teaching, marvel at His rare form of wisdom to perform mighty works, and to question the authenticity and authority of His teaching. But all these things were down to one thing – the wisdom of God. In John's revelation, the angels, living creatures and elders ascribe wisdom to the Lamb of God (Rev. 5:12; 7:12). Divine wisdom was a vital virtue in the life, ministry, and identity of Christ.

Equipping his disciples for their persecution in the end times, Jesus promised to give them *a mouth and wisdom which all their adversaries will not be able to contradict or resist* (Luke 21:15, NKJV). Regardless of the academic, political, religious, royal, or social standing of their enemies, heavenly wisdom overruns the wisdom and schemes of the world. We have access to a rare form of wisdom that is superior to human wisdom. The combination of a mouth, righteous heart and wisdom commissioned by God produces a lethal weapon, which our adversaries cannot contradict or resist. God has assured us that when we are brought before earthly judges or arbiters, He will put a word in our mouths that will confound earthly wisdom.

Every child of God who walks in paths of righteousness must possess wisdom. God expects us to operate in His wisdom. Solomon asserts that God stores up sound wisdom for the upright (Prov. 2:7, KJV). His wisdom is authentic, accompanied by godly knowledge, understanding, discretion, and common sense. Every Christian must have it. James cites wisdom as a key factor in a believer's ability to achieve perfection and completeness in his walk with God. He instructs believers who lack wisdom to ask God in faith and He gives liberally and without reproach.

Solomon demonstrated his newly acquired divine wisdom in a case involving two harlots sharing a house, who came to him for arbitration in a case of disputed ownership of a surviving son after one of them laid over hers and killed him. Passing judgment, Solomon said, *Bring me a sword. ... Divide the living child in two, and give a half to one, and half to the other* (1 Kings 3:23-25, NKJV). However, the owner of the son asked the king to give her son to the woman who killed her own, but the murderer insisted on the baby being divided into two halves. King Solomon, passing the final judgment, said, *Give the first woman the living child, and by no means kill him, she is his mother* (1 Kings 3:27, NKJV). Wow, what a monumental judgment it was! No wonder, when the news spread in Israel, they feared the king because they saw that he had the wisdom of God to administer justice. Solomon admonishes all believers to search for and acquire this kind of wisdom.

Drawing from his experience, Solomon shares some features and benefits of wisdom. He reveals that people endowed with godly wisdom: dwell with prudence, knowledge and discretion (Prov. 8:12); have access to godly counsel and practice sound judgment (Prov. 8:14); have riches, honor, enduring wealth and prosperity (Prov. 8:18); walk in the way of insight (Prov. 9:6); love those that rebuke them (Prov. 9:8); accept the commands of God (Prov. 10:8); inherit substance (Prov. 8:21); are wise, happy, blessed, rewarded and find life and favor with God (Prov. 8:32-35); are lifted/promoted and honored when they value wisdom (Prov. 4:8); live for many years (Prov. 4:10); and dwell safely and will be secure, without fear of evil (Prov. 1:33).

When we acquire the wisdom of God: we understand righteousness, justice, equity and a good path (Prov. 2:9); discretion preserves us (Prov. 2:11); we set our hearts on the right path (Prov. 23:19); we walk on the way of righteousness along paths of justice, enjoying a rich inheritance on those who love her, making their treasures full (Prov. 8:20-21); we speak the truth and righteous words (Prov. 8:7-8); and we have a virtue that outweighs all human desires (Prov. 8:11). A wise person is an oasis of peace, pleasant and is a tree of life to those that interact with him or her. Solomon stresses that wisdom leads in a straight path and follows the course of righteousness along the paths of justice (Prov. 8:20, KJV).

Wisdom is an integral component of our nature and identity. Solomon admonishes us to watch daily at wisdom's gates and wait at the posts of her door. God and humanity need wisdom to fulfill God's plan for the earth and its inhabitants. No one can walk with God without wisdom. For Enoch and Noah who walked with God in their generations, wisdom was an integral virtue of their lives. Their prolonged walk with God enabled them to gain unmatched divine wisdom. We now understand that our patriarchs understood their inadequacies and sought God's wisdom, which sailed them into God's presence and paths of righteousness.

Walking with God involves dwelling in Him and He in us

Walking with God involves dwelling in Him and God dwelling in us permanently. Living in Him means living as Christ did. Enoch and Noah walked with God and they understood what it meant to live in God and He in them. Jesus used the metaphor of the vine and its branches to describe His relationship with believers: *I am the vine, you are the branches. He who abides in Me, and I in Him bears much fruit; for without Me you can do nothing* (John 15:5, NKJV). There are several salient features of this relationship. First, the vine and the branches are two parts of the same plant, and they are organically united and interdependent. When a person is saved, there a spiritual union between Christ and the believer mediated by the Holy Spirit. This union guarantees continuous presence of Christ in us.

Abiding in Christ means that there is never a moment when Christ is not in us. It involves transformation from a visitor to a permanent resident in God's presence. This is a difficult thing to practice. Several utterances by believers show that we do not fully understand the permanency of abiding in God. When praying, why do we ask the Lord to come in our presence? Why do we invite the Holy Spirit if He lives in us? Why do we ask the Lord to be with us when He lives in us? Such prayers are justified if we believe we have deserted God or if we do not (fully) understand that God lives in us.

Second, the vine and the branches have different responsibilities, which may not be functionally equal. In a typical vine, the stem provides mechanical support to branches to ensure they receive adequate sunshine, provides physiological support by providing water and nutrients, and transports hormones to different plant parts. Jesus Christ likens His spiritual functions to what the vine does to support the branch. He is the author of our salvation and the Word that cleans, heals, strengthens, teaches, trains, corrects, and builds us. As we dwell in Him, He becomes our ark, refuge, and access route to our father.

The vinedresser expects the branches to produce and support fruits, produce and release hormones, transpire and cool the plant, and to produce food and share it with other parts of the plant. Jesus Christ expects us to bear the fruit of the Spirit, win souls, care for His creation, reproduce and grow, and perform every good work that our discerning hearts instruct us to do. He instructs us to remain in Him and in His Word to feed our spiritual and physical needs. Third, our ability to bear fruit is conditional upon abiding in Christ. He warns us that if we detach ourselves from Him, we cannot do anything.

If we live in God and He lives in us, we will exhibit, among others, the following attributes.

(i) We will obey God's commandments: *Now he who keeps His commandments abides in Him, and He in him* (1 John 3:24a; 1 John 4:7, 12, NKJV). The two great commandments on which the Law and the Prophets hang require us to love God and our neighbor. Since love is God's nature and His domain is saturated with love, everyone who practices love lives in Him.

(ii) We are one with other believers as God the Father is in Christ, and He in the Father. A believer lives in union with Jesus Christ, who is united with the Father (John 10:38). Jesus prayed for relationships between God and believers, which include a union of all believers, every believer living in the Father, the Son, and the Holy Spirit, and all the three persons of God dwelling in every believer (John 14:15-17; 20).

(iii) We abide in love: *God is love, he who abides in love abides in God, and God in Him* (1 John 4:16, NKJV). Children of God consistently dwell in love. They know, see, and fellowship with God and fellow believers through the lens of love. When God lavishes His love on us, we love Him and His creation.

(iv) We eat the flesh of Christ and drink His blood (John 6:54-55), which represent new life through His death and resurrection, a new blood covenant, fellowship with Him and a memorial until He returns. This fellowship meal symbolically unites believers in, and with, Christ and reflects our life in Christ and His in us.

(v) Whenever a person or an animal eats food or drinks water, the body absorbs the substances. They are integrated in the body; they become one with the body. This is a metaphorical union of Christ and people that can never be separated. Thus, Christ is in us and we are in Him even as He sits at the right hand of God.

(vi) The Holy Spirit, who lives in us, guides and counsels us (Rom. 8:9, 14, KJV). He knows the mind, the plan and purpose of God concerning man, and the universe and everything it. The Holy Spirit provides godly counsel, gives wisdom, knowledge and understanding, reveals wondrous truths in the Word of God, and leads the believer on paths of righteousness. He consistently guides us on paths of righteousness and to make wise judgments when required to.

(vii) We know God. John said, *Now by this we know that we know Him, if we keep His commandments* (1 John 2:3, NKJV). Keeping God's commandments is a litmus test to determine whether we know Him. They represent an outflow of God's nature, character, purpose, will, and pleasures. For us to know, keep and practice commandments, we must have sought God to reveal His knowledge. This shows that we abide in Him and He abides in us.

(viii) We keep God's Word and His love is truly perfected in us (1 John 2:5, 24): As the Word builds up in our hearts, so does His love. Abiding in God and He in us reflects a perfection of love in God, a sign that we are in Him.

(ix) We walk as Jesus walked (1 John 2:6, KJV). Abiding in Jesus Christ involves a living union between Christ and a believer. If we receive, keep, and practice the teachings about the life, ministry, death and resurrection of Christ, our lives are modeled after Christ. The sanctifying work of the Holy Spirit enables us to walk as Jesus did.

(x) We confess that Jesus Christ is the Son of God. According to John, *whoever confesses that Jesus is the Son of God, God abides in Him, and he in God* (1 John 4:15, NKJV). Such a confession originates from a deep understanding and conviction of who Jesus is and of His life, ministry, death, and resurrection. Apostles believed this and were martyred for it. Our confession is the knowledge of an adopted son, an insider in the household of God. It is an expression of someone who abides in God.

(xi) We are temples in which the Spirit of God dwells (1 Cor. 3:16). The moment we are saved, we are sealed with the Holy Spirit as a guarantee of the promises to come and as a sign that we are children of God. We become the permanent residence of the Holy Spirit and He is always available to help us.

(xii) We do not continue in sin: *Whoever abides in Him does not sin.* (1 John 3:6, NKJV). Anyone born of God is a new creation with a nature that disposes one to loathe and hate sin. We carry a seed that constantly abides in the Christ and cannot characteristically and habitually sin. Sin has no place in us because of the spiritual union with Christ with.

(xiii) Our hearts are at rest in God's presence (1 John 3:19). This is like a baby resting peacefully in the arms of her parents. We need to define two terms, heart and rest, before exploring what it means to rest one's heart in God's presence. While science treats the heart as merely an organ that sustains blood circulation in the body and supports other body functions, Bruce K. Walke explains that it has a bigger role in the Bible. The heart is a person's center of physical activity and hidden emotional-intellectual-moral activity. It is a morally sensitive device for understanding, discerning, and gaining insight.

Walke summarizes the Biblical and ancient understanding of the heart as a central organ that moves the rest of the body; a figure of remoteness and inaccessibility; a hidden entity whose secrets are betrayed by the mouth; dependent on the ears as the filter of what it receives and stores; needing to be educated by filling it with God's word; a device that functions as the conscience; a device that plans, makes commitments, and decides; the inner forum where decisions are made after deliberation; here a person engages in self-talk; representing a conscious commitment to the Lord; and constituting a conscious decision to follow his instructions. The heart describes an inner self that defines an individual's identity.

The term "rest" has several meanings. The Merriam-Weber Dictionary defines rest as: *a bodily state characterized by minimal functional and metabolic activities; freedom from activity or labor; a state of motionless or inactivity; a place for resting or lodging; or a peace of mind or spirit.* Other dictionaries define rest as: *ceasing to work or move in order to relax sleep or recover strength; as a state of peace or tranquility; depending on being based on; being supported to remain in a specific position.*

The definitions of rest refer to states of repose, dependence, rootedness, tranquility, peace of mind or spirit, being supported, belonging to a place, security, trust, relaxation, reduced work rate, and refreshment. These physical, physiological, and mental states define a key requirement of a healthy and productive life. It is a component of the action-rest rhythm in living things. There are also spiritual equivalents of these states, which characterize the heart at rest in God's presence. It assumes a broader role in the life of a believer.

A person who loves others belongs to the truth and rests his/her heart in God. Such a heart maintains its vitality and is productive (1 John 3:18-20). The phrase *set our hearts at rest in His presence* (1 John 3:20, KJV) has been paraphrased in some Bible versions to read: *feel at ease in the presence of God; assure our hearts before Him; having peace with God; persuade our hearts before Him; to be confident in God's presence; reassure our hearts before Him; convince our conscience in His presence; have our hearts certified before Him; and put our hearts at rest.* Resting is a consistent state of releasing one's heart to God to draw from His nature and qualities. Our lives in Christ involve physical, physiological, mental, and spiritual activities that drain us and we need an ambience, a place, and a resource that keeps us fresh functional.

When we love our neighbor, we are expressing a heart that rests in the presence of God. Such a heart draws its confidence, tranquility, peace, conscience, security, strength, wisdom, knowledge, and understanding from God. As our hearts abide in God's presence, His nature and virtues permeate our heart to resource and restock us for life on earth. Setting our hearts at rest in His presence is living God's reality. We need to remain in the presence of God to soak His nature and qualities.

Therefore, walking with God involves recognizing that our full expression of the image of God can only be realized when we are fully grafted in Christ and He fully abides in us. As Christians, we need to consistently remind ourselves that we have no life outside Christ. It involves sharing the same soul, body, mind, and Spirit with Christ. When you walk with Christ, people should only see one footprint and hear one voice.

CHAPTER 5

What should I do in my walk with God?

Walking with God involves a commitment to Christian principles and practices to consistently live a disciplined life by faith in Christ. A life devoted to God requires us to do certain activities in line with the duty of every man or woman to fear God and keep His commandments. When Enoch and Noah walked with God, they did not rely on God to do everything for them. They still played a part in nurturing their relationships with Him. Similarly, every Christian walking with God must individually do certain activities to abide in His presence. But what are these activities?

Walking with God requires letting go of anything that would distract us

Anything that interferes with our walk with God is a distraction. In most countries, national laws prohibit drivers from speaking on the phone while driving because the act compromises the driver's concentration and sense of judgment. The mobile phone distracts the driver from his/her commitment to drive the car with full awareness of fellow road users and the general environment. Similarly, walking with God requires a full commitment to keeping His commandments.

Jesus Christ was very blunt in explaining the cost of discipleship when He asked two people to join His team of disciples. He asked a man to follow Him. In response, he said, *Lord, let me first go and bury my father.* Jesus said to him, *Let the dead bury their own dead, but you go and preach the kingdom of God.* Another person said, *Lord, I will follow You, but let me first go and bid them farewell who are at my house.* Jesus said to him, *No one who put his hand to the plough, and looking back, is fit for the kingdom of God* (Luke 9:59-62, NKJV). Jesus Christ taught them that the primary commitment of His followers was to preach the Kingdom of God.

The two men whom Jesus invited to join His disciples were shocked by Jesus' responses to what they considered were very serious family commitments. In our society, a father is a very important person in a family. When he dies, the family, the Church, the government, and even private companies would expect a son to attend his funeral. In company and government policies, there are provisions for an employ to bury his or her close relatives. The Church also supports people who lose their parents. But Jesus told the men to put the kingdom business above all else. Followers of Jesus must seek the Kingdom of God first and everything else is secondary.

In the parable of the Sower, Jesus said, *some seeds fell among the thorns, and the thorns sprang up and choked them* (Matt. 13:7, NIV). Interpreting this portion of the parable, He stressed that *he who received the seed among the thorns is he who hears the word, and the cares of this world and the deceitfulness of riches choke the word, and he becomes unfruitful* (Matt.13:22, NIV). Jesus identified cares of the world and deceitfulness of riches as major distractions in receiving, keeping, and practicing the commandments of God.

We can be so preoccupied with the things of the world that God's work is viewed as a distraction. We worry about children, careers, aging parents, clothes, physical appearance, relationships, marriage, social status, promotion, and accommodation. For many, these thorns have become so sharp and prickly that our Christian faith and commitment to God's work have been seriously compromised. We are faced with several questions: Should I attend a Church service or work an extra shift to increase family finances? How can I support my aging parents on such a low income? If God loves me why is my spouse so worldly and violent? What wrong have I done for my children to walk away from the Lord? How can I climb my career ladder if I must commit to Church activities? How will I feed and clothe my family if I don't have a stable income? How can I secure decent accommodation to fit my status? These and several other concerns have become serious distractions in our lives. While we do not deny that have needs, Jesus tells us to put them in their right position. He instructs us not to worry about life and its accessories, but to seek first the Kingdom of God and His righteousness first and He will deal with all the cares of our lives.

Jesus unveils the deceitfulness of riches as a distraction. We have access to wisdom to create wealth. God made us to rule over His earthly creation including means of creating wealth. God's formula for wealth creation is seeking His kingdom first and His righteousness so that wealth is added to our lives. Solomon asked God for wisdom, but God also gave him wealth. But we are seeking the riches first hoping that God will add His Kingdom and righteousness to us.

Instead of a Christ-centred life attracting wealth as God's provision, there is an emerging trend of considering the great commission as secondary to wealth creation and prosperity. This model of wealth creation may result in Christians worshipping wealth rather than God. There are two implications of this problem: riches or wealth colour and shape our perception of the gospel; and wealth becomes the key indicator of Church growth. While the real measure of Church growth is the number of saved souls added to the kingdom of God and spiritual progress, the economic indicator can be achieved without necessarily adding any soul. Let me use an example from the agricultural industry.

Considering that the world population is likely to hit 9 billion by 2050, FAO estimates that food production must increase by 70%, approximately double the current level of production although available land seems to be decreasing. One of the proposed interventions is to increase output per hectare of agricultural land by narrowing the crop productivity gap. This assumes that the current production per hectare of agricultural land is at its best 30% below optimal yield. Therefore, narrowing the yield gap through resource use efficiency and other technologies would increase agricultural yield without clearing fresh land. Similarly, members of the body of Christ still have a giving capacity that has not been fully exploited. Encouraging Christians to give more would still increase Church income without necessarily winning more souls. This represents financial growth even without numerical or spiritual growth. Every believer needs to earnestly strive to sustain an intimate fellowship with God and to filter out distortions in Christian doctrinal teachings. Testing the teachings against the Word of God will ensure that believers are fed pure spiritual food, especially in an era with increasing false teachings.

Unfortunately, there are spiritual leaders who focus on riches much more that spiritual health of the flock. When parameters other than spirituality are used to measure the health status of the Church or individual believers, the indicator is deceptive. It distorts spiritual reality.

At times we hold on to fleshly desires while trying to walk with God. We bring wrong habits, sins, worldly entertainments, or unhealthy relationships. I am not in any way suggesting that new believers should break off all habits upon conversion. However, we are expected work out our salvation with fear and trembling. This involves studying the word of God and meditating on it, extracting its instructions, and prayerfully breaking off sinful habits. But we cannot continue to live in sin and walk with God at the same time.

A Christian newsletter featured different stories on Christian leaders, including pastors, who are addicted to different vices, including watching pornography, abusing children and sexual immorality. If sin persists in our lives despite our spiritual efforts to get rid of it, seeking help from trustworthy Church leaders is strongly advised. Anyone walking with God resists the cares of this world and the deceitful riches or vices that erode integrity.

Walking with God involves pleasing Him

Pleasure has been associated with fundamental and higher-level emotional experiences in humans and animals. Pleasure has been defined as: a feeling of happy satisfaction and enjoyment derived from something to one's liking, gratification and delight (CITE); a broad class of mental states of humans and other animals experience as positive, enjoyable or worth seeking; freedom from pain in the body and freedom of turmoil in the soul (Epiculius); or an effective positivity of all joy, gladness, liking, and enjoyment (Stanford Encyclopaedia of

Philosophy). The International Standard Bible Encyclopaedia refers to pleasure as good thought and will or every desire of goodness. W.L. Walker, reviewing the New Testament, explains that pleasure means: to think that it seems good to me; to take or have pleasure (Luke 12:32, NKJV); sweetness (Luke 8:14, KJV); wish (*thelema*); favour (Acts 24:27, NKJV); and to live delicately or luxuriously. It refers to mean mental states of God, man and other creatures experience as positive, enjoyable, joyful, and worth seeking.

Pleasure is a desirable emotional trait which God and his creation exhibit when exposed to certain positive circumstances. God is the origin of all forms of godly pleasure, and it is part of His nature. He has a trait to please, and to derive pleasure from, His creation. God has used His pleasure as a framework for certain courses of action. *With all wisdom and understanding, He made known to us the mystery of His will according to His good pleasure, which He purposed in Christ, to be put into effect when the times reach their fulfilment – to bring unity to all things in heaven and on earth under Christ* (Eph. 1:8-10, NIV). God's revelation of the mystery of His will to Christians, rather than the prophets, was based on His good pleasure. This emotional experience undergirds acts of conceiving, creating, and sustaining His creation. When God spoke different creatures into existence in Genesis 1, He examined and saw that they were good – He was pleased with the work of His hands. Good pleasure was an expression of satisfaction with what He had made.

God derives pleasure from His creation, and He made creatures with intrinsic capabilities to please Him. God has deposited in every creature traits to please Him and His creation. He has also created us to generate activities that have potential to please God, humanity and other creatures. Paul told the Ephesians that, *we are God's handiwork, created in Christ Jesus to do good works, which God prepared in advance for us to do* (Eph. 2:10, NIV). God prepared good works before we were born and then designed and created us in Christ to have qualities to do good works that please Him.

David said, *you created my inmost being; you knit me together in my mother's womb* (Psa. 139:13, NIV). The art of designing different parts of my body, and of weaving them together produces a Christian with all abilities to do all the good works. Good works please God if a Christian with the right specifications does them. Anytime we fail to do a good work we deny God, our neighbour or creation pleasure.

Believers discover the desire within them to do things that please God, people, and creation. Have you ever considered why some people love domesticated animals, plants, wild animals, and other aspects of nature? When people spend huge sums of money and travel long distances to visit different natural attractions, we explain that in terms of natural tourism, but we never consider the traits God has deposited in nature to please humanity and in humans to derive pleasure from nature.

At times we accuse people of being obsessed with their pets or other sources of pleasure. In some cases, our inner being tells us to either act to please people or other creatures, but we suppress this urge. Created in the image of God, He has given us every resource to please Him and His creatures and to respond to sources of our pleasure.

Christians know how to thank God for his providence but are not very good at expressing pleasure from things God has gifted to them. God has given us biological pleasures including food, water, sex for married couples, and children as primary sources of joy and happiness on earth. Other sources include plants and animals, neighbours, careers, education, and entertainment. Unfortunately, some cultures teach us not to express or even derive joy from these gifts. But to rejoice when they come out of a difficult situation because either a miracle has happened, or the condition has changed from negative to positive.

Wealth is another obvious source of pleasure for many. In Psalm 145, David expresses his desire to praise God every day and to meditate on His wonderful works. He praises God because there is always a temptation to look beyond ourselves for great works and yet the power of His mighty acts clearly manifests in our homes. Although God has designed us to pick signals of His good activities to trigger pleasure in us, some sensors are dysfunctional, blocked, suppressed, or disabled.

Believers who walk with God quickly discover the importance and the secret of pleasing God. Enoch and Noah understood this and did it well: Enoch was commended as one who pleased God (Heb. 11:5); and Noah found favour in the sight of God (Gen. 6:8). These men did their homework and knew how to press into the presence of God wisely and effectively by presenting Him with pleasures.

God as the origin of pleasure has the full capacity to please humanity and all other creatures, the ability to derive pleasure from His creation, and to use pleasure to fulfil His other divine plans, purposes, and functions. He has access to, and full control of pleasure in its various forms. The problem is with humanity and by extension other creatures on earth. While other creatures have instincts to do certain things to please God, we need to discover what God has placed at our disposal to please Him. But how can Christians please God as they walk with Him?

Christians need to know how to please God and then seek Him fervently. David sought to please God through his meditation (Psa. 104:34). Sinking deep into the word of God in solitude enables a believer to discover the wondrous truth, gain a deeper understanding of God, have an intimate fellowship with God, and to express how much one values God. This practice elevates God above all else and pleases Him.

Paul encouraged the Church at Corinth to aim to always please God, whether at home in the body or away from it (2 Cor. 5:9-10). He also instructed the Thessalonians how to walk or live to please God (1 Thes. 4:1-3). Other practices that please God include: faithful actions; blameless life; living by faith; doing everything heartily (Col. 3:23); doing the will of God; praying everywhere without anger or quarrelling (1 Tim. 2:8); cheerfully using the gift God has deposited in you according to the faith and grace God has given you (Rom. 12:3-8); a pure heart (Luke 16:15); expressing the fruit of the Spirit (Gal. 5:22-23); and walking in the fear of God (Neh. 5:9).

God is pleased with a believer who: prays in righteousness; abides in Christ; has a wise heart and lips that speak what is right; witnesses for Christ and proclaims repentance and forgiveness; grows in stature and godliness (1 Sam. 2:26); detests worldliness; is faithful to his or her spouse; obeys God's commandments; trusts in the Lord with all his/her heart and acknowledges Him in all ways (Prov. 3:5-6); has a rich and godly thought pattern (Philip. 4:8); seeks God's interests (Philip. 2:21); and offers acceptable sacrifices. Worship pleases God. A. W. Tozer encourages every Christian to live in a state of unbroken worship.

God created the universe and everything in it and, in their original state, all creatures pleased Him. He sustains and loves them, and is pleased with them (Gen. 1, 2; 8). Created in His image, humans please God when they rule the earth. Anything we do to dress the earth and keep it pleases God.

Some Christians believe that the responsibility of humans to care for God's creation ceased with the fall of humanity. However, despite the fall God still expects us to care for His earth if we inhabit it. When the children of Israel defrauded the land of its rest (Sabbaths), God was not pleased. Moses confirms this in Leviticus 26:34-36: *Then the land shall enjoy its Sabbaths, as long as it lies desolate, as you are in your enemy's land, and the land shall rest and enjoy its Sabbaths. As long as it lies desolate, it shall rest – for the time it did not rest on your Sabbaths when you dwelt in it.* God expected the Children of Israel to rest the land, but they never did. God further demonstrated that humans need to care for His creation when He appointed Noah to build an ark to preserve wildlife breeding stock based on His instructions. God is still pleased when believers care for His creation.

God hates sin and it displeases Him. However, despite God's desire that we live lives that please Him, we often displease Him because of our disobedience. When the children of Israel focused on building their houses and neglected the temple of God in Jerusalem after returning from exile, God was displeased, and He instructed Prophet Haggai to tell them to consider their ways (Hag. 1, NIV). But God made provision for restoration of relationships for His pleasure before the creation of the world. He is pleased when we confess our sins and are reconciled to Him.

Walking with God requires clothing ourselves with humility

Walking with God requires humility (maintaining a modest self-opinion), an integral element of God's nature and character. Humility may be defined as the fear of God (Prov 22:4), lowliness of mind (Phil. 2:3), the state of absolute bankruptcy of spiritual worth (Matt. 5:3), a modest estimate of one's worth or absence of self-exultation (Matt. 10:39) or meekness (Eph. 4:2; Col. 3:12). It is a heart attitude that precludes selfish ambition, conceit, and the strife that comes with self-justification and self-defence. It is not merely an outward demeanor, but an expression of a true perception of your personal status and identity.

Humility enables us to recognize our identity that rarely measures up to God's nature and character as our yardstick. If only we could fully understand who we are, we would be the best followers of Christ. This perception of humility should help us to live a life aligned to God's perception of who we are. The humble believer is willing to put aside selfishness and submit to God and His Word. True humility produces godliness, contentment, and security. When we understand our spiritual bankruptcy and the purity of God, we will humble ourselves and value other people above self. Humility is a hallmark of God's children, holy and dearly loved.

When we understand who we are and approach God with humility, He sees His attributes in us because it is grounded in His nature. Our Father demonstrates humility by seeking sinners and stooping down to redeem them. How can the omnipresent, omnipotent, and omniscient God search for a stubborn and stiff-necked sinner? Yet He is patient to see His wayward child return to Him. David understood God when he said, "*When I consider heaven, the work of Your fingers, the moon, and the stars, which you have ordained, what is man that You are mindful of him, and the son of man that You visit Him?* (Psa. 8:3-4). If you know God as the creator and sustainer of the universe, then He is greater than the greatest scientist, wiser that the wisest human being, richer than the richest man, and holier than any godliest man. Surely, His status is way beyond human understanding and yet He chases after mortals like us.

Consider this, all things were created through Christ. Which mortal qualifies to come near such a powerful, holy, righteous, and wise Son of God? Yet, Jesus demonstrated humility from the manger to the cross. But a believer who is joined with the Lord is one with Him. We are also sealed with the Holy Spirit and the fullness of God dwells in us through the Holy Spirit.

Humility defies social classes. It is also a foundational hook on which spiritual worship and service hang. Fully understanding the humility of God and His desire for humans to express this attribute toward Him and other people, Peter said, *All of you, clothe yourselves with humility toward one another, because God opposes the proud but shows favor to the humble* (1Pet. 5:5). We ought to exhibit humility in the way we relate to others. It commits us to serving others in all lowliness of mind, always valuing other people above self. Humility recognizes that it is not possible to accomplish anything in this world without God enabling and sustaining us. This attitude pleases God and attracts His favor.

Humility is a lever that God uses to exalt His children (Jam. 4:10). But, pride fails to recognize our spiritual and moral gaps. This inflated self-worth irritates God and He fiercely opposes it. But how do you know that someone is humble? John Piper taught that humility starts with a sense of subordination to God in Christ. It does not feel entitled to a better treatment than what Jesus received. It asserts truth and does not bolster ego with control or with triumphs in debate. Humility refers to service to Christ and love to the adversary. When we understand that humility is fallible and is dependent on grace for all knowing and believing, we will value criticism and learn from it.

Humility knows that God has made provision for human redemption and that he calls us to persuade others. Understanding that God reached out to us in our state of spiritual poverty, we ought to join Christ in search for lost souls. The conviction to win souls for the Kingdom of God is deeply rooted in humility. Noah and Enoch were humble, and this attracted the presence of God. We need to humble ourselves to walk with God as the patriarchs did.

Walking with God involves living by faith

We cannot walk with God if we cannot live by faith. For without faith, no one can please Him. Faith is not merely an intellectual assent to a doctrine or acceptance of divine commands. Moses Silva's Bible dictionary defines faith as belief, trust, or loyalty. Faith is utter confidence in the faithfulness of God, our personal commitment to Him, and consequent loving obedience to His will. The Bible also has several references to faith. It defines faith as *the substance of things hoped for, the evidence of things not seen* (Heb. 11:1). Faith perceives as reality what has not yet happened and what has not yet been revealed to our physical senses. It is the ability to see things coming far in the future. Faith is having complete trust in God that He will fulfil His promise. It is the basic structural frame of our relationship with God and is foundational to the Christian belief system. As we walk with God, He will promise us things in this life and beyond the grave. Faith gives us the confidence that He will fulfil everything He tells us. Isaiah equates faith with existence. It is the confident trust in God based on His promises in His word.

Faith is the spiritual access code to God and the basic structural component of everything thing that pleases Him. It frames the pre-existent reality of the Word of God which becomes the evidence of the unseen. This unique attribute of God enabled the Word to frame the worlds and enables Christians to come to Him believing that He is. It is therefore impossible to please God without faith (Heb. 11:6). Noah and Enoch pleased God because they lived by faith. It enabled them to enter and abide in His presence. Faith also sustains our communion with Him. God has designed faith as a believer's precursor of products that please Him. God has given you and I the ability to trust Him as we walk with Him.

God is faithful and His creation is an act of faith. He envisioned the universe and everything in it and believed that at His word things would come into existence. Genesis 1 and 2 present creative acts of faith which demonstrate God's conviction of things He hoped for, the evidence of things not seen. Jesus Christ had faith in the Father and it pleased Him. A faithful Christian trusts and obeys God just as Jesus did nothing except what His Father taught Him (John 8:28). Jesus is the author and finisher of our faith (Heb. 12:2). Apart from believing in His creative activities which we encounter as we walk with Him, God expects us to engage in acts of faith every day. Our faith should motivate and empower us to study the Word, pray, and seek God's way to realize prophecies and promises of God.

Faith helps us to understand that the universe was framed and created by the Word of God. The Bible provides a catalogue of servants of God who gained approval because of their faith in God. Hebrew 11 asserts that: by faith Abraham was ready to sacrifice his only son despite God's pledge to him that through his offspring, his descendants would be called; by faith Moses was hidden for the first three months of his life; by faith the Israelites kept the Passover and sprinkled blood on lintels and door posts so that the angel of death would pass over; by faith the Israelites crossed the Red Sea as though passing on dry land; by faith the wall of Jericho fell when the Israelites shouted and blew trumpets; and by faith Rahab, the prostitute, was saved because she welcomed the spies in peace. Faith is the medium for execution of God's creative acts and sustenance of His creation.

Our patriarchs demonstrated great faith when they walked with God. Enoch walked with God and pleased Him, while Noah built an ark that saved his family and wildlife. By faith, Abraham heeded the call of God and left his country for an unknown place of inheritance. His wife conceived and gave birth to a son in old age. God's servants trusted Him for things they hoped for that would not materialize in their lifetime. When we take God at His word, we can do supernatural things.

Faith empowers us to do great works as we walk with God. Hebrews 11 recognizes Gideon, Barak, Jephthah, David, Samuel, and prophets whose acts of faith included subduing kingdoms, administering justice, receiving promised blessings, closing mouths of lions, subduing the power of fire, killing the prophets of Baal, escaping the edge of the sword, victory in battle, putting enemy forces to flight, and raising the dead. In the New Testament, by faith the disciples, Paul, Barnabas, and John the Baptist did great works including preaching the gospel, teaching the Word of God, healing the sick, raising the dead, making the lame to walk, casting out demons, and setting the captives free. We also have the potential to do great works by faith as we walk with Him.

Faith gives us courage to endure adversities as we walk with God. By faith the disciples of Christ were arrested, tried, mocked, flogged, chained, imprisoned, beheaded, stoned to death, crucified, and tortured to death for their faith. Others were sawn in two, put to death by the sword, utterly destitute, oppressed, cruelly treated and they wondered in deserts, mountains, caves, and holes in the ground. As we walk with God, faith gives us steely confidence in God amid difficulties. Whatever storms you are experiencing, trust God who will walk with you through them all. Walking with God does not guarantee a trouble-free life. But faith assures us that God will save us from the curse of decay.

Faith is the basic operating system of God, which couples a believer's heart to the heart of God to initiate and sustain the flow of ideas and resources which we need to access everything we need for life and godliness. It is a medium for communion with God. Faith and its works have an inherent ability to please God, a quality He looks for in believers. *By faith, God has predestinated us to be adopted as His children through Jesus Christ according to the good pleasure of His will* (Eph. 1:5, KJV). Faith enables

Christians to align their lives with the life of Christ and the pleasure of His will.

As God's workmanship created in Christ Jesus, Christians must do good works He planned for them in advance. When faith drives us to do these good works that are conceived according to the good pleasure of His will, we please Him. *But without faith, it is impossible to please Him* (Heb. 11:6, NKJV). Faith provides a framework for recognition and interpretation of the work God has done in us and we must trust Him to help us live it out as we walk with Him. Whatever God planned for you to do can only materialize if you have faith to accomplish it.

Believing in the resurrection of Jesus Christ from the dead is central to the Christian faith and our walk with Him. While God gives every believer a full measure of faith to fulfill a God-given purpose, its manifestation may vary on a continuum from zero to full faith. Our expressions of faith include lack of faith - zero faith or unbelief (Mark 16:14); little faith (Matt. 6:30) or faith as small as a mustard seed (Matt. 17:20); great or strong faith (Matt. 8:10; Acts 11:24); and full faith (Acts 6:5). But there is a threshold of faith below which it cannot produce any fruit. When the disciples failed to heal an epileptic boy, Jesus Christ described them as faithless (Matt. 17:17) and taught them that if they had faith as little as a mustard seed, they could move mountains and nothing would be impossible to them (Matt. 17:20). We must work towards full faith.

Faith is organic because it can grow, increase, and can be strengthened. However, it can also shrivel (Rom. 4:13), fail, can be abandoned or shipwrecked (Acts 27:25; 1 Tim. 1:19) and it can die (James 2:14; 1 Tim. 4:1). Walking with God requires a measure of faith that will translate God's instructions into activities that yield products, and honor and please Him. Consistent communion with Him enables our faith to grow and sustain our discipline of discipleship. As we walk with God, we learn how to examine ourselves to ensure we are keeping the faith, and to test whether it is sincere, sound, or genuine.

Faith is an entry permit to the Kingdom of God. In a city with salvation as a perimeter wall, Christians present faith at city gates to access the Kingdom. No one can become a citizen of the Kingdom of God without faith because salvation is the reward of faith (1 Pet. 1:9). Without faith your entry and resident permit for the Kingdom of God can never be processed. Faith is an access code to the Kingdom of God and its rights and privileges, and products and services. We need faith to start and maintain our walk with God and to dwell in His presence.

Paul refers to the gospel that produces faith as a 'door of faith': *On arriving there, they gathered the Church together and began to report everything that God had done with them and how He had opened to the gentiles a door of faith* (Acts 14:27, NIV). A door of faith does not only open the heart of a person to God, but also opens the door to the throne of God. It breaks down the dividing walls between an individual and God, reconciling us to God. How else can we approach God, except by faith? *Through faith in Jesus Christ, we approach boldly and confidently into God's presence* (Eph. 3:12, NIV). What gives us the boldness and confidence is a suite of credentials wrapped in faith. Through faith in Jesus Christ, we are confident that God is whoever He says He is and will do whatever He has promised to do. The love that obligated God to sacrifice His Son to redeem us from our sinful nature drives me into His open arms and settles me in His presence. His Word promises me life, shelter, peace, joy, love, providence, protection, comfort, health, and deliverance. Does this sound too good to be true? Yet, He has assured us that He is the good Shepherd and we shall not want.

Faith gives us access to the grace of God. Paul assures the Church in Rome that *we have peace with God through our Lord Jesus Christ, by whom also we have access by faith into this grace in which we stand, …* (Rom. 5:2, NKJV). The grace of God, accessed through faith, motivates Him to give us things and the royal treatment we do not deserve. Our walk with God includes standing in His grace. If for a moment, God decided to treat us based on our godless life, would He find anything to merit what He has lavishly given us as we stroll with Him? Grace overrides our deficiencies in meeting the standard of God. While God does not glory in our sin, His grace enables us to access things we need while we go through the refiner's fire.

Declaring an ungodly person righteous based on faith is the most gratuitous act of God, which is overwhelming if one fully understands what it means. Paul, writing to the Roman Church, said, *But to one who does not work, but believes and completely trusts in Him who justifies the ungodly, his faith is credited to him as righteousness.* (Rom. 4:5, NKJV); *For the promise to Abraham or to his descendants that he would be the heir of the world was not through the Law, but through the righteousness of faith* (Rom. 4:13, NKJV). Faith is the gateway to righteousness and a godly life. We are declared righteous through our faith in Jesus Christ who shed His blood for the remission of our sins. An ungodly person who believes and completely trusts in God is declared free from the guilt of sin and its penalty and is placed in right standing with Him. The righteousness of faith is credited to us by faith alone. God's promise to give Abraham and his descendants the whole earth as their inheritance was not based on his obedience of the law or good works, but on the right relationship with God, which comes by faith. Abraham was counted as righteous because of His faith. We cannot walk with God unless we believe and completely trust in Christ who justifies the ungodly.

Contrast justification by faith with justification by the law as pursued by the Israelites. Paul taught the Roman Church that, *the Gentiles who did not seek righteousness, have obtained righteousness which is produced by faith; whereas Israel pursuing the law of righteousness did not succeed in fulfilling the law. And why not? Because it was not by faith, but as though it was by works. They stumbled over the stumbling Stone* (Rom. 9:30-32, NIV). Satisfying the requirement for justification by the Law requires observing all the laws to the letter and no finite being has ever achieved this. We can walk with God because He sees the righteousness of faith in us by virtue of the completed work of Christ on the cross and His resurrection.

Recognizing the lack of capacity to fully obey the Law, God has given us an alternative route for satisfying the requirement for righteousness through faith in Jesus Christ. The Gentiles, who never pursued righteousness, obtained it by faith in Christ. Israel's attempt to attain righteousness by observing the Law failed. By rejecting righteousness by faith in the Son of God, He became her Stumbling Stone. It is only by faith in Christ that we are freed from the prison of the Law.

Justification by faith changes the verdict of the ungodly from 'guilty of sin' to 'not guilty of sin and its penalty', which accompanies the declaration of our right standing with God. Once justified by faith in Jesus Christ, we acquire a new identity and live by faith. Paul sums up the new life this way, *I have been crucified with Christ; it is no longer I who live, but Christ lives in me. The life I live now in the body I live by faith in the Son of God, who loved me and gave Himself up for me* (Gal. 2:20, NKJV). Our sinful nature has been crucified with Jesus giving rise to a righteous man or woman, who lives by faith in Christ. Our walk with God is based on the condition that we are crucified with Christ and are dead to self but alive in Christ, with faith as our foundation.

The righteous have life, which they live by faith (Rom. 1:7). Those who are in right standing with God are grafted on Christ, the vine, and draw their life-supporting resources from Him by faith. Righteousness anchors us in Christ and gives us access to what we need for life and godliness. He gives us His righteousness in exchange for our faith. But we need abiding faith to sustain the righteousness of God which is the source of life. Thus, our faith in Jesus Christ becomes the basis of life for those who are justified. The righteous man who puts his trust in God shall live. God enables us to grow in faith and in His image and likeness as we are cleaned by His Word. Faith is thus a framework through which believers live their lives in obedience to instructions of God. As we walk with Him, our abiding faith sustains the righteousness of God and our life in Him.

As Christians we have a unique access to the power of God that enables us to operate in the supernatural realm through Jesus Christ. Paul assured the saints in Rome that *Christ has redeemed us from the curse of the law, having become a curse for us that the blessing of Abraham might come upon the Gentiles in Christ Jesus, that we might receive the promise of the Spirit through faith."* (Gal. 3:13-14, NKJV). Faith enables believers to access the blessings of Abraham and to avert the curse of the law through Jesus Christ. We have also received the Holy Spirit, who empowers us to live by faith (Hab. 2:4), to witness for Christ on earth (Acts 1:8), and to do good works, which God prepared beforehand for us to do (Eph. 2:10). We need God's power to walk with God on paths of righteousness.

Faith has works as demonstrated by the acts of the apostles and other servants of God. The type of faith that these Christians exhibited was so effective that we are taught to imitate them (Heb. 6:12) and to share it to enter the rest that God has prepared for us (Heb. 4:2). The Bible also highlights following benefits of faith

a) *Faith, in the armory of a believer, is a defensive weapon in our walk with God*: We must wear the full armor of God, which has the shield of faith to stop all burning arrows from the Devil (Eph. 6:16). Every believer needs to study the Word to build faith and trust in God. He instructed the Israelites to keep the book of the Law in their mouths and to meditate on it to prosper and have good success (Josh. 1:8). This enables believers to receive the instructions which guide us in our walk with God.

Meditation is likened to rumination in animals such as sheep and cattle. When grazing, they ingest grass but the nutrients are not accessible to the animal when the feed is intact. To extract the nutrients, the animal must break down the grass into minute particles through chewing and digestion by enzymes. Similarly, we must study the Word of God and meditate on it to extract spiritual nutrients (doctrine, promises, prophecies, teachings), which believers must absorb to prosper have good success. Just as rumination involves breaking down the grass repeatedly to extract as many units of nutrients as we can, we must also repeatedly reflect on Scripture to extract the wondrous truth in it.

When we study the Word and meditate on it, we build components of faith, which collectively produce and sustain the shield of faith. James said, I will show my faith by what I do (Jam. 2:18). We must use the shield of faith as we walk with God. Jesus also applied this principle when He was tempted by the Devil after 40 days of fasting in the wilderness. Each time the Devil tempted Him, He quoted the Law (Luke 4:4, 8, 11). He demonstrated His ability to meditate upon the law and to apply it when tempted. When we walk with God, we become premium targets of the enemy. We need the shield of faith to quench the fiery arrows of the Devil.

b) When we excel in our test of faith, we grow and mature spiritually. Writing to the twelve tribes of Israel, James said, *My brethren, count it all joy when you fall into various trials, knowing that the testing of faith produces patience, but let patience have its perfect work, that you may be perfect and complete lacking nothing* (Jam. 1:2-4, NKJV). Very few people derive joy from trials. We tend to associate trials with judgment of sin, a curse, or poor decisions. People facing trials may even doubt their faith and God's love for them. If we understood what James is asking us to do, we would gladly share his joy in trials. The ultimate goal of a believer is to be perfect and complete, lacking nothing. Trials are mills that process raw Christian converts into mature believers. Count yourself blessed to be a candidate for the refiner's fire, which brings out the pure and perfect godly nature in us. Trials are an essential recipe for our progression to spiritual growth and maturity.

Think of Daniel in the lions' den, Meshach, Shadrach and Abednego in the fiery furnace, and Joseph, Peter, Paul, and Silas in prison. These were not pleasant experiences. But, we must count it all joy when we fall into such trials because they test our faith and produce patience. We need patience to build our pure and perfect God-centered life. Trials test three areas of our faith: knowledge (*notitia*) – content of our faith, fundamental truths (doctrinal content of faith) and propositions that are central to our Christian beliefs; assent (*assensus*) - intellectual conviction that the knowledge we have is factually true and meets our needs; and our trust (*fiducia*) in Jesus as offered in the gospel and complete reliance upon him for salvation. We need to grow and exercise this three-dimensional faith in our walk with God.

As Christians, we must apply a complete three-dimensional faith (comprising knowledge, assent and trust) in all situations. James reminds us that even demons know and believe there is one God (Jam. 2:19, NKJV), but they do not trust Him. In the 1850s, Charles Blondin walked across the Niagara Falls on a wire and people watched him do it several times. One day, he asked the crowd whether they believed he could carry somebody on his back across the Falls. The crowd responded that he could. However, when he asked for a volunteer, he could carry across the Falls, no one was willing to step forward. Trust is the most difficult and distinctive virtue of faith. As we walk with God, He expects us to exercise an all-rounded faith.

Consider these people: a believer whose child is stabbed to death; a woman of God who is divorced because of her faith; a Christian brother who loses his job; a woman who has believed God for a fruit the womb for forty years and yet does not conceive; and a person diagnosed with cancer, among others. These real life trials test our faith for constitution, consistency, commitment, obedience, and our dependence on God. These situations could result in anxiety, depression, frustration, anger, or walking away from faith. Alternatively, they could draw us closer to God. The trials we face reveal strengths and weaknesses, and gaps in our faith. Walking with God exposes our frailties because we are preferred targets of the enemy but God is always ready to steer us through these challenges.

Trials must draw us closer to God through prayers, studying the Word of God, fellowship with the Holy Spirit and the fellowship of believers. These Christian practices help us to understand that there are situations that are beyond our control and to detect gaps in our faith which our God fills. Although trials may appear devastating initially, they help us to eventually calm down and productively reflect on our relationship with God. This process enables us to develop our capacity to use God-given resources to find solutions to our challenges, to rely on God to walk us through the fiery furnace, and to depend on Him to handle trials and their effects. This builds our patience and the capacity to accept or tolerate delays, problems or suffering without becoming annoyed or anxious.

Testing of our faith produces patience, which stabilizes believers as they wait for the promises of God to be fulfilled. The life of a believer needs patience to save the soul (Luke 21:19, KJV) and to keep it focused and stable, steering it through every stormy situation. Faced with trials, patience, and the comfort of Scripture ground us in our hope to inherit the promises of God. A believer who lives by faith needs patience to gradually build and strengthen his faith. The process of building faith through trials and perseverance may involve pain and suffering, but we must allow patience to complete its work to make us perfect and complete.

Without understanding the work of patience or perseverance, believers have naively prayed against, and labored to prematurely terminate this desirable process. James counsels believers to *let patience have its perfect work, that they may be perfect and complete lacking nothing* (Jam. 1:2-4, NKJV). Trials are a desirable component of a believer's process of sanctification and believers should be ready for them as they seek to grow and mature in faith. When we walk with God, our faith is continually tested. Every believer must learn the discipline of managing trials for perfection and completeness of Christian virtues.

c) *Faith-packed prayer brings healing:* God's will for His children is that they enjoy good physical, mental, and spiritual health. When this desired state of health is altered through physical injury, undesirable mental condition, spiritual malaise, infection of the body, or abnormal functioning of body parts, our welfare is compromised. Our faith enables us to recognize God as Jehovah Rapha who heals our diseases. Jeremiah reassured the Israelites that God would restore their health and heal their wounds (Jer. 30:17, NKJV) if they trusted and obeyed Him. They cried to their God in their trouble and *God sent His Word and healed them and delivered them from their destructions* (Psa. 107:20, NKJV). The afflicted Israelites cried to God and He restored their health. Their cry to God was a cry of faith. John also prayed for the saints that they might prosper in all things and in health, just as their souls prospered (3 John 1:2, KJV). But we can only access this healing by faith.

Faith gives us the confidence to pray and fast for healing and deliverance. James encouraged believers to confess their sins to each other and to pray for each other for healing because the prayer of a righteous person is powerful and effective (Jam. 5:14-16, KJV). Faith is the sensor and receptor of the healing power of God. When Jesus saw the faith of the four men who brought their paralytic friend to Him, He told the paralytic that his sins were forgiven and healed his disease (Mark 2:5; Acts 14:9, KJV). Discretely approaching the Lord by faith, the woman with the issue of blood also believed that if only she touched the hem of the cloth of Jesus, she would be healed (Mark 5:28, 34, KJV). Faith gave her the confidence to expect a miraculous healing after touching the hem of the Lord's garment.

Healing has several triggers: the faith of the person praying for the sick; the faith of the people bringing the sick to Jesus; the faith of the person who needs healing; trusting in the finished work of Jesus Christ; believing that Jesus was wounded for our transgressions, bruised for our iniquities, the chastisement for our peace was laid upon Him and by His stripes we have been healed (Isa. 53:5); faith that trusts the Holy Spirit to intercede for us with groanings beyond expression; and faith that recognizes the anointing to heal demonstrated by the Godhead, prophets, disciples and Spirit-filled children of God. This faith releases the healing power of God.

God and His Ambassadors use the healing power differently: God can speak to a condition or send his Word to heal the sick; Jesus used the sense of touch and saliva to heal a blind man; handkerchiefs and aprons that touched Paul were taken to the sick and their illnesses were cured and evil spirits left them (Acts 19:12, NKJV), while the woman with issue of blood touched the cloak of Jesus; a believer can lay hands upon the sick (Jam. 5:14-16, KJV); and the shadow of Peter healed the sick. We must be attentive to the Holy Spirit to tell us what to do.

The different ways of healing demonstrate a unique attribute of the healing power. It works like radioactive material. Jesus Christ carried power that permeated every part of His body, including His clothes. As such, His Word, saliva, shadow, and body carried power that healed diseases. Can you imagine, before Jesus spoke a Word, the demons manifested? The disciples demonstrated these powers by faith and God can still perform miracles through us today.

d) *Faith dares people to launch into the unknown*: Complete trust in God enables us to venture into unknown territories. Children usually trust their parents so much that if they are told to jump into their arms, they instantly do so. Abraham totally trusted God so much that he left his own nation and people for an unknown destination where his inheritance lay (Heb. 11:8, KJV). Abraham was convinced that God would fulfill His promise. Contrast this with our age of meticulous planning in which we want full details of the itinerary, accommodation, food, and the nature and duration of the assignment before we leave their home. Thomas doubted the resurrection of Jesus (John 20:25-28, KJV). His fellow disciples' testimony of the risen Christ was a fairytale until he personally examined Him. We sometimes behave like Thomas when God gives us instructions. If we believe without seeing the evidence, we are blessed.

e) *Faithful service is an offering to God.* Work or service founded on faith is a pleasant offering to God. When we trust God, our job description is derived from His plan of work. *For we are God's workmanship created in Christ Jesus for good works, which God prepared beforehand that we should walk in them* (Eph. 2:10, NKJV). Before we are saved, we do not know our real identity and job description. Citizens of the Kingdom of Satan are assigned duties that satisfy his will, which are different from God's assignments for Christians.

Sinners cannot discern the good works that God has prepared for them because they are inaccessible. However, when we receive Christ and are justified by faith in Christ, we become a new creation. We receive the Holy Spirit by faith, who unlocks our true identity, reveals the good works that God has prepared for us, and empowers us to do them. God has designed us with qualities that match the good works we are meant to do.

Paul prayed that God would give believers power to fulfill every desire for goodness and to complete every work of faith (2 Thes. 1:11). God also gives believers gifts, which they must use according to the measure of faith apportioned to them (Rom. 12:6). Faithful believers discern every good work and use their spiritual gifts to do their work which pleases God.

f) *Faith protects until total salvation is accomplished.* Faith protects believers in their walk with the Lord until final salvation of the soul when the Lord returns (1 Pet. 1:9). When we wholeheartedly believe in the Lord, He fills us with inexplicable joy that does not fluctuate with changes in circumstances, with salvation of the soul as a reward. Faith permeates and controls our every sphere of life, consistently enabling us to live according to the Lord's teachings. God is committed to keep our souls daily by His power until we are totally saved when He returns.

Walking with God means loving Him unconditionally

God is love and He loves us unconditionally. Regardless of our academic, marital, mental, religious, or social status He loves us. Created in the image of God, we are expected to love Him as He loves us. When an expert in religious law asked Jesus which commandment was the greatest, He said, *Love the Lord your God with all your heart and with all your soul and with all your mind"* ... *and the second command is "Love your neighbor as yourself* (Matt. 22:37-39, NKJV). God wants us to engage our whole being (heart, soul and mind) in loving Him and our neighbors.

The mind refers to the portion of a person where the thought process takes place and perceptions and decisions to do good or evil are made. It includes intellect, reason, understanding, or worldview. The mind is associated with intellectual and emotional dimensions of life from the perspective of the whole person. The term soul refers to the spiritual and immaterial part of a person regarded as immortal. It also refers to the whole person, whether physically alive or in the afterlife. The soul is animate, the seat of senses, desires, affections, and appetites. The heart, soul and mind collectively embody the entirety of human life. God knows that we can love Him unconditionally because we have the mind of Christ. Paul instructs believers to transform their minds to do what is good, acceptable, and perfect will of God.

The heart is a library of the Word of God, storing everything love holds. With redeemed heart, soul, and mind, we are commanded to love God completely with everything that makes us alive. If we fully understand how God loves us and how we should love Him, we can then love ourselves according to the measure of love the will of God has apportioned to us. Our love for self becomes the standard for how we love others. Any deviation from this standard distorts measure of love we appropriate to our neighbor. In our walk with God, we enjoy His presence when we love Him and fellow believers according to His standard.

Walking with God means fearing and obeying God

The fear of the Lord is key to cultivating an intimate relationship with God. Moses told Israelites what the Lord required of them: to fear the LORD their God; to walk in His ways and love Him; to serve Him wholly with heart, mind, and soul; to keep His commandments and statutes (Deut. 10:12, NKJV) and to fear God and obey His commandment (Eccl. 12:13, KJV). This is the hallmark of Christian living and our walk with God. Paul said that the Churches he had established were edified and walking in the fear of the Lord (Acts 9:31, KJV). The fear of the LORD should shape our lifestyles. Walking in the fear of God requires us to revere, honor, or respect Him.

Pastor Dr Stuart Pattico stresses that the fear of God is so important that there are at least 144 references to fearing God in the Bible, with 19 of those appearing in the New Testament. What is fear in a Christian context? Some of the definitions are captured here:

- John Parsons defined the fear of the LORD as: *what you have when you receive the revelation of how awesome and powerful God is; walking in the awareness of how awesome and powerful God is, and not daring to sin against Him; an overwhelming sense of glory, worth, and beauty of the true God; and as the sense of awe and respect for the majesty of God.*
- The Institute in Basic Life Principles (www.iblp.org) defines the fear of the LORD as: *the awareness that you are in the presence of a holy, just, and Almighty God, and that He will hold you accountable for your motives, thoughts, words, and actions; and as the desire to live in harmony with his righteous standards and to honor Him in all what you do.*
- The Bible refers to the fear of God as the beginning of wisdom, hatred for evil (Prov. 8:13), wisdom (Job 28:28), and as the fountain of life (Prov. 14:27).

There are several Old Testament references instructing believers to fear the LORD (Deut. 10:20; Neh. 5:9; Prov. 3:7). The fear of the Lord is an essential attribute of a saint. Isaiah prophesied that the Messiah would receive the Spirit of knowledge and fear of the *LORD* (Isa. 11:2). The Holy Spirit leads Christians to fear the Lord. We need to learn and internalize the fear of the Lord, and to grow, live and serve in it. God also instructs believers not to fear.

In the Old and New Testaments, there are instructions and commands not to fear or to be afraid of creatures and other destructive things: do not fear (Jer. 30:10; 46:27, 28; Psa. 23:4); fear not (Isa. 41:10; Deut. 31:6; Job 5:22); and do not be afraid (1 Chron. 28:20; Isa. 41:13b; Deut. 31:6). The Word of God instructs believers not to be afraid, frightened, or scared of creatures and events. The Lord who created and sustains the universe and everything in it watches over us.

The courage and confidence to declare that we are not afraid comes from the LORD our God. Since we live in God and He lives in us, He always provides for us, fights our battles, and walks us through all the storms of life. There is no created being, object or situation that should instill fear in us. Financial difficulties, illnesses, unemployment, business failure, poverty, persecution, marital disputes, ministerial challenges, or family issues should not frighten us.

We must fear God because He disciplines us when we disobey Him, albeit with love. Jesus instructed His disciples not to fear those who kill the body but cannot kill the soul. We should rather fear God who is able to destroy both soul and body in hell (Matt. 10:28). Our fear must be rooted in knowing His ability to discipline and its severity. When the Israelites witnessed the thundering, lightning flashes, the sound of the trumpet, and the mountain smoking as God gave them commandments, they were so terrified that they told Moses to speak to them rather than God or they would die.

Moses said to them, *Do not fear; for God has come to test you, and that His fear may be before you, so that you may not sin* (Exod. 20:20, NKJV). This verse seems to be referring to two different types of fear. Understanding the difference between these two phrases is key to living out the fear of the LORD. The word "fear" is derived from the Hebrew words 'Yirah' and "Yare", which refer to anxiety, terror, dread or worry (Prov. 1:7; 9:10; Psa. 2:11) that comes with the anticipation of pain. But it can also mean wonder, amazement, astonishment, gratitude, glory, worth, and worship. Bakya Ibn Pakuda characterized two types of fears: lower fear of punishment or fear of harm and higher fear of divine glory or awe or fear of greatness.

Martin Luther made a distinction between servile and filial fear. Servile fear refers to dreadful anxiety, fright, terror or worry that grips someone because of a clear and present danger that is represented by another creature (human, beast, microbes) or condition (disease, unemployment, failure). This is the type of fear expressed by a prisoner in a torture chamber or by a slave facing a malicious master who comes with a whip to torment him. John Mallon refers to this as "the fear of getting in trouble." Sinners have every reason to fear God's judgment.

Luther and Mallon refer to the second type of fear as filial fear. The term *filial*, derived from a Latin word which means relating to a son or daughter or concerning a parent-child relationship. This is the type of fear expressed by a child who has tremendous respect and love for the father or mother and who dearly wants to please them. The child fears offending the one he loves, not because he fears torture or even punishment, but he is afraid of displeasing the one who is the source of security and love.

C.S. Lewis describes filial fear as fear filled with awe, in which one feels "wonder and certain shrinking" or a sense of inadequacy to cope with such a visitant or a prostration before Him." Abraham Herschel defines awe as an intuition for the dignity of all things, that things are not only what they are, but also stand, however remotely, for something supreme. Asserting that awe is a sense of transcendence, for the mystery beyond all things,

Parsons explains that when we see life as it is, we will be filled with wonder and awe about the glory of it all. Every bush will be aflame with the presence of God and the ground we walk on will be perceived as holy. The theologian Rudolf Otto refers to filial love as "numinous" to express the type of fear one has for the LORD based on his respect and love for Him.

John Parsons describes another model of fear in the Jewish tradition, which claims that there are three levels of Yirah (fear): the fear of unpleasant consequences accompanied by anticipation of pain and the desire to flee; the fear of breaking God's Law, which motivates people to do good things because they are afraid God will punish them – the believer's motive may be mixed with a genuine desire to honor God or to avoid God's righteous judgment; and the fear based on profound love for God that enables a believer to discern the presence of God in all things, holding God's glory and majesty in all things.

Reverential fear of the LORD elevates believers to a level of awareness, holy affection, and genuine communion with the Holy Spirit. It is anchored in love, which creates spiritual antipathy toward evil, and conversely hatred of evil is a way of fearing God (Prov. 8:13, NKJV). Which type of fear would be most appropriate for a believer?

John Mallow argues that the "fear of the Lord" should be understood as "filial fear"; the fear of offending someone whom one loves. Robert B. Trample says, *There is a convergence of awe, reverence, adoration, honor, worship, confidence, thankfulness, love, and yes, fear of judgment.* Chofetz Chaim also acknowledges that *dreadful fear may deter believers from sin in the short term, but by itself, it is insufficient for spiritual life since it is based on an incomplete idea about God, who is a consuming fire, but also a comforter and a loving God.*

Rabbi Toba Spitzer shares the Hasidic teaching, which claims that Rabbi Simcha Bunem of Pershyscha carried two slips of paper, one in each pocket. On one he wrote, *For my sake the world was created.* On the second, the Rabbi wrote, *I am but dust and ashes.* He would take out each slip, as necessary, as a reminder to himself.

Parson contends that both senses of Yirah are called for in our hearts. We must fear the Lord as our judge and yet be in awe of the cost of redemption. He stresses that we should be afraid of stumbling and dishonoring God with our lives, and hence we should be vigilant, alert, awake, mindful and attentive to the presence of God in all things. Everyone who stands before us is created in the image of God and Martin Buber regards such a person as a reminder of God's presence. Parson concludes that a reverent and focused attitude means "practicing the presence of God in our daily lives".

How did Jesus handle fear? Isaiah prophesied that He would receive the Spirit of knowledge and fear of the LORD. Was Jesus Christ afraid of the LORD? No, He wasn't. Did He fear the LORD? Yes, He revered, adored, honored, worshipped, thanked, and loved, and had confidence in, and stood in awe of the LORD. While we fear judgment, we are not expected to be afraid of the LORD, but to reverently fear Him as a child fears a loving father. But just as Christ was aware of the fear of the LORD, we also ought to be aware of judgment that comes with disobedience.

Jesus relied on the Holy Spirit to fear God and hate evil. Jacques Forget asserts that the gift of the Holy Spirit fills us with sovereign respect for God, and makes us dread, above all things, to offend. We are invited to call Him Abba Father and to have personal intimacy with Him, but we should know that God could be frightening. John writes, *There is no fear in love; but love casts out fear, because fear involves torment* (1 John 4:18, NKJV). Jesus Christ was judged for our sins and His perfect love in us casts out fear. Our love for God drives away our desire to commit sin.

Anybody who fears the LORD hates evil, keeps God's commandments, is wise and confident, stands in awe of God and serves in the fear of God, rules in the fear of God, is a fountain of life, has access to the mercy of God and the secrets of God, lacks nothing, walks in His ways, fears no evil and is always with God. Believers who fear God are delivered from all fears, cast all their anxieties on Jesus, trust in the LORD, are rich in God's everlasting mercy and are blessed. They delight in God's commands and are never put to shame. When we fear God, we will forget the shame of our youth because we are adopted sons and daughters of God. The fear of God embodies trusting Him, intimate fellowship and knowing His name.

Every disciple of Jesus Christ is instructed in the fear of God and is not afraid when destruction strikes. Such believers are not afraid of the beasts of the earth and speak up without the fear of man. As they fear the splendor of God, they are honored and fulfilled. With a fear-free heart, they are not afraid of bad news or the terror of the night but enjoy communion with God. As they delight in the fear of the Lord, their hearts are secure in His name. These selected features characterize the nature and attributes of a believer who fears God.

The fear of the LORD should start with a reverent heart that feeds every sphere of a believer's life with the right type of fear. A life lived in the fear of the LORD firmly secures our position in the presence of God.

Walking with God means living a life contentment

Any believer walking with God must learn to be content in life regardless of the circumstances. This contradicts worldly culture. Jeff Manion, the author of a book, *Satisfied*, asked a very difficult question 'Is there ever a point when we become satisfied with who we are, what we have, and even what we do not have?" Several scholars have grappled with this question and concluded that human wants and needs can never be satisfied.

Adam Smith and Lionel Robbins assert that humans never get enough things because natural resources are too little to meet unlimited human needs. An anonymous scholar argues that *Throughout history, there is no documented case of anyone ever becoming completely and absolutely satisfied.* He concludes that when unlimited needs and wants are matched with limited natural resources, a fundamental problem of scarcity arises.

To address the problem of scarcity, Smith suggested that we should *optimally combine* different resources to produce enough goods and services to meet diverse human needs. Other scholars have urged humans to *choose* what they really want and what is necessary in life and be happy with it. Despite all efforts to satisfy unlimited human needs, many scholars have concluded that limited natural resources cannot meet all the human needs and wants. Will humanity ever resolve this problem?

The issue of scarcity of resources has been compounded by the fact that humans are not the only inhabitants of the earth. Moreover, we live in consumer-driven, debt-ridden, and advertisement-saturated culture, which strives to lure people into buying things that were not originally in their budgets. The world, especially in its advertisements, is pushing the overuse of our appetites all the time. When we turn on the television, we are bombarded with commercial advertisements of products and services. However, the ability of nature to provide for humanity has been undermined through overharvesting of resources (water, plants, animals, fish), pollution, land degradation, and climate change or environmental decay.

Is it true that throughout history there are no cases of satisfaction of human needs? No, it is not true. Paul, Job, and Jesus lived lives of contentment. They and several other believers understood the secret of living a satisfied life regardless of the circumstances. What can we learn from them? Jesus Christ said, *Watch out and guard yourselves against every form of greed; for one's life does not consist in abundance of things he possesses* (Luke 12:15, NIV). Jesus totally agrees with secular scholars that human needs and wants can never be met from resources that nature provides because they were not designed to meet all the needs defined by the fallen nature of humanity.

Jesus pinpoints the problem with Smith's approach to meeting the human needs, which is three-fold: no amount of riches or abundance of possessions can ever satisfy all human needs; expressed needs are only part of what man needs; and the secular perception of human needs and wants is coloured by greed. Human needs quantified by secular scholars are inflated or exaggerated by greed– they are not a true reflection of what humans need.

Jesus teaches us that Adam Smith and other scholars are addressing the wrong question because the full set of human needs consists of biological/psychological and spiritual needs. Needs are biological/psychological requirements for maintaining life (such as food and water, shelter, and clothes), while wants are psychological desires (such as movies, music, jewels) that are not essential for life, but that make life more enjoyable. Humanity must embrace all types of needs to reach a required level of satisfaction. We will look at these issues separately.

Jesus warned a young rich man (Matt. 19:16-22) and other people to watch out and guard against greed. What is this greed and why should we guard against it?

> Greed is a selfish or excessive desire for more of something than needed. (Merriam-Webster Dictionary)

> Greed is inordinate and insatiable longing, especially for wealth, status or power. (Anonymous)

> Greed is an inordinate desire to acquire and possess more than one needs. (Wikipedia)
>
> Greed is a bottomless pit, which exhausts a person in an endless effort to satisfy the need without ever reaching satisfaction. (Enrich Fromm)
>
> Greed is a state of restlessness of the heart, and it consists mainly of craving for power, possessions, or status. (Meher Baba)
>
> Greed is a sin against God, just as all mortal sins, in as much as man condemns things eternal for the sake of temporal things. (Thomas Aquinas)

The definitions of greed given above have one thing in common: craving for more things than we need. The degree of craving is related to inability to control the formulation of wants once the desired needs are met. This is complicated by the fact that whatever we do to fulfill our needs always results in partial fulfillment of desires. The partially unsatisfied needs fan and increase the flame of inordinate desires instead of extinguishing them.

Greed may result in inability to sustain the costs or burdens associated with what has been or is being accumulated, which could backfire or lead to self-destruction or ruining other things or people. Paul said, *But those who want to get rich fall into temptation and are caught in a trap of many foolish and harmful lusts, which pull them down to ruin and destruction. For the love of money is a root of all sorts of evil, and some by longing for it have wandered away from faith and pierced themselves with many sorrows* (1 Tim. 6:9-10, NIV). People who crave for riches are easily tempted to indulge in sinful acts to satisfy their inordinate desires.

We tend to accumulate things that we don't need. A comedian, George

Calin, once said, "*a house is just a pile of stuff with a cover on it. We place our stuff in the house and leave it while we go out and get more stuff.*" Let us look at our wardrobes, shoe racks, houseware, appliances, and other possessions in our homes. Do we really need all these things? Do we have decent clothes which no longer fit but are just there in our wardrobes for admiration? If not restrained, our fallen nature tends to scavenge and hoard materials or objects. Greed can drive us to defraud, steal, trick or manipulate people and authorities to satisfy our greed.

Greed can lead people to afflict themselves with many sorrows. Think of businessmen or women who so desperately want to win a contract that they are willing to bribe someone. Consider the desires of an employee who steals from the employer to buy landed properties.

What makes a married man or woman commit adultery? What would drive somebody to buy three flat screen TV sets when s(he) only needs one or two? What would make a person buy food that will end up in the bin? Why buy clothes that you may not wear? Such inordinate desires do not only abuse resources, but they also deprive others of their goods and services.

A BBC News report suggested that if everyone on the planet consumed as much as the average US citizen, four Earths would be needed to sustain us. Can you imagine a world where people buy or use only what they need? Mahatma Gandhi said, "There is sufficiency in the world for man's need, but not for man's greed." Greed is a cancer that is destroying God's creation. After the rich young man failed the disciples' test, Jesus knew how troubled his heart was, and hence warned those craving for riches to guard against greed. How must believers address the problem of unlimited human needs?

We need to deal with greed. But humans are trapped in a bubble of greed and cannot free themselves. This is an age-old problem that even the early Church grappled with. In Ephesus, one of the wealthiest cities and a renowned center of learning, the first generation of Christians wrestled with commercial advertisements of goods and the vice of greed. They had to learn how to live a contented, deeply satisfied life while they were bombarded with spending options.

Freedom from the grip of greed will take nothing less than a total transformation to adopt the heart and mind of Jesus regarding what we have, what we need and what we want. The heart, attitude, and mind determine how we formulate our wants once needs are met.

Jesus Christ teaches us to understand that true life is not derived from the abundance of things. A few decades ago, societies in some African countries assessed the net worth of an individual based on three things: a car, a house, and money. Jesus Christ overturns this mentality. He taught his audience that he who lays up treasure for himself but is not rich toward God is like a rich fool. He demonstrates that contentment is having a heart that is satisfied and alive with God.

Our culture of consumerism tells us to amass things and every effort is expended on devising means and technologies to achieve this, but Jesus considers this as fraud. He provides us with the only genuine and effective way of meeting human needs (Matthew 6:33). His model teaches us several things. Firstly, our priority should be to seek God's kingdom and His righteousness. Once we become citizens of the Kingdom of God, He provides for us, while we reverence Him and obey His commandments. This involves knowing our identity as God's workmanship, discerning good works we are created to do and doing them. We use the gift God has given us to do good works according to His grace and the measure of faith given to us.

When we seek first the kingdom of God and His righteousness, *all other things* are be added to us. The phrase "all other things" refers to everything a believer needs to live a fulfilled life. Contrary to our cultural belief that unlimited human wants can never be met in full, Christ assures us that all our needs and wants perceived through the lens of the Kingdom of God and His righteousness will be added to the life of a believer. All things relating to every sphere of life including family, education, ministry, business, career, and marriage will be added to you if you follow the teaching of Jesus Christ.

Peter assured the saints that God's *divine power has given to us all things that pertain to life and godliness, through the knowledge of Him who has called us by His glory and virtue, by which have been given to us exceedingly great and precious promises, that through these we might be partakers of the divine nature, having escaped the corruption that is in the world through lust* (2 Peter 1:3-4, NKJV). The power of God has provided believers with everything they need to meet their biological/psychological needs. This is possible through our knowledge of God who has called us and given us promises to partake of the divine DNA of God. However, the divine power of God has rescued us from the corruption of the world through lust. Having escaped the corruption of the world, we no longer perceive needs and wants through greed.

Thirdly, when we seek first the Kingdom of God and His righteousness, all other things shall be *added* to us. God adds all things (riches and righteousness) to a believer's portfolio of assets. Possessions are the products or fruits of a life lived by faith. They are blessings that God bestows on those who live a life yielded to the Lord. Can a farmer harvest a crop of maize if he never tilled the land, planted maize, and nurtured the crop? Will a businessman expect a profit from an enterprise he has never invested in?

Moses outlines the blessings that accompany acts of obedience when he says, says, *Now it shall come to pass, if you diligently obey the voice of the LORD your God, to observe carefully all his commandments, which I command you today, that the LORD your God will set you high above all nations of the earth. And all these blessings shall come upon you and overtake you, because you obey the voice of the LORD your God* (Deut. 28:1-2, NKJV). This Word summarizes the source of riches: they are blessings that come upon God's children because they obey the voice of the LORD their God. God reminded Israelites that He gives power to earn wealth that He may establish His covenant, which He swore to their fathers (Deut.

8:18, KJV). Christians, like Israelites, are guaranteed blessings as adopted descendants of Abraham through the covenant He made with him. If this is the established way of getting wealth, all other means the world uses are illegitimate and hence the failure to meet all human needs and wants.

Riches do not control a heart yielded to Christ. But a heart filled with love for wealth has no room for God. Jesus teaches that true life does not consist of earthly riches, but reverence for God. What does it mean to be contented or satisfied?

Paul's description of contentment is sobering. *Now godliness with contentment is great gain. For we brought nothing into this world, and it is certain we can carry nothing. And having food and clothing, with these we shall be content* (1 Tim. 6:6-8, NKJV). Contentment comes from a sense of confidence based on the abiding presence and sufficiency of God in the life of a believer is great gain. True contentment is derived from the image of God in us and not from the external environment of a believer because man brings nothing on earth and will take nothing when he dies. With this attitude, we should be content if we have food and clothing.

Paul shares his secret of contentment in his letter to the saints at Philippi when he said, *Not that I speak in regard to need, for I have learned in whatever state I am, to be content. I know how to be abased, and I know how to abound. Everywhere and in all things, I have learned both to be full and to be hungry, both to abound and to suffer. I can do all things through Christ who strengthens me* (Phil. 4:11-13, NKJV). Paul shares salient features of contentment. Firstly, contentment is neither inherited nor naturally acquired. Paul *learned* to be satisfied with what he had. We can be satisfied in all situations. Whether we have or do not have money and whether hungry or full, ill, or well, rich or poor, married or single, president or a sweeper, whether able-bodied or disabled, we should be content with what we have, who we are and where we are if we are in Christ.

Secondly, contentment is realistically attainable. This contradicts economic theories that suggest that human wants are unlimited and cannot be fully satisfied. Thirdly, both to be full and to be hungry, both to abound and to suffer, are part of the life cycle of a contented believer. Some modern theologians teach that poverty, hunger, and suffering are indicators of sin, while abundance or prosperity is a sign of a healthy Christian life. However, Paul explains that believers can experience both poverty and wealth depending on what the Lord's purpose for our condition is. He can use both to test our allegiance to him. If Paul was always contented in all situations, his satisfaction was not determined by circumstances. He learned to live above all circumstances.

Fourthly, contentment always and in all situations is not a state that a human being can achieve in his own strength. Christ is the only source of strength that can carry a believer through cycles of abundance and lack. Paul's declaration, *I can do all things through Christ who strengthens me* (Phil. 4:13, NKJV), implies that he mastered both lack and abundance through Christ. It is not surprising that the world thinks satisfaction is an illusion because it does not have access to divine power. Fifth, Paul learned to be satisfied with what he had. True contentment is not having all you want, but wanting only what you have. This extinguishes the flame of craving for more. But what brought Paul to this level of satisfaction?

Paul redefined his identity and his course of life to gain what he valued most, Christ. He said, *I count all things but loss for the excellence of the knowledge of Christ Jesus my Lord; for whom I have suffered the loss of all things, and count them but dung, that I may win Christ"* (Philip. 3:8, NKJV). This is what drastically transformed Paul to gain victory over different life situations. Paul shed off all things that could constitute needs in his culture in exchange for the excellence of knowledge of Christ his Lord. The things that the world values most (wealth, status, power) became worthless.

When we live our lives in union with Christ, we are so filled with Christ that we no longer live, but Christ lives in us. Contrary to craving for unlimited wants the world strives to satisfy we give up everything to gain the infinite knowledge of Christ in our hearts. Abiding in Christ and His abiding in us means that no condition that we face comes up without the approval of Christ. We are also guaranteed divine power to face any condition at any time. We derive our satisfaction from gaining the excellence of knowledge of Christ. Our sole desire should be to win Christ, the source of our contentment.

For Paul, Christ was the need. Do we see the attitude of Christ in Paul? After Jesus had finished talking to the Samaritan woman at the well, the disciples returned from their errand and had a chat with Him. When the disciples asked Jesus Christ to eat, He said to them, *I have food to eat of which you do not know. ..., "My food is to do the will of Him who sent Me, and to finish His work* (John 4:31-34, NKJV). Jonh suggests that: disciples were surprised that Jesus Christ was not keen to eat; His main preoccupation and source of contentment was doing the will of the Father and to finish His work. He was so full of His Father that He literally lived out His will. Anyone who desires to walk with God must learn the secret of contentment.

Walking with God involves stewardship

As we walk with Him, God expects us to steward His earthly creation. God made man in His image, after His likeness, to primarily rule over the works of His hands in the air, on the land and in the sea. The Godhead gave humans the cultural mandate to rule over the earth and everything in it when they said, *Let us make man in Our image, according to Our likeness; let them have dominion over the fish of the sea, over the birds of the air and over the cattle, over all the earth and over every creeping thing that creeps on the earth* (Gen. 1:26 NKJV). After six days of creative activities, God saw everything He had made, and indeed it was very good (Gen. 1:31). As the creator of the earth and everything in it, God owns and loves His creation, but He delegated its care to humankind.

David, in his Psalm, reiterated this mandate when he said, *You have made him to have dominion over the works of your hands; You have put all things under his feet* (Psa. 8:6). But the mandate to have 'dominion' over God's creation does not mean that humans can use or manage creation as they will. The term 'dominion', in this context, means loving and caring for creation as the owner would. Genesis 2:15 emphasises this aspect when it says, *the LORD God took man and put him in the garden of Eden to tend and keep it* (Gen. 2:15 NKJV). Similarly, humans had to till the ground and it had to rain before any plant of the field was in the earth and before any herb of the field could grow (Gen. 2:4-5). Christians have a mandate to keep and care for creation as they walk with God.

Walking with God involves knowing Him and seeking Him diligently

Ask anyone who has sustained a stable and vibrant relationship with God, and they will stress the importance of knowing Him well. Simply knowing about God is not adequate for a life with Him. We must know Him personally. When we know about God, we have an abstract or speculative thought concerning God or mystical experiences based on limited knowledge and understanding of who God is, and His likes and dislikes.

The package of eternal life includes knowing the LORD our God and Jesus Christ. John underlined the significance of knowing God as an eternal principle when he said, *this is eternal life, that they may know You, the only true God, and Jesus Christ whom You have sent* (John 17:3). It refers to God-man experiential relationship. Humans are wired to know God. Knowing Him is not optional for saints.

Knowing God begins when we become alive to God by turning away from our sins and trusting in Jesus and His atoning death on the cross for the forgiveness our sins. When we are born of the Spirit into God's Kingdom, we can see, perceive, understand, or know God. As we walk with Him, we grow to know Him more deeply after new birth. A new convert to Christianity goes through a development cycle of knowing God from an infant to a mature believer in Christ (1 Cor. 2:6; 3:1). John identifies three types of believers in this cycle: little children who know God but not very well; young men or women progressing toward maturity; and fathers or mothers in Christ, mature believers who have faithfully walked with

God for decades and whose life is characterized by seeking God diligently (1 John 2:12-14). On Mount Sinai, Moses cried out to God, *If I have found favour in your sight, please show me now your ways, that I may know you* (Exod. 33:13).

Knowing God deeply is not automatic. It takes time and effort. Paul had known Christ for many years, yet but his passion was to know Him better. He revealed this when he said, *Not that I have already obtained this or am already perfect, but I press on to make it my own* (Philip. 3:12). God has made a provision for us to know Him through His Son - whoever has seen me has seen the Father; and through creation – He has revealed His invisible qualities (His eternal power and divine nature) through the earth, the sky and all that He has made.

Straining and pressing on to know God is embedded in the deep work of God in our hearts, arousing hunger and desire and drawing us to engage our will and strength to seek Him. Paul urged the Philippians to work out their own salvation with fear and trembling, for it is God who works in us both to will and to work for his good pleasure (Philip. 2:12–13). This can only happen when the Holy Spirit empowers us to transcend the greatest earthly desires.

God told Israel that, *You will seek me and find me, when you seek me with all your heart* (Jer. 29:13). *Ask, and it will be given to you; seek, and you will find; knock, and it will be opened to you* (Matt. 7:7). Jesus assured His disciples that those who seek God will find Him. He gives everything we need to grow into deeper fellowship with Him and His Son, but we must embrace it. The Lord gives us the Word, but we must study it. Yielding to the power and authority of the Holy Spirit allows Him to teach, nurture, guide, and encourage us to know God. He reveals Christ and our Father to us in ever-deeper ways.

The Scriptures are our only reliable source of knowledge about who God is; what He is like; what His will is; what His plans and purposes are; what He has done in the past; what He will do in the future; who we are; what life is all about; how we can know, love, and serve Him; and His promises how they will be fulfilled. Apart from providing building components of our faith in Him,

Scriptures are God's ultimate and final authority for what we are to believe and how we are to behave. They are our lifeline in this fallen world.

Walking with God involves recognizing that He is a personal God who created us for Himself and longs for an intimate relationship with us. Through prayer we spend time alone with Him, communicate with him, and trust and follow him daily. A prayerful saint will know the mind of God because we need to pray according to His will. As we walk with God, we continue to develop a relationship with Him enabling us to stand in His grace.

An answered prayer is an affirmation of the convergence of the will of man with the will of God. Whether God's answer is a 'yes', 'wait' or a 'no', it draws us closer to Him and enables us to understand the things He approves, those that need to wait for the right time of execution, and those He disapproves. C.S. Lewis said prayer doesn't change God, it changes us. Through prayer, God directs our lives, reveals the purpose for our lives, and guides us to discern and do good works He prepared for us before time. Apart from helping us to draw near to God and to commune with Him, prayer invites the Holy Spirit into our lives to reveal the Godhead, His will, His love, His power and glory, and His majesty to us. This mode of communication with God: helps us to gain an understanding of God's nature; helps saints to become like Jesus and to develop a relationship with Him and our heavenly Father; and invokes the power of God through His miraculous workings. It unleashes and displays His omnipotence. We must pray to know God better.

Every human being created in the image and likeness of God has an inert potential to seek and know God. Awakened by our salvation through faith in Jesus Christ, our deep-seated passion to know God is activated. The LORD also yearns for us to seek Him. The author of Chronicles urged the children of God to look to the LORD and his strength and to seek his face always (1 Chron. 16:11). He also said, *Now devote your heart and soul to seeking the LORD your God....* (1 Chron. 22:19). Nearing the end of his ministry, Paul's greatest passion was to know Christ and the power of his resurrection and to share his sufferings

(Phil. 3:10). He still longed to know God deeply. Regardless of how long or how well we have known the Lord, there is always room to know Him more.

Knowing God more deeply has not been the privilege of only a few luminaries in the Old and New Testament times. God calls all His people to know Him personally and love Him supremely with heartfelt devotion. God delights in His people who truly know Him, love Him, and enjoy the blessings of His faithful love, justice, and righteousness. In our daily lives, we can know God better by committing ourselves to: worship God every Sunday in an orthodox church; meditatively study and live out Scriptures daily; maintain a disciplined life of prayer and fasting; to be filled with the Holy Spirit each day; seek to walk in the Spirit and manifest the fruit of His presence in your life; spend time with the Lord whether in need or in time of blessings; and embed yourself in the fellowship of believers; and read books and articles that are likely to help you know God better.

Walking with God involves committing ourselves to a disciplined and God-centred life. We must strive to understand His desires and values so that we are moulded to express His will and purpose for our lives. As we walk with Him, we learn to observe His principles and the discipline of discipleship.

CHAPTER 6

What is God's commitment as we walk with Him?

Walking with God is a privilege as a believer must live in and with God. The Lord desires that our walk with Him is fruitful and enjoyable. He invests in the life of a believer to ensure that a rich and loving relationship continues to grow. He sovereignly does certain things to reveal Himself to us and ensure our walk with Him is pleasant and honourable. His works, which build and sustain us in our walk, are briefly explained.

God cleans man with the blood of Jesus and His Word. Once we were alienated from God and were enemies in our minds because of our sins. We were helplessly destined for eternal hell fire because the law requires that nearly everything is cleansed with blood and without the shedding of the blood there is no forgiveness of sins. But the LORD sacrificed His Son and cleansed us from our sins with His blood. The blood of Jesus, which gives us access to the presence of God, also cleanses our consciouses (Heb. 9:14), purifies us from sin (1 John 1:7), makes atonement for our lives, and makes us holy (Heb. 12:13).

The Word of God also cleanses us from our sins. Jesus told His disciples that they were clean because of the word that He had spoken to them (John 15:3). Paul also charged Timothy to continue in what he had learned and become convinced of. He stressed that *all Scripture is God-breathed and is useful for teaching, rebuking, correcting, and training so that the man of God may be thoroughly equipped for every good work* (2 Tim. 3:16). As we walk with the Lord, He uses the Word to teach us Kingdom principles and practices, rebuke and correct us when we stray from our paths of righteousness, and to train and equip us to do good work in His vineyard. Everyone who walks with God is cleansed with the blood of Jesus and the Word of God.

God deposits an imperishable seed through the living and enduring word of God. God has deposited a precious treasure in the life of every believer who walks with Him. This gift of immeasurable value is the incorruptible seed that abides forever (1 Pet. 1:23, NKJV). A seed is a reproductive unit, which carries hereditary material from its parents. In our natural environment governed by natural laws, human 'seed' eventually dies because its source is perishable. The Word of God, the expressed will and creative thought, carries the eternal germ of life that begets a child of God with eternal life.

God is eternal and that which flows directly from His being into human soul, through truth, has an eternal nature. God gives His children His Word and the Holy Spirit to dwell in them and they engender eternity in the life of a believer. God seals believers with the Holy Spirit *who is the guarantee of inheritance until the redemption of the purchased possession, to the praise of His glory"* (Eph. 1:13, NKJV). The Holy Spirit is an instalment of the inheritance to come and a sign that we are His children. Believers who walk with God carry the incorruptible seed of God.

God chooses potential believers according to His foreknowledge. Believers who walk with God do not stumble into Him, but they are a product of God's long-term plan for human redemption. Writing to the Church at Ephesus, Paul said, *Just as He chose us in Him before the foundation of the world, that we should be holy and without blame before Him in love, having predestined us to adoption as sons by Jesus Christ to Himself, according to the good pleasure of His will* (Eph. 1:4-5, NKJV). This Scripture does not imply that God has favorites. He chose His children before the foundation of the earth based on his prior knowledge of the response of every human being to his invitation for adoption as His children through Christ.

In union with Christ God chose every believer to be holy and blameless just as He is. He made a provision for us to attain this level of spirituality through the sacrificial death and resurrection of Christ and the ministry of the Holy Spirit. God predestined us to be His adopted sons through Jesus Christ according to His pleasure and will. As we walk with God, we should remember that it was God's initiative to choose us, adopt us as His sons, and to sanctify us. What a privilege!

God protects believers who walk with Him: A major privilege of believers who walk with God is His guaranteed protection in His presence. While encouraging the saints to thank God for the living hope in rich blessings which God has kept for them in heaven, Peter also said, *They are for you, who are kept by the power of God through faith for salvation ready to be revealed in the last time.* (1 Pet. 1:5, NKJV). This Scripture underlines four key truths. First, there are rich blessings that God is keeping in heaven for His people. They are secure and cannot rot, spoil, or fade away. Second, believers are protected by God's power against all forces of evil that would destroy their lives (2 Tim. 4:18; Jude 1:24, KJV). Amid persecution of believers in his audience, Peter assured them of God's protection. Believers take refuge under God's canopy of protection.

Third, God protects believers who have faith in Him. His protective power is only accessible by faith. Living faith in Christ is an essential condition for enjoying God's continued protection. Fourth, the goal of God's protection of believer is salvation to be revealed when He returns. The eyes of the Lord watch over the ways of the righteous (Psa. 1:6, NIV).

God shepherds those who walk with him. When a person walks with God, he or she accepts the LORD as the Shepherd. David confidently declared that he would never lack anything because the LORD was his Shepherd. God is caring, loving, merciful, selfless, compassionate, and generous to his own flock. He knows every sheep by name and always gives us a sense of worth and belonging.

With the welfare of sheep as His primary concern, the Shepherd sacrifices His comfort and fights for their welfare. He always stays with them giving them the best care they need. When they are stressed, He comforts, calms, encourages, instructs, protects, and blesses them beyond measure. When the sheep disobey His instructions, He lovingly corrects and disciplines them. In the Middle East the shepherd tends his flock, identifying and meeting their needs. The welfare of sheep entirely depends on the nature and character of the Shepherd.

The Bible provides several examples of a good shepherd. A major responsibility in caring for the flock is the feeding and watering of lambs and sheep. Equipping His disciples for ministry Jesus Christ stressed these responsibilities of a good shepherd when he spoke to Peter after having breakfast with His disciples (John 21:15-17, NIV). Jesus Christ asked Peter to feed His lambs and to tend and feed His sheep.

Jesus places so much value on His followers that it becomes the criterion for measuring Peter's love for Him. How committed are we in teaching our children, young believers, and other followers of Christ the Word of God? How devoted are we in tending God's flock as shepherds - pastors, deacons, elders, group leaders, husbands, wives, parents, managers, heads of department, and any type of leader?

David knows that the Shepherd makes the sheep to lie in green pastures (Psa. 23:1), a source of fresh, nutritious and succulent feed, and a place of tranquil and rest where the sheep can ruminate. God feeds His children on the truth with potential to satisfy our every need. After grazing, the Shepherd leads sheep to the still waters because they need water to digest their food and absorb nutrients in their stomachs. The 'water' is a metaphor of the Holy Spirit that removes the filler of the Word to expose the wondrous truth, the active ingredient a believer needs to live by faith.

When the soul is distressed, the Shepherd restores it (Psa. 23:3, KJV) by encouraging, comforting, affirming, and soothing it through the Word and counselling of the Holy Spirit. The Shepherd leads the sheep in paths of righteousness by teaching and guiding them to do what is right on all its trails. There are different spheres of our life that need to comply with the way of the Lord, including instructions regarding salvation and sanctification, relationship with God, family relationships, marriage, bringing up children, giving, business, career, and ministry, among others. The Shepherd watches over all spheres of our lives.

The great Shepherd guards His sheep and guarantees their peace and freedom as they walk on dangerous trails frequented by predators, using his rod and shepherd's crook (Psa. 23:4, KJV). As Christians, we face different challenges in life, but God is always guiding us to take right decisions as we pass through the storms of life. God uses the rod of authority to protect, guide and keep the sheep on the trail. He also uses the staff to rescue sheep that fall into pits and to catch sheep that need attention or treatment.

The Shepherd provides safety, freedom and peace as sheep pass through fire and troubled waters. The shepherd prepares food for his sheep amid their enemies. The pastures are not naturally found in enemy-free zones. They are carved out of territories that harbour enemies as well. The Shepherd prepares the table – finds, manages, and secures fresh pastures and water for sheep amid their predators.

The enemies (bears, lions, cheetahs, leopards) watch as the sheep rest in the pastures, but they can't attack them because the Shepherd is there to protect them. He is ready to fight and lay down his life for sheep (John 10:11) and to rescue them from the jaws of their enemies. As Christians, we are always stalked by the devil in our marriages, families, businesses, colleges, and even in the Church, but the Shepherd secures our table.

David acknowledges that the Shepherd anoints him with oil and His cup overflows (Psa. 23:5, NIV). The oil serves three functions: it expresses the great value of the anointed; bestows authority and power derived from the source of the anointing; and protects the anointed. Oil is also a valuable health remedy for sheep. Shepherds apply oil and spices on the heads of sheep to protect them against harmful insects. When the Shepherd prepares the table for His sheep, provisions always exceed the sheep's requirements and hence the cup overflows.

The shepherd ensures that sheep are in good health. In the early stages of my career, I learned how to diagnose sheep diseases and parasites, and how to treat them. Using the Shepherd crook, I would restrain sheep by their hind legs to examine them for different health conditions: parasites and diseases, injuries, and overgrown hooves. Based on the diagnosis, I would treat them for diagnosed diseases and parasites. Similarly, our good Shepherd always examines us for any biological, psychological, and spiritual conditions that affect His flock and treats them.

Every sheep is so precious that when it strays from the flock, the shepherd leaves the rest to search for the lost one and greatly rejoices once he finds it. His desire is to always gather the flock and ensure it is intact. God values us regardless of our social status and He is always searching for lost souls to bring them back to the fold. Whenever shepherds neglect their sheep, they easily scatter and become food for beasts. Any genuine shepherd will detest the loss of any of his lambs or sheep, and the Great Shepherd is no exception. God, speaking through the Prophet Isaiah, said,

> *"Woe to the shepherds of Israel who feed themselves! Should not the shepherds feed the flock? You eat the fat and clothe yourselves with wool; you slaughter fatlings, but you do not feed the flock. The diseased have you not strengthened, neither have you healed that which was sick, neither have you bound up that which was broken, neither have you brought again that which was driven away, neither have you sought that which was lost; but with force and with cruelty have you ruled them. So, they were scattered because there was no shepherd and they became food for beasts of the fields when they were scattered."*

(Ezek. 34:1-5, NKJV).

God was angry with the shepherds of Israel for they exploited the flock. Unfortunately, this problem still exists in the Church today. There are shepherds who feed themselves on sheep and their resources but neglect their spiritual and physical needs. The diseased and the broken-hearted do not receive the care they need. The shepherds rule over them with force and brutality that leaves the sheep utterly distraught and vulnerable. Some of the victims have become so disillusioned by the exploitative behaviour of their shepherds that they have become an easy prey for predators or have abandoned the faith. God pledged to seek out His flock that the shepherds of Israel scattered and to deliver them from all places where they were scattered. He vowed to bring them to their own land and feed them in good pasture. As under shepherds, how have we tended or scattered God's flock? For flocks that have been scattered through negligent and exploitative behaviour of unfaithful shepherds, there is hope because our good Shepherd values every lost sheep, and he will find you and place you on His green pastures.

CHAPTER 7

Noah preserves human and wildlife as he walks with God

Have you ever considered seriously the fate of innocent Christians who are persecuted for practising their faith? Have you ever been frowned upon when doing God's work and warning people against disobeying God's commandments? Noah walked with God in a wicked generation and built a sanctuary for preservation of human and wildlife during the flood. As people watched Noah building the ark, they mocked him and could not listen to his message of hope asking them to return to the LORD. What did Noah do as he walked with God in this perverse generation?

Noah walked with God in a wicked world

Noah's generation was so wicked that God was filled with indignation and regretted having made people on earth (Gen. 6:1-6). The primary function of humans was to rule over the fish in the sea, the birds in the sky, the livestock, and wild animals, all the earth, and over all creatures that move along the ground. But this mandate was compromised because of human wickedness including worshipping pagan gods, sexual immorality, oppressing the poor, and cruelty in warfare. The Israelites abused God's blessing on humanity to be fruitful and increase in number, and to fill the earth and steward it.

Intermarriages between descendants of Seth (sons of God) and female descendants of Cain (daughters of men) resulted in a corrupt and violent earth. The humans, livestock, and wildlife, which were part of the very good universe God created to praise, worship, and glorify Him were so corrupted that their original purpose was greatly compromised. God's response to desecration of His creation was that of grief, regret, and judgment. But, amid this wicked generation, Noah worshipped and served God.

What distinguished Noah from the rest of his generation?

Amid widespread wickedness of those days, Noah found favour in the eyes of

God (Gen. 6:8). There are two ways of explaining this favour. First, Noah enjoyed divine favor because of his righteous and blameless disposition. *These are the ones I look on with favor: those who are humble and contrite in spirit, and who tremble at my word* (Isa. 66:2, NIV). This view suggests that Noah's pleasant character attracted God's favor. However, some theologians and believers argue that this theory contradicts biblical passages (Psa. 14:1-3; Rom. 3:9-18, NIV), which declare that no one is righteous. So, did Moses contradict the rest of the Bible?

Second, God's favor produced a good character in Noah. He was a very good man, but the good attributes were no better than what the grace of God made in him. Mark Driscoll and Henry M. Morris III suggest that everyone one, including Noah, was a sinner in those days, just like we are today. Noah was not an exemplary individual because he bypassed the fallen nature we possess.

Morris believes that the vignette of Noah's drunkenness recorded in Genesis 9:20-27 (NIV) was not the only instance of impropriety, Noah was born with a sinful nature like any of us. However, God's grace upon Noah accounts for divine favor toward him, without which he would have perished with other sinners during the flood. Nonetheless, Noah was keen to love and worship God. This gives us hope that God can favor any of us if we are open to commune with Him.

The two theories explaining God's favor toward Noah are not mutually exclusive. God still saw something in Noah that glorified and honored Him. Mark Driscoll stresses that Noah found grace in God's eyes because he was actively looking for it.

Noah, a righteous man (Gen. 6:9, KJV), was justified by faith in the promised Messiah. He is revered as one of the exceptionally righteous in the history of God's people. Twice God declares that Noah, Daniel and Job are men who could be saved by their righteousness in a sinful country if He judged by the sword, plague, famine or wild beast that kills people and their animals (Ezek.

14, KJV). However, there are two types of righteousness in the Bible: absolute righteousness, which the Lord demands for anyone to stand before Him in glory and only those who precisely obey all His commandments at all times belong to this class. Only God is absolutely righteous (Rom. 2:21-22, KJV).

The second type of righteousness is given to believers by virtue of their salvation and sanctification. Noah's faith in God made him righteous relative to the condition of his generation. He was a preacher of righteousness who courageously called people to repent and avert the approaching destruction. However, people rejected Noah's call, and only his wife, and three sons and their wives boarded the ark with him.

Noah was a perfect (blameless) man among the people of his time (Gen. 6:9). God loves people whose lives are upright: *For the eyes of the Lord run to and fro throughout the whole earth to show himself strong on behalf of those who are perfect toward Him"* (2 Chron. 16:9, NKJV). The Matthew Henry Commentary stresses that '*He was perfect, not with sinless perfection, but a perfection of sincerity."* By virtue of the covenant of grace based on the righteousness of the Messiah, sincerity is accepted as perfection.' Augustine, in his book *In the City of God* (15.26), says *Noah was not perfect in his generation – not indeed with the perfection of the citizens of the city of God in that immortal condition in which they equal the angels, but in so far as they can be perfect in the sojourn in the world. It is Noah's openness, humility, and selfless giving of his all to God that allows Him to direct him.*' God pursues us as our hearts are given to a life of integrity.

Noah walked with God (Gen. 6:9, KJV) and communed with Him. He lived a God-centered life, resembling our true vine – branch relationship in Christ (John 15:1-8, NKJV). Noah's walk with God was a product of surrendering his life to God and allowing Him to live in and through him. Genesis 4-6 describes his lifestyle, which demonstrates God's grace and mercy, righteousness, obedience to God's law, justice, and unconditional love for the Father. As a faithful and trustworthy servant of God, he actively communicated with God, sharing knowledge and experiences. As God's creation, Noah offered acceptable sacrifices and observed His covenants. He diligently obeyed the voice of God and His commandments.

As Noah faithfully walked with God, he was entrusted with the responsibility of building an ark for preservation of selected humans, livestock, and wildlife for repopulating the earth after the flood. He was expected to carry out God's work in an environment that was hostile to his faith. It is easy to live a God-centered life when Christianity is in fashion, but Noah constructed the ark regardless of the hostile environment.

Noah was a just man. Morris III says, even in a wicked world that disgusted God the creator, Noah was justified by his equitable dealings with others. Apart from charging reasonable prices for his work, he offered his employees good conditions of service. Noah's honest dealings contributed to his influence in his community.

John Calvin said, *They are called just not who are in every respect perfect, but who cultivate righteousness, purely and from their hearts* (Logonier Ministries – Teaching of the Fellowship of R.C. Sproul). From God's perspective, Noah was a man of no condemnation, above reproach despite the opposition he might have faced from people in his own generation.

Noah was a faithful man (Heb. 11, KJV). He is included in the "Faith Hall of Fame", an indication that he was considered as a role model of faithfulness and that his faith pleased God (Heb. 11:6, NKJV). *By faith, Noah being warned by God of events as yet unseen, in reverent fear constructed an ark for saving of his household. By this he condemned the world and became an heir of righteousness that comes by faith* (Heb. 11:7, NKJV). Noah built the ark in about 100 years because God who revealed the unseen future event to him was the object of his faith. Noah had every reason to doubt God's command to build the Ark. The task pertained to a very distant future event and there was no visible evidence that what Noah believed would occur. The course of things (weather, life, matter, and natural laws) was very much against what Noah believed. However, he trusted God and believed that the ecological catastrophe He had predicted would happen. Noah's reverence for God convinced him to construct the ark for keeping his family and wildlife. His trust in God and his preparation for the flood showed Noah's wisdom and the folly of the rest of his generation. Through this act He obtained an inheritance that comes by faith.

Noah was God's confidant (Gen. 6, KJV). God made him the man of His counsel, sharing with him His plan and purpose of destroying the wicked world by floodwater just as He revealed to Abraham His resolution to destroy Sodom and Gomorrah. Amos concludes, *Surely the Sovereign Lord does nothing, unless He reveals His secret to His servants the prophets* (Amos 3:7, NIV). The Holy Spirit reveals plans and purpose of God's activities to those who walk with Him.

God trusted Noah as a friend and shared with Him his heartache about the wicked earth, His plan was to bring the floodwater to destroy all life, and to preserve his family and pairs of animals of every species on earth. The responsibility of undertaking the most complex wildlife preservation project ever assigned to an individual showed the highest level of trust, confidence, and faith that God had in Noah.

Noah was obedient to God (Gen. 6:22). Noah followed all the instructions God gave him to build the ark, gather food to feed his family and wildlife during the flood and to keep selected wildlife with him. As a descendant of Seth, he was a product of generational obedience and faithfulness toward God. While he lived amid the most heinously evil society the world had ever known, he showed that humans could obey God in any environment. Have we found ourselves in situations where God has asked us to do what appears to be a very complex task?

Noah worshipped God (Gen. 8:20). After the flood, Noah built an altar and offered a burnt offering from every clean animal and bird species. He worshipped God as soon as his family and all the wildlife got off the ark emphasizing the primacy of worship. His decision to build an altar before constructing his own dwelling place, to sacrifice unblemished clean animals and birds, and his desire to worship God resulted into a smooth aroma in the nostrils of God. This quality sacrifice made God to vow never to curse the ground for man's sake. If we were to model our lives after Noah, we would seek the Kingdom of God first (Matt. 6:33) after a major rescue.

Noah was a man of God's covenant (Gen. 6:18-21). Never had God entered a formal covenant with humankind as He did with Noah. The substance and terms of conditions of the covenant employed Noah and his descendants to preserve humankind, livestock, and wildlife species during and after the flood. The covenant would ensure that the course of nature continued beyond end times, and by God's grace, He would be God to Noah and that out of his seed, He would take a people for Himself.

God spared Noah as a vessel for fulfillment of His plan to send the Messiah and to redeem the wicked world. God made Noah a great blessing to the world – a form of messiah. God transits humanity from the unwritten covenant of works with Adam in the Garden of Eden to the covenant of grace with Noah, knowing that the human heart is inclined toward evil at all times. We, like Noah, are products of the covenant of grace through Jesus Christ.

Noah as God's conservationist

When God looked at the wicked world, He was so enraged that He decided to destroy humankind and all wildlife He had made on earth. He employed Noah to preserve his family and at least a male and female of all species of wildlife on earth to repopulate it after the flood. What was the significance of the flood and the role of Noah in God's rescue plan for humanity and wildlife?

The depraved human mind corrupted the earth

The wickedness of humankind corrupted God's creation. A disorganized, evil, and violent human government ruined and distorted the nature and the functions of the land, livestock, and wildlife. Everything stood in sharpest contradiction with that good state which God the creator had established. Moral and spiritual degeneration in Noah's world undermined creation's ability to praise, worship and glorify God. A depraved human race does not only destroy itself, but also degrades wildlife and its habitats.

A wicked human heart rebels against God, disregards and dishonors fellow human beings, and abuses God's creation. At the core of environmental crises, wars, oppression, slavery, moral decay, and injustice is the inclination of the human heart toward evil. In the 21st century scientists claim that unprecedented human pressure has undermined the stability of the earth and its ability to support human development.

In 2009, scientists introduced nine planetary environmental boundaries which define safe zones of human development: climate change; ozone depletion; ocean acidification, biogeochemical flows; Biosphere integrity; atmospheric aerosol loading; land use change; freshwater change; and chemical pollution. We have already exceeded the boundaries of climate change, land system change, biosphere integrity, fresh water change, biogeochemical flows, and novel entities.

Our planet is amid its sixth mass extinction of plants and animals. Scientists estimate that we are losing species at 1000 – 10,000 times the natural background extinction rate of one – five species per year. At this rate, 30-50% of species could be heading for a mass extinction by mid-century.

Development, especially in the West, has come at the expense of the poor. In 2017, 689 million people (9.2%) of the world's population lived on less than US$1.90/day, did not have access to clean water (UN, 2017), and went to bed hungry (FAO, 2015). Industrialization has polluted water, air, and land, and adversely affected humans and wildlife.

The current global average concentration of carbon dioxide (CO_2) in the atmosphere is 421 ppm as of May 2022 (0.04%) compared to pre-industrial value of 280 ppm in the mid-18th century (NOAA, 2022). The effects of environmental and socially unjust development, and climate change are disproportionately borne by poor people, especially those in the developing world.

In the Old Testament, prophets attributed ecological catastrophes (e.g. droughts and famines) to human disobedience to God and abuse of His creation. Creation groans as humans continue to implement development economic models, which reduce God's creatures to mere raw materials for human development and dehumanize poor people. Just as the corrupted human race in Noah's time abused God's creation, western civilizations have in the last 500 years placed people at the center of development.

Within the societies, there are glaring inequalities resulting in a huge gap between the rich and the poor. The richest 1 percent account for nearly two-thirds of all new wealth worth ($42 trillion) created since 2020, almost twice as much money as the bottom 99 percent of the world's population (Oxfarm, 2023). While ordinary people are making daily sacrifices on essentials like food, the super-rich have outdone even their wildest dreams. It concludes that this concentration of wealth at the top is holding back the fight to end global poverty.

Business and economic models of human development have removed creation care from the centre of our vocation and numbed our sensitivities to the needs of the poor, loss of species and destruction of God's creation. While scientists believe that a radical shift in our mindset from a linear to a non-linear approach to human development will address environmental crises, Scriptures trace the origin of these crises to the thoughts of the human heart that are always inclined toward evil. Most of the issues humanity is facing in the 21st century stem from rebellion against God.

God's judgment of the corrupt human race and the earth

God who created a very good earth and its inhabitants saw that it was so defiled in Noah's time that it had lost its original purpose. From the time Adam and Eve started their family outside the Garden two distinct lines of descendants, Sethites (godly people) and Cainites (wicked people) emerged. However, Sethites abandoned their worship of the Lord, opening themselves to intermarriages with Cainites. The wickedness in Noah's time was so heinous that God decided to destroy the humans, livestock, and the defiled wildlife.

The Sovereign LORD could have commanded the earth and its inhabitants into extinction, erasing the entire creation. But He chose to purge and keep the earth, and to preserve Noah's family and at least a pair of every species of living things with life in them. Neither did God destroy Adam and Eve and the non-human creation after the fall in the Garden. These two episodes suggest that God's desire has been to keep His creation despite its scars. God never abandoned His creation despite the rebellious nature of His people. Even when it was defiled by human corruption, He still chooses to preserve the seed of human, livestock, and wildlife species.

Despite bringing floodwaters to the earth to destroy all flesh that had breath in it, God looked forward to its ultimate salvation through the death and resurrection of His Son. The flood would cleanse the earth of the evil human race and wildlife to allow for a fresh start. The submerged earth is symbolically cleansed and baptized. The flood allows Noah and his family to witness the fate of a corrupt earth and to gather testimonials about God's love and mercy to preserve, and His wrath on disobedient descendants.

Noah, God's conservationist

God's desire was to keep selected human, livestock, and wild animal genetic material to repopulate the earth after the flood. Noah, a righteous and faithful servant, is the God's ordained conservationist to rescue human and animal species from the flood. God employed Noah to implement His conservation plan and his family to assume the role of a custodian of His creation. This was the most complex conservation project ever undertaken by a human being and yet it was effectively delivered. How did Noah achieve this?

Construction of the ark: God instructed Noah to construct the ark according to his specifications. It was designed to ensure conditions (space, ventilation, feeding and drinking facilities, sanitation, temperature) were suitable for keeping his family, and selected livestock and wildlife indoors for a year while the earth was flooded. This massive structure, constructed over a period of about 100 years amid insults and violence tested Noah's faith, but he obeyed everything God commanded him to do. As Noah built the ark, he also warned people of the coming judgment, but it never made sense to them. This monumental symbol of mercy and salvation was despised just as people reject Christ and the evidence of His judgment today. We need to consider the signs of His coming.

Gathering of food for people and animals on the ark: God instructed Noah to gather enough food to feed his family of eight and pairs of every species of livestock and wildlife for the duration of the flood. Building such a food store required knowledge of types, quantities, and quality of food/feed for each species. I believe Noah needed to feed these animals well to keep them in good health and reproductive state. Can you imagine how challenging this task was? Yet Noah did it.

God invited Noah to board the ark with his family, livestock, and wildlife. As the Captain of the ark, he gathered and brought with him humans and animals according to the checklist God gave him (Genesis 7:2-3, KJV). God's conservation strategy was to maintain genetic diversity of all livestock and wildlife species; keep all species of both clean and unclean animals, stressing that every species is valuable and precious in His sight; He instructed Noah to keep more pairs of clean animals and birds than unclean animals based on the numbers used for sacrifice; and Noah preserved quality breeding stock of birds and animals to repopulate the whole earth after the flood.

God renewed the mandate given to Adam to care for birds, livestock, and wildlife. Noah brings with him his family in the ark to preserve the human species. God starts afresh with the only family that obeyed and trusted Him and entrusts it with care for representatives of current biodiversity. This family would reorient creation to glorify God.

For one lunar year, Noah and his family cared for all livestock and wildlife on the ark. They fed them and ensured that conditions were suitable for their growth and maintenance. I believe the family learned the behavior and individual management requirements of the animals. God allowed them to know, appreciate and love them and their habitats. The experience they acquired on the ark would be useful in their care for creation after the flood. Livestock and wildlife, which suffered abuse in a wicked world, are now looked after by a righteous and faithful family enabling them to worship God.

After spending a year in the ark, Noah's family, livestock, and wildlife safely disembarked from the ark. Every human being and animal that had sought refuge on the ark with him survived the flood just as everyone who abides in Christ will overcome the world and will survive His judgment. God opened the door of the ark to release human and animal species on a purged earth, but dramatic events happen to mark the reoccupation of the earth. After leaving the ark, Noah built an altar to the LORD and offered burnt offerings of some of all clean animals and clean birds on it (Gen. 8:20) of his own free will. He offered the highest order of a sacrifice in the OT rituals to acknowledge the sinful nature of humanity and renew a relationship between humanity and the holy God.

The sacrifice was complete satisfaction of God's righteous requirement of substitutionary atonement of sin. This was a foreshadow of Jesus Christ, the perfect sacrifice for sin. The smell from the altar ascended as pleasant aroma, which made God vow never to curse the ground and to destroy all living things although every inclination of the human heart is evil from childhood. God commits himself to sustain the earth and its systems by His mercy and grace.

Second, God pronounces a blessing on Noah and his sons to be fruitful, increase in number and fill the earth, just as he blessed Adam. He places the beasts of the earth, birds in the sky, every creature that moves on the ground, and all the fish in the sea in the hands of Noah and his sons. God also provides guidelines on human food. God's desire is to restore the community that existed before humans rebelled against God just as He always wants us to care for His creation.

Third, God establishes His covenant with Noah and his descendants, and with every creature that was with him in the ark, that He would never again destroy life and the earth by floodwaters (Gen. 9:8-11). He makes an unconditional pledge to sustain His creation. While humans are to care for creation, God establishes a covenant with each species to stress that ultimate preservation of species is not to be tied to the behavior of humans. He seals His covenant with a rainbow, a symbol of hope for human and non-human creation. The descendants of Noah entered into a covenant with God at Mount Sinai, while we have one with Christ.

God has always demonstrated His desire for a righteous human race to care for His creation (Gen. 1:26-28; 2:5, 15). In a world that strives for human-centered development, the true value of the rest of creation is elusive. Everything exists because the Creator loves and sustains it, and His Son died for all creation to be reconciled to Him. The neglect of creation in Noah's time and the 21st century provides credible evidence of the effect of human wickedness on creation. Unfortunately, the Church has not quite grasped a holistic gospel that views the death and resurrection of Christ as God's initiative for restoration of both human and non-human creation.

PART 3
What are the challenges facing Christians in the 21st century?

Christians in the 21st century are facing unprecedented challenges. Advances in science, technology, and multimedia have improved the quality of human life. But these developments have come with serious challenges to Christian life. Dechristianisation of institutions, secularisation of nations, persecution of Christians, pursuit of pleasure, antichristian ideologies, antichristian environment propped by science, technology, and media, among others, have contributed to persecution of Church. The situation is compounded by false teachings and divisions within the body of Christ. In the Western world, these challenges are haemorrhaging the Church. Understanding this environment in which Christians practice their faith is key to living a faithful life. What are these challenges and how do they impact Christian life in the 21st century?

PART 3
What are the challenges for the Christians in the 21st century

CHAPTER 8

Science, technology, and multimedia: a challenge to the Christian faith

Science as a lens for what is good for society

The shift in the balance of power from a faith-led to a science-led society has, in many countries, created a hostile environment for devout Christians. We are living in a society, which views science as the filter to determine what is true and good for humanity. Western civilization argues that decisions must be based on verifiable evidence and dismisses Christianity as an unreliable, destructive, and retrogressive worldview. Science has become a convenient resource atheists and the media are using to dispute the existence of God, the deity of Jesus Christ, and the authority of the Bible.

Some people believe that God's existence should be proved using empirical studies by testing hypotheses. Without such evidence, the credibility of the Church is questioned, and godly principles, values and spiritual concepts are brutally dismissed as myths or illusions. In a society obsessed with science, people easily embrace propositions tagged with scientific principles.

At its inception in 1660, the Royal Society adopted as its motto "*Nullius in verba*', which means 'take nobody's word for it." This motto expresses the desire of the founding fellows of the Society in the UK to counter political and religious authorities and stresses the need to verify all statements by an appeal to facts determined by experiments. This evidence-based approach to decision-making has increasingly filtered into different professions (e.g. education, law, medicine, and business) and institutions. Some of the world's eminent scientists have claimed that science can explain everything while faith cannot explain reality.

Philosophers such as David Hume and Immanuel Kant argued against the existence and nature of God based on alleged lack of empirical evidence. David

Hume provided two standard questions for testing any proposition: *Does the proposition contain any abstract reasoning concerning quantity or number? Does the proposition contain experimental reasoning concerning fact or evidence?* If the answer to these questions is No, such propositions needed to be committed to fire because they were merely sophistry and illusions.

Hume also argued that all knowledge is reducible to two things, knowledge or propositions generated through sensation and reflections on ideas in the mind. How does this view relate to Christian faith, existence of God, the authority of the Bible, or God's revelation through creation? It rejects Christian truths because they can't allegedly be empirically verified.

Can science test the existence of God?

My understanding of science and Christianity persuades me to argue that the two areas are not mutually exclusive. I believe that science is a tool that God has given us to explore, understand, and keep wonderful creation, which He has entrusted to our care. We are only one of the creatures in the universe and our understanding of nature is limited unless God equips us to study and understand it. Science was not designed to test metaphysical hypotheses to prove or disprove the existence of God, deity of Jesus Christ or the authority of the Bible.

The division between science and faith is a social construct, which hinders our holistic understanding of nature. In God's vocabulary, there is neither a scientist nor a theologian. God created humans in His image and likeness to think and act like Him. We are either fallen or saved individuals. The false dichotomy between science and faith could be attributed to the fact that 'sinners do both science and theology and are prone to mistakes'.

Mechanical approaches to theological investigations have yielded knowledge, which has sometimes contradicted Scriptures because the assumptions are flawed. Scientific studies are based on existing matter and hypotheses restricted by human boundaries of matter, natural laws and logic associated with the existence and functioning of natural elements. These limit us to things we can feel, see, taste, hear, and touch. Understanding God and His creation involves studying the physical nature and metaphysical reality which is beyond what science can explain.

Both scientists and theologians understand very little about the earth we inhabit, let alone the rest of the universe. All our studies are conducted within the time and space of created nature. Our scientific theories and principles are based mostly on samples of matter, which do not always give the full picture of what exists. While science explains some natural elements and processes, it is only one of the tools. It would be tragic to consider science as 'the' tool for understanding reality.

My experience with science is that discoveries come with hidden layers of unexplained effects, which surface after a while. Consider DDT, a chemical that was first synthesized in 1874 and used in World War II to control insects that carried malaria and typhus. After the war, DDT was promoted as a wonder-chemical capable of controlling different agricultural pests. In recognition of his discovery of the high efficiency of DDT as a contact poison against several types of insects, Muller was awarded the Nobel Prize in Physiology or Medicine in 1948.

As a secondary school pupil in Zambia, I learned in my agricultural science lessons that DDT was a very effective pesticide against various potato beetles, codling moths, maize earworm, cotton bollworm, and tobacco budworm, among others. Agricultural extension workers in many parts of Africa advised farmers to use DDT to control pests. Little did we know that the wonder-chemical had adverse effects on human health and nature. It was not until Rachel Carson published the book *Silent Spring* in 1962 that environmental impacts of indiscriminate use of DDT in the USA were catalogued and the logic of releasing large amounts of this potentially dangerous chemical in the environment was questioned.

Scientists later discovered that DDT had devastating effects on human health and was finally banned for agricultural uses worldwide under the

Stockholm Convention on Organic Pollutants in 2001. Forty years after banning this chemical, people in the US were still living with its long-lasting effects. Its breakdown products were present in several foodstuffs and in 99% of tested human blood samples. Studies by the President's Cancer Panel revealed that girls exposed to DDT before puberty were five times more likely to develop breast cancer in middle age.

There are several other major discoveries which have contributed to global environmental crises: fossil fuels are now blamed for climate change; chemicals in refrigeration appliances were responsible for depletion of the ozone layer; and industrialized agriculture increased agricultural yields, but at the expense of soil, vegetation, water, and air quality. These major scientific and technological developments have ended up harming humans, plants and animals, and their environment. As the number of discoveries increases, our intellectual inadequacies also increase.

We should also be aware of scientists whose major objective is to prove that God does not exist, and the Bible is just a storybook. They have invested a lot of resources in peddling falsified scientific knowledge, which does little to provide credible evidence for or against the existence of God. There are credible academic theologians (e.g. David Wilkinson, John Polkinghorne, William Lane Craig, Alistair McGrath) who seek to provide in-depth understanding of theology. But atheists (e.g. Richard Dawkins, Sam Harris, Christopher Hichens, Stephen Hawking, Susan Blackmore) and agnostics (e.g. Jennifer Michael Hecht, Paul Zachary Myers, Dan Barker) purposefully use science to advance anti-Christian views.

The 21st century is churning out many scientific breakthroughs, which could be used to challenge Christian beliefs. While science is a useful tool for understanding nature, it is not the only tool for understanding reality. We also need methods for exploring metaphysical reality. A major challenge is recognizing the benefits of constructive science, while recognizing its limitations.

Toxic literature against Christianity

The 21st century is witnessing an increased circulation of very hostile literature aimed at undermining Christian beliefs and values. As knowledge increases, considerable volumes of literature are offloaded in the public domain; these challenge the authenticity of the Bible, the deity of Jesus Christ and the existence of God. Apart from unbelievers who have invested vast resources to discredit Christianity, some theological writings also challenge this worldview. They counter the comfort of commonplace Christian ideas, principles, values, and practices.

Critics of Christianity and the Church understand that literature is one of the most effective ways to engage culture. We also know that reading literary works allows us to test all things (1 Thes. 8:21, NKJV) and to hold on to what is good. What motivates critics to challenge Christianity and the Church? They argue that challenging Christianity achieves four things. First, criticisms reveal biases and blind spots of Christianity. Critics allege that faith is a metaphysical sleight of hand, in which a believer's prejudices are smuggled away into the supernatural world to avoid criticisms. They use our psyche to explain the complexity of the universe, which blurs our perception of natural reality. Analysis of Abrahamic faiths provides a glimpse of the psychological architecture of humans.

Second, challenging the Christian worldview is seen as a noble duty of every citizen to bring out the truth and expose falsehood. Third, criticizing Christianity is intellectually rewarding to sceptics who derive pleasure from dealing with the difficult issues. Finally, there are people who absolutely hate Christianity and are determined to discredit it.

Some writings portray Christianity as a violent, corrupt, superstitious, polytheistic, stubborn, and intolerant faith. Politicians, philosophers, ideologists, and some theologians have criticised traditional Christian doctrines, beliefs, and practices feeding into the secularist agenda. Scholars who apply to Biblical documents the same analytical methods applied to literary and philosophical text have produced controversial literature questioning the validity of biblical texts.

In a culture that systematically seeks to discredit Christ, the *Da Vinci Code*, serves this purpose. Dr Erwin Lutzer observes that this novel is the most serious assault against Christianity that he has ever witnessed. What made him arrive at this conclusion? Dan Brown, the author of the novel, makes two very serious conspiracy theories. First, he alleges that Jesus Christ married Mary Magdalene. After the death of Jesus Christ, Mary supposedly flees with their child, who later becomes a symbol of the "sacred feminine" of paganism.

Second, Brown asserts that the cannon (Bible) was put together under the direction of the Roman Emperor. He alleges that the Roman Emperor Constantine sifted through the ancient gospels and chose the ones that suited his political agenda, creating what we have as the Bible. Lutzer identifies major flaws in this conspiracy theory. The author totally overlooks the fact that the Nicene Council of Augustine, which chose the gospels in the Bible sat after Constantine's death.

The *Da Vinci Code* researchers admit that the study of gospels faced serious methodological constraints: "In order to find them (facts), we realized, we would be obliged to read between lines, fill in certain gaps, account for certain caesuras and ellipses. We would have to deal with omissions, with innuendos, with references that were, at best oblique." Although Brown claims that, "all descriptions of artwork, architecture, documents, and secret rituals in this novel are accurate," the novel contains serious factual inaccuracies and is grossly misleading.

Let me also briefly refer to Friedrich Nietzsche's atheism, which was viewed as complex and the most comprehensive critique of religion ever assembled. He hated Christianity and his writings were described as extremely violent, hateful, and corrosive. Nietzsche sees Christianity as:

- fundamentally anti-scientific, based on obscuring and denying physical truth: a power premise for avoiding all threatening questions of scientific nature.
- emphasizing wrong values for mankind, preferring weakness, a herd mentality, or a false morality, individual genius, and honesty.

- a religion formed by the refuse, castoffs, and disenfranchised rabble.
- a degenerate movement composed of reject and refuse elements of every kind.
- a religion that is steepened in sickness and illness.
- a sacrifice of freedom, all pride, and self-confidence - subjection, self-derision, and self-mutilation.
- a religion that is entirely metaphysical, tainted with fundamental dishonesty in the face of the physical world.
- a great curse and the one great innermost corruption.
- the triumph of the unthinking lowest classes of the herd - domestic animal, herd animal, the sick human – animal, the Christian.

Nietzsche believed the Roman Empire might still be standing today had its progress not been derailed or undermined by the early Christians, who brought inevitable dark ages to Europe. He also bemoaned the unprecedented tragedy that the emergence of Christianity ruined many of the ancient world's scientific achievements. What sparks such derogatory views about Christianity?

At times people attack the Church because it cannot endorse activities or practices that contradict its doctrines, values, and principles. In a culture that teaches us that the meaning of life is found primarily in sexual fulfilment and satisfaction, biblical prohibitions on homosexuality are considered harsh and cruel.

Occasionally, academic and research platforms have been used to advance personal anti-Christian agenda. The problem is that the innocent people who read publications from such dishonest authors fall prey to their destructive ideologies. Many people reading publications that dismiss Christianity as a misguided and oppressive religion have no time and ability to investigate the factors fuelling animosity against the Church.

There are authors who have carved out theological niches that generate a body of literature, which neither supports nor disputes the existence of God.

This category of literature provides theological arguments that question certain aspects of Christian beliefs, but seem to accept others, sending mixed messages. This position leaves some readers in a dilemma.

Some critics provide erroneous Biblical interpretations to fuel academic debates, which they use to advance their own agenda. Society is presented with complex theological narratives and contradictions. Such writings have not only confused Christians but have also justified false theological ideologies and countered the Christian faith. Not only have these arguments fortified the resistance of unbelievers to the gospel of Jesus Christ but have also prompted some Christians to doubt the existence of God. This happens when eminent people in the Church and society, who have a large following, champion controversial views. The conspiracy theories plant seeds of doubt in the reader's mind about God and the Bible, a direct assault against Christianity.

At times theologians and Christians criticize mediocre work of fiction and secular publications but they also publish literature that teaches that God's Word can't be trusted in all the 66 books, especially Genesis. The sad truth is that not every reader has the capability to objectively analyse the anti-Christian narratives and to weigh the evidence against the Word of God. Some people are desperate for an excuse not to believe in God and His Word. As Christians we are facing this toxic body of literature every day.

Abuse of technological advancements

The current generation is witnessing the fastest technological developments that humanity has ever seen, which are increasingly idolised by unsuspecting and vulnerable people. The aggressive electronic and print media, entertainment industry, social media and gaming industry are robbing society of its life. Television networks have a variety of programmes to keep children and adults glued to the screen for 24 hours. If you love sports, there are enough events on TV for the whole week, but Christian programmes are very few. These activities usually replace quality family communion. We have become slaves of our own technology development. These entertainments have disrupted family associations, devotions, academic activities, and togetherness.

Apart from reduced time of interactions between spouses in homes, children have developed their own technosphere, creating a relational distance between them and their parents. The devices that are keeping our children busy include computers, TV, Xbox, PlayStation, Nintendo, mobile phones, and iPads, among others. Many children lock themselves up in their bedrooms to play these games. Some of these gadgets allow them to play remotely with their friends and hence develop their own virtual world that totally excludes parents and siblings, who are viewed as intruders.

Many children, especially in western countries, are so addicted to gaming that it has become their default life. At school, they discuss games they played the previous night and update each other on the latest games on the market and those about to be launched. As soon as they get home, they cannot wait to switch on their gadgets and everything else becomes immaterial.

Some children love movies so much that they have bought or rented them using their parents' bankcards without permission. For others, music is their hobby, and they spend much of their time searching for free downloadable music. These different forms of entertainment keep vulnerable children away from the gospel or from activities that enrich their Christian faith.

Spending long hours watching TV and playing games with minimum interaction with people has serious implications for the social development of children. A study conducted by Ohio state University researchers, reported in the Daily Mail (November 23, 2013:21), concluded that television may have a direct effect on mind development by presenting the child with superficial portraits of characters and situations that only require superficial processing to understand. The bad news is that children watching such portraits while minimally interacting with people take longer to develop an understanding of other people's thoughts and emotions.

Stunted social and mental development means that children do not actively participate in social relationships and could easily resort to aggression as a means of achieving their goals. Children develop their theory of mind to attribute mental states — beliefs, intents, desires, emotions, and knowledge — to themselves and others. When they achieve their theory of mind, they can engage in more sensitive, cooperative interactions with other children and are less likely to resort to aggression as a means of getting what they want. Can we speak to our children about the programmes they watch to ensure they interact with diversified groups?

The problem of children spending hours glued to television, android, and iPad screens alone in their rooms is increasingly becoming a common feature in a busy career world. The gadgets occupy the child while parents do their work. Some parents use social screens as pacifiers, babysitters or to stop tantrums. The more parents become engrossed in their work than family relationships, the more we bring up children who are aggressive and emotionally brittle. The irony is that they may grow up detesting anything to do with people living or working together. This, unfortunately, affects how they respond to the gospel of Christ.

Assessing the impact of smartphones on the health of children, Jonathan Haidt (2024) explained that smartphones are addictive, disrupt sleep, fragment attention, and deprive people of real-world interactions. He argues that brains of youngters who use them during the vulnerable developmental stage of puberty are changed as a result, causing an epidemic of mental illness in the young. There is a strong link between heavy social media use and illnesses, especially in girls. But tech companies are designing a firehose of addictive content that has displaced physical play and in-person socialising.

Many teenagers consistently interact with their peers on mobile phones and other electronic gadgets. In her Evening Standard article (22 March 2024), Anna Davis explained that heavy social media users receive on average one interruption every minute. Even when they are meant to be doing their homework, they frequently take their eyes off books or laptops to send a message, take a call, or exchange e-mails with their colleagues. As they wash dishes, hover in the house, or clear the table after a meal, they often take breaks to check or send text messages. A task that would normally take less than 30 minutes may take almost an hour. Anna Davis argues that this constant fragmentation of attention takes a toll on adolescents' ability to think and may leave permanent marks in their rapidly reconfiguring brains. Parents may have to closely monitor their children to ensure that they are not completely overtaken by the winds of civilization.

Children are not the only victims of new technology. In 2014, a newspaper featured a very disturbing story about a woman who fell off a pier because she was so glued to her phone that she didn't realise she had walked to the edge. It took the skills of the lifeguards to rescue her. This is not an isolated case. Another woman in Beijing was so busy texting that she walked straight into a fountain and fell into the water.

The social media has posed a very serious challenge to parents because it is very difficult to closely monitor what children can access. Meta-Facebook, You Tube, WeChat, Tik Tok and WhatsApp are some of the platforms people use to quickly share useful information. However, they are also used to share materials that could corrupt our minds. Some people have followed their children, family members, celebrities, and even colleagues on Facebook and twitter, and only to discover very distasteful messages and photographs, which clearly antagonize our Christian faith.

As Church leaders, we have been alerted of cases involving members of our Christian community who posted photographs and videos of youth parties and activities that were not only seductive, but also obscene. However, the power of the media in such circumstances has been devastating to the morality of our society. As the social media options increase and technology advances, the users become more vulnerable to predators who use electronic sophistry and their predatory instincts to attack the unsuspecting users.

Aggressive media industry

In this age of a liberalised media and publishing industry, distribution of sexually explicit materials has thrived on the pretext of protection of human rights and freedoms. Internet providers have capitalised on weak legislation and indifferent regulations to populate the media with spiritually immoral materials, which are known to increase traffic to such sites. In cases where Internet providers have installed software to restrict access to these sites, campaigners have labelled it as censorship, which they have fiercely fought using existing rights.

In some countries, software for censoring materials for public viewing are easily breached and corrupted leading to people unintentionally straying into sites with inappropriate materials. Sometimes, merely opening such sites has resulted in persistent pop ups of unsolicited adult materials, which are reportedly difficult to remove from computers without engaging specialists.

Some websites thrive in the 'cult of celebrity' culture, which portrays indecent exposure as a totally acceptable way of displaying unique identities of models, and as a benign way of promoting products. Attractive commercial fees for posing naked or promoting unconventional ways of luring people into buying certain products feed this culture. What is disheartening is the ease with which distasteful sexual materials are circulated or accessed.

At times, apparently benign stories can corrupt the minds of unsuspecting Christians and unbelievers. Certain public places, including barber shops, illustrate this practice. They tend to display a wide range of hairstyles promoted mostly by celebrities as if to tell other people that any hairstyle that a celebrity chooses is automatically a state of the art and a must have cut. Close examination of certain styles shows that they have been designed to make the person conspicuous in any group or setting, and many people choose the styles based on the celebrity rather than their own appearance and conscience.

Another example that has perplexed me is the practice wearing trousers (pants) with the rim either mid-way or below their buttocks, leaving the underwear partially or fully exposed. If you asked most of the youths or adults where they learned that style of dressing, they may not have a clue. In an article on the Internet, someone explained the origin of this dressing style. The author reveals that this form of dressing is common in prisons for two reasons. Firstly, inmates surrender their belts to the prison authorities for security reasons and therefore loose pairs of trousers or pants sag. Secondly, male inmates also use this practice to invite other men for sex. This article left me wondering whether people on the streets who dress this way understand the origin of this dressing style. When the media circulates such practices, especially if they associated with celebrities, some people easily embrace them.

Disguised spiritual bombs

Christians are faced with increasingly difficult decisions because individuals and institutions are developing subtle ways of shunting Christians away from their paths of righteousness. The Devil knows that if he gives us destructive devices in their original form, even unbelievers would avoid them. The strategy is to disguise the spiritual grenades using deceitfully attractive wrappers.

In the 1970's when Zambia hosted freedom fighters from neighbouring countries, the colonial armies in former Southern Rhodesia, South-west Africa, and South Africa, used a variety of military arsenal to attack freedom fighter camps and the innocent people in Zambia. The most popular and effective way to kill and maim children was using cluster bombs concealed in objects that appealed to children. The mercenaries strategically placed nicely decorated toy cars, footballs, trains, puppies, kettles, and other objects, which contained bombs in places frequented by children. Out of curiosity, children picked up the objects designed to explode when disturbed. Many children died and it took several months for them to learn that there were evil people who were determined to kill or maim them.

In our age, our children and vulnerable adults are tempted to embrace spiritually deadly devices, which have manifested in form of government policies, heresies, rules and regulations, and norms and values that legitimize sin. They are presented as genuine and beneficial accessories of normal life. But they have hidden stingers capable of destroying our Christian faith.

The Devil uses conventional teaching aids to spread spiritually inappropriate materials. In September 2013, my son's college in Cambridge introduced iPads as a learning aid in class and at home. But, two months later, most of the parents were concerned that their children were also using the device to access adult websites. The matter was so serious that the school and parents had to consider different options to restrict access to non-educational sites. The Devil wrapped his weapon in the iPad. Many paedophiles are also exploiting technology to attack our children.

While parents often use basic functions on modern gadgets including computers, iPads, kindles, phones and other electronic gadgets, many children can utilise nearly all the functions. The intergenerational gap in technological competencies limits parental control or guidance on appropriate use of electronic gadgets. Many parents have limited knowledge about what the children are doing on the Internet. Children have accessed websites containing unsuitable materials and have exposed themselves to predators resulting in tragic events, such as rape, suicide, and depression. But new versions of androids and their applications are entering the market almost every month. Our challenge is to keep abreast with these changes and to help children to know their God.

The unforgiving media

As societies promote freedom of information and develop advanced investigative tools, heinous crimes committed by unbelievers and believers are gradually unearthed. In many countries, abuse of children by clergy in the Church has seriously undermined the trust that many people have in the Church. The irony of the matter is that some people believe that the Church authorities knew about these crimes but swept them under the carpet hoping that they would never be discovered. The problem with this is that the authorities never addressed the matter and Church leaders supposedly chose to act in favour of those who abused the children.

Men of God who were supposed to protect the children ended up preying on them. In some countries, the revelation of these scandals has affected the life of the Church, and the reputational damage has been huge. In our fast-developing societies, people have access to this information more readily than in the past decades and some of these developments have reinforced the argument for secularization of systems.

Natural disasters have become too frequent

Natural disasters, which have become more frequent and devastating than they were in the past few decades, are playing into the secularization debate. The tsunamis, wildfires, floods and landslides, hurricanes, typhoons, volcanic eruptions and several other events have left a trail of destruction and recorded large numbers of fatalities. As people watch these events unfold using satellite images, television, and social media, it is becoming clear that these events are beyond what man can do to either minimize damage to property or reduce deaths.

Atheists and critics of Christianity use natural disasters to argue that either God who created the world has lost control, God does not care about the earth, or God doesn't exist otherwise he would not allow such catastrophic loss of property and precious human lives. While Christians attempt to explain the faithfulness, power, and loving kindness of God, some people easily swallow the bait of sceptics who deceitfully blame God for the problems on earth.

In sharp contrast to natural disasters, there are human-induced events that are destroying lives and infrastructure on a massive scale. Some countries have been plunged in ruinous wars to protect the interests of a few individuals. When people look at the number of lives lost and consider the afflictions of innocent civilians who are tortured, forced into exile, deprived of decent livelihoods, subjected to inhuman treatments, and forcibly separated from their loved ones, they question whether there is a supreme being who can bring these events to an end.

Humanity is witnessing several other human-mediated global issues including economic disasters, biodiversity loss, climate change, land use system change, biosphere change, freshwater change, novel entities, and others. At the centre of all this is greed or the desire for economic and political dominance, which overrides the need for social justice and love for fellow human beings.

As nations compete for global leadership, respect for human life is trivialised. The spirit of 'love thyself more than thy neighbour' seems to rule in many human transactions. This foul spirit lifts its ugly head in many spheres of life and demeans God's creation. Taking human life has become a lot easier now than in the recent past.

In western countries where people are generally more affluent than their counterparts in the south, wealth has become a stumbling block to their belief in the sovereign God. Many people in the west can largely afford the basic needs of life and hence many do not see any need for God. In some countries, the social benefit system ensures that everyone, including those that are not employed, has access to basic needs of life - accommodation, food, and clothes. The fact that people do not struggle to get these things has blinded them from believing that the earth is the Lords and everything that is in it.

Science, technology, and multimedia have been weaponised to fight Christianity. They have also created a false sense of security, enslaved the human mind numbing our God-consciousness, and facilitated the dissemination of false ideologies. The scientific, technological, and multimedia sophistry of the 21st century poses serious challenges to Christian living and to spreading the gospel of Jesus Christ.

CHAPTER 9

Socio-cultural challenges facing Christians in the 21st century

Christians practise their faith in a sociocultural milieu defined by their set of beliefs, customs, practices, and behaviour within a society. As societies adjust their beliefs and guiding principles in response to the new worldviews, their perception of Christianity and behavioural practices change. Most of the current ideologies and related wisdom challenge various Christian beliefs, principles, values, and practices. What is the impact of these sociocultural challenges on Christian living in the 21st century?

The desire to be accepted by other people

There is a consistent pressure on both believers and unbelievers to conform to changing beliefs, principles and values as society responds to new ideologies and philosophies. This desire to be accepted or look like the most dynamic group of people tempts us to embrace behaviour supposedly perceived to be unique. Celebrities have promoted strange behavioural practices (fashions, haircuts, facial make ups, sexual expositions, dancing styles, language, cars, ornaments, and pets) to display their allegedly unique identities. These practices erode Christian beliefs and values of young believers who idolise and imitate celebrities. The 21st century is yet to experience many more of morally bankrupt lifestyles.

Major social events are increasingly taking place on Sunday

Many institutions are staging major events on Sundays, competing with Sunday Church services. Whenever major golf, cricket, lawn tennis, horse racing, boxing, athletic, football, and other sporting events are staged on Sunday, many Christians are distracted. Some believers miss Church services to watch or participate in these events, watch events on electronic devices while in the Church service, or follow the game during the service by monitoring updates.

Some Christians choose not to use electronic gadgets to follow events but their attention during the Church service is compromised until they know the result. The information vacuum psychologically traumatizes them although they are physically present in the service. If they must attend the event after service, they may spend part of the time in the service planning how to get there or speculating the outcome.

Apart from sports, there are several other things that compete for time with our Christian programmes. For example, we live in a society that believes shops should remain open for seven days a week although there are still countries where shops and other business houses are closed to the public on this day. Sadly, some of these countries are changing their marketing strategies to open their business houses on Sunday as well. Apart from denying Christian employees the opportunity to worship their God on Sunday, they lure people into believing that the best day to go shopping is on Sunday. As countries adopt secular values, the urge to conduct business on Sundays is becoming more attractive than rest. What has happened to our Sabbath?

The enemy subtly dangles programmes that appeal to our fleshly desires to distract us from activities that build our Christian faith and our relationship with God. As the events increase in frequency and complexity, and as technology advances, people are increasingly faced with hard choices, which are likely to affect our Christian faith.

Human rights and civil liberties as potential instruments for eroding Christian values

The secularization of society and public institutions in the 21st century is a huge challenge. In many western countries, including the USA and UK, the Bible shaped public life and provided operational guidelines for different institutions for many centuries. Is it not amazing that the Bible has been used in the coronation of sovereigns and swearing-in of presidents and other senior public servants?

In some schools, reading the Bible during an assembly was the norm rather an exception. However, as systems are liberalised to embrace multiple faiths, human rights, and secular principles, Christian principles are being openly challenged and forcibly squeezed out of many institutions. In many schools, Bibles have been removed and children are taught different faiths and encouraged to choose what they are comfortable with.

In some working places, discussing the Word of God is prohibited. In some countries, Christians are prohibited from wearing any symbol of their faith in workplaces. In others, opponents of Christianity have become so powerful that they have blocked broadcasting of Christian programmes on TV. The anti-Christ spirit has infiltrated our institutions to the extent that Christians are not only portrayed in some societies as infidels, but also regarded as divisive elements that create unnecessary trouble. If anything, Christians are increasingly becoming an endangered species in some societies.

A major source of controversy in our society in recent times has been the whole issue of lesbian, gay, bisexual, and transgender (LGBTQ2) relationships. Conservative Christians who oppose these relationships are viewed as obstacles to total liberation of humanity because their beliefs counter human rights and freedoms in some societies, especially in some western countries, and believers are accused of wrongly applying hermeneutical and exegetical principles of biblical interpretation.

Critics allege that opposition to same sex marriages clearly undermines principles of justice, reconciliation, and inclusion, which are at the heart of the gospel of Jesus Christ. In legalizing same sex marriages, Her Majesty's Government in the United Kingdom asserted that this decision ensured that the ancient institution remained relevant in this century. They argue that the Church needs to review its belief systems to accommodate the legal and policy changes relating to LGBTQ2.

The February 2013 issue of Christianity Magazine featured several articles on the current debate on the 'Bible and Homosexuality'. Steve Chalke, a London-based Baptist Minister, argues that permanent, faithful, stable homosexual relationships aren't sinful, according to his understanding of the Bible. He further contends that Christians should take the same principle that we readily apply to the role of women, slavery, and numerous other issues, and apply it to our understanding of permanent, faithful, homosexual relationships.

The rapidly increasing numbers of self-confessed homosexuals in the Church, and Church Ministers supporting such relationships, in these times signifies a significant theological paradigm shift in some sections of the Church on this issue. Greg Downes (2013) further observes that it is not surprising therefore that this theological shift is mirroring a massive cultural shift in society at large where in a space of one generation attitudes to homosexuality have changed from prohibition to tolerance, and now to celebration.

This generation must survive in a society, which strives for a diversified sexual ethic demanding a high degree of tolerance for any dissenting views. What is equally frightening is the fact many people do not know what is true when they hear conflicting voices from people who command our respect within the evangelical community.

The noises have become so loud that Biblical texts are treated like abominations in some sectors of society. For example, in Leviticus 18:22 (NIV), the Lord God Almighty said 'Do not have sex with man as you would have sex with a woman. That is detestable.' Observing this law is seen as an infringement of human rights and freedoms, discrimination against minority groups and as lack of understanding of the biological conditions of a disadvantaged group of people lacking a voice. Apart from laws passed to legalise same sex marriages, there are prominent preachers who claim that the Bible has provision for these relationships. Even some high-profile clergy, who strongly upheld the Biblical commandments for decades, have changed their position in support of same sex marriages. This is a challenge that any disciple of Christ will face in this century.

Persecution of the body of Christ

Christians of the 21st century are persecuted in greater numbers than any other faith group on the earth. Several organizations monitoring their welfare globally have reported disturbing statistics of hostilities against this minority group. In 2008, Christian owners of a bed and breakfast in Cornwall, in the UK, were forced to sell their hotel for refusing to let a gay couple to stay in one of their double bedrooms. As Christians, the couple operated a strict policy of letting only married heterosexual couples share a room, but they were fined £3,600 in damages for violating the 2007 Equalities Act. Despite arguing their case that their policy was not targeted at sexual orientation, but the sexual practice because of their belief that sex outside a heterosexual marriage is sin, the couple lost the case.

Similarly, several traumatic stories of Christian persecution rocked the world media in the first half of 2015. In Sudan, two Pastors, Michael Yat and Peter Yen Reith, were arrested and accused of crimes against the state including espionage, 'offending Islamic beliefs', promoting hatred amongst sects and undermining the constitutional system. We thank God they were released. If the state had found them guilty, they could have faced the death penalty or life imprisonment. Other cases included: abduction of 88 Eritrean, 12 Kenyan, 220 Syrian, over 200 Nigerian, and Iraq Christians; and execution of Ethiopian, North Korean, Kenyan, Egyptian, Kenyan, and Syrian Christians, among others. Recorded cases of beheadings, torture, rape, kidnappings, mass killings, forced starvation, forced labor, imprisonment and even crucifixions prove that the persecution of Christians did not end at the foot of the cross or the closed gates of the Roman Coliseum, they are still growing in number globally. Current trends show that Christian principles and values that have always been considered as normal fibres of everyday life are being aggressively challenged, and these cases are likely to increase in their frequency and intensity.

Although Open Doors cited the year 2014 as going down in history for having the highest level of global persecution of Christians in the modern era, current statistics suggest that the number of Christians currently facing abuse and persecution in China, India, Iran, Nigeria, Somalia, Pakistan, Eritrea, Libya, Somalia, Sudan, and Yemen has increased tremendously. One in seven Christians worldwide faces high levels of persecution and discrimination for their faith; that is equivalent to 365 million Christians (Open Door, 2023). Islamic extremism was identified as the main source of persecution of the Church. It is disheartening to know that Christians have been forced to flee from their home areas turning into refugees.

Dysfunctional marriages on the increase

Our dynamic society is creating situations that pose serious threats to bringing up children in a Christian home. As spouses exercise their rights and freedoms, heterosexual marriages have been grossly undermined and this has contributed to an increase in divorce rates, especially in western countries. The UK Office of National Statistics (2020) reported that that 42% of marriages in England and Wales ended in divorce. This represented a 3% decline compared to the rate (45%) for 2005.

High divorce rates and decreasing heterosexual marriages and cohabiting have a negative impact on children. God designed heterosexual marriage as a perfect environment for bringing up children, but single parents are raising many children. A major challenge with the broken marriages is that the family altar is usually broken because the original design of the unit is clearly undermined. Even in cases where the single parent is committed to teaching the children the Word of God, children are likely to question the authenticity of the Christian faith because the Bible says God hates divorce.

The negative impact of divorce on the upbringing of children has been extensively researched. A judge, presiding on a multi-million-pound divorce case in the United Kingdom once retorted that, "A marital breakdown is distressing enough for any child, but for the divorce to be played out in the full glare of the public eye is appalling to them." He concluded that "marital breakdown and the fall out that follows are not child focused."

As children grow up in a broken marriage, they are usually confused because they fail to see love in a dysfunctional relationship between their parents, especially if they can clearly feel the animosity. The trauma of witnessing a relationship between two parents degenerate into an ugly row or court case, which reveals disgraceful and image-shattering facts, is emotionally draining. Many children consider legal battles embarrassing, distasteful and disgusting.

Damaged familial relationships can impact negatively on the social and psychological welfare of the children. As a way of avoiding embarrassments, such children may choose to withdraw from their friends, especially if they come from stable families. Some children have argued that if Christianity is based on the love of God, they question the gospel because they cannot experience godly love in a divorce. Children missing one of the parents in the house may become bitter with one of the parents and their lifelong relationship may be permanently damaged.

The emotional trauma experienced by children caught in a marital crossfire creates a permanent dent on their social, physical, and spiritual development. As the divorce rate increases, the number of children in this situation is also increasing and their perception of God's love is different from that of children raised up in a stable, love-centred godly family.

Bringing up children in a broken home also breeds other problems. Where parents realise that the children are missing their company, the tendency is to make up for their absence by lavishly spending on them. In this age, the temptation is to buy items that entertain them and keep them busy. Such items have encouraged the children to spend most of their time in isolation.

Divorce may create a dilemma for children who find it difficult to decide which parent to follow and some do not accept the decision of their parents to live apart. In trying to appease both parents, the children are emotionally distressed. The children also miss one of the role models. In cases where a mother brings up children singlehandedly, the father figure is missing and vice versa.

The absence of one of the parents in the upbringing of children manifests in their latter life. The 21st century will continue to see a large number of such troubled children. Bitterness resulting from such troubled families greatly influence people's perception of God.

The impact of role models

As many nations become increasingly secular, children are finding it difficult to find trustworthy role models. In a society where the cult-of-celebrity culture is flourishing, people are increasingly looking up to prominent public figures, including sportsmen and women, politicians, actors, and professionals, to provide examples of exemplary lives. In our society today, we have celebrities who have made admirable contributions to the welfare of humanity. For example, there are, scientists, engineers, technologists, political leaders, and theologians who have generated novel ideas, which have earned them Nobel prizes, knighthoods and damehoods. Unfortunately, these achievements are not celebrated much beyond their communities. They are unknown to millions of young people who need their inspirational leadership.

The Honourable Michael Gove (MP), once the Educational Secretary in the Coalition UK government, responded to what he termed as a very damaging message that Simon Cowel, an X-factor judge, sent to our young people. This famous X-factor celebrity said, *Forget about hard work at school, getting good exam grades and all that nonsense – just leave it all to life's lottery and hope you get a golden ticket to one of the X-factor shows. I didn't work hard when I was at school. I left at 16 and didn't have any qualifications. I was useless. The secret is to be useless at school and then get lucky.*" (Michael Gove, Daily Mail, November 23, 2013: 16-17). Simon Cowel has a very large following among young people worldwide. Although not everyone will believe this, there are some of his followers who hold him in such high esteem that whatever he says is treated as the gospel truth.

In his essay "*How Simon Cowel is inflicting such terrible damage on children's education*", The Hon Gove explains that our society increasingly prefers to bow down before a new golden calf and worship a new cult of celebrity instead of celebrating progressive virtues – hard work, academic rigour, intellectual ambition, and creative excellence. He argues that the young generation in the western world is engrossed in the celebrity culture dictated by personalities with questionable influence. The then Education Secretary further observes that we are living in a world that is becoming increasingly competitive and where the future belongs to those who work hard, enjoy the best education, and pursue the most rigorous qualifications.

Honourable Michael Gove stresses that in Shanghai, South Korea, and Taiwan, young people are working harder, for longer, to acquire mathematical and scientific knowledge that will enable them to shape their future. It is not surprising therefore that popular after school clubs in these countries are rooted in mathematics and sciences. With this contrasting mindset, who would these young people be looking up to as their role models? Their heroes and heroines are teachers, academics, and researchers, who occupy the most prestigious positions in universities, the engineers, scientists, architects, lawyers, theologians, great writers and artists, who embody high cultural ambitions.

By contrast, the figures, who populate our children's imaginations, mostly in the western culture, and embody their ambitions, are reality show winners, footballers and their wives, cover stars of celebrity magazines, and sports personalities. Michael Gove concludes that the future belongs to young people who have that work ethic, appetite for excellence, and innate sense of admiration for intellectual adventure and creative ambition. In this celebrity culture, the quest for fame and wealth, in most cases, overshadows development of our true personal identity. How can Christians effectively reach this generation largely influenced by such influential celebrities?

Although some celebrities appear to have very successful professions, behind the scenes, many are hurting. There are many people who have invested a lot of resources to join the club of celebrities. For every celebrity, there are thousands of candidates who fall by the wayside. Contestants invest several days to years and other resources to enrol for a big brother, X-factor, film audition, and premier league football trials, but never make it.

For some the scrabble towards celebrity status involves conforming to the expectation about body image, marketing themselves as commodities, posting provocative photographs of themselves doing something daring on social media, humiliations played out on the public stage, being paraded for amusement, inviting the public to laugh and gawk at vulnerable contestants as they display gaps between their desperate urge to be famous and their lack of discernible talent. The celebrity culture has attracted good and decent people who have been encouraged to perform songs they cannot sing or lines they cannot master, and they have been labelled as failures or unlucky.

The irony is that several thousands of people scramble for a few positions. For many of these young people, failure to qualify for this 'elite' status is interpreted as the end of the world. The value they place on this opportunity cannot be compared to anything else in life. As the population increases and more complex celebrity roles are released, the number of people aspiring to become famous will increase. The chase for fame has gripped many 21st century youths to the detriment of their faith.

Some celebrities undermine Christian principles and values. While young people admire the charisma and fame of their celebrities, their lives come with baggage that could easily destroy the moral fibre of their followers. Some celebrities command so much trust and respect that their failings are accepted as part of the normal life.

A celebrity can have a child out of wedlock, engage in adultery, deny the existence of God, insult people in authority, commit traffic offences, divorce and remarry several times, or batter a spouse, yet most of the followers will still accommodate the mischief. Most of their followers openly defend their idols, while a few are utterly disappointed and lose their trust in their idol. There are reported cases of celebrities who rejected God and yet received a Christian burial. It is this ability to maintain large followings despite their failings, which misleads many people in our society because they can subtly promote immorality.

Have you considered how politicians influence society? In many countries, the impact of political lies on the electorate has been profound. To win the votes of the electorates, some politicians have made false promises, which they have never fulfilled in their full terms of office. For example, many political candidates have promised to reduce tax, introduce free education, reduce university fees, and abolish some controversial laws. It is not uncommon for aspiring politicians to pledge to turn the economy around within 90 days of being voted into the office. However, once elected, they have pursued their own political agenda. How does this role model impact Christianity? People who are battered in other spheres of life find it difficult to trust other people including Christians.

Christians will continue to face even more challenging situations as society embraces more secular lifestyles than witnessed in the last few decades. Secular societies trust worldly political, economic, and social systems to meet all their needs. However, when these systems fail, they have no safety net, and the results are catastrophic. Based on "robust economic models", several western economies grew astronomically and formed an exclusive club of developed economies validated by different rating agencies. For many years these countries have dictated world policies and economic development patterns. Surprisingly, when the world economy shrunk, the major economies also experienced recessions.

In the last decade who would have predicted that the United States of America and the United Kingdom would have their financial ratings downgraded? What happened to the elite economic models that shaped these economies? The impact of these economic crises is being felt by the young generation which faced with high rates of unemployment, difficulties in climbing on the property ladder, and withdrawal of certain social benefits. These gruelling situations force some people to question the existence of God.

What about poverty?

It is a common belief that poverty in many developing countries has been the most effective recipe for the spread of the gospel of our Lord Jesus Christ. Many theologians and sceptics have argued that desperate people who cannot afford necessities of life are ready to do anything to survive. It is argued that poor people who are desperate of coming out of the poverty trap embrace faith either as Church leaders seeking a source of income or mere congregants believing in God's miraculous intervention. This argument holds to some extent.

Poverty has forced individuals to engage in activities they would never have thought about if they had not found themselves in such situations. On 18th December 2013, my wife and our two sons were sharing an evening meal while watching a BBC documentary on women in Yemen. What caught our attention was the confession of a very poor woman who explained how she gave away two under-15 daughters in marriage for a bridal price of £150 per head because she did not have any resources to feed her family. When asked how she felt, one of her daughters explained that her aspiration was to complete her education and study medicine, but her plans were prematurely terminated when she was forced by her family to get married. I could feel the agony of a mother and daughter who were utterly helpless because of poverty.

As a postgraduate student in Ghana, I learned that some poor people in rural communities in West Africa were forced to accept Islam because the institution provided water reticulation, education, and health facilities. It also provided university scholarships to Islam converts and many students from poor families were ready to identify with this faith to access these educational opportunities.

Considering that some of these students were Christians, but accepted scholarships to simply further their education, I was keen to know how they would dissociate themselves from Islam after completing their education. Many students who found themselves in such a predicament ended up leaving the country and settling overseas to ensure they were not pursued by the system.

This, I felt, was a high price to pay because of their socioeconomic status. But it is not just the poor people in developing countries that are ready to give anything to get out of poverty. Students in some elite western universities have engaged in work, and others in prostitution, to raise money to supplement their grants. The degree of depravity is higher in developing than developed countries.

The desire for riches and fame has forced some Christians to engage in ungodly business transactions, which compromise Christian ethics. In a world where people idolize the rich and famous, people are ready to do anything to outdo others. In sports, match fixing is a familiar vice. Men and women have used performance-enhancing drugs to increase their chances of winning medals at major events. In the recent past, culprits have included cyclists, footballers, basketball players, and boxers, to name a few.

Some testimonies and writings have suggested that the source of wealth of some of the celebrities has been traced back to unholy covenants with the dark world. Some have very strong links to satanic altars and have sacrificed lives in exchange for wealth. Unfortunately, the quest for wealth and fame has also trapped some Christian leaders who have bowed to foreign gods to make it in ministry. The unbridled quest for riches and fame is increasingly drawing people away from God. As people fight for recognition, the temptation to contract ungodly power to make it to the top is becoming increasingly attractive to many.

Busy lifestyles in civilized societies seem to undermine marriages. Recent studies have revealed that the sexual behaviour of an average middle-class couple has significantly changed with most couples having less sex than previously reported. As both husbands and wives work hard and longer hours to meet household needs, their sexual drives are significantly reduced.

Apart from economic hardships, changing societal values have resulted in women having a larger number of sexual partners before marriage than men, a decrease in the number of couples living together, greater approval of non-exclusive sexual relationships (one-night stand), higher incidence of infidelity among married couples, greater acceptance of same-sex relationships, and less acceptance of lasting relationships.

We are experiencing extremely fragile and less valued heterosexual relationships, and some people prefer loose and non-committal relationships, which they can establish and dissolve without the need for accountability. This sexual behaviour has also been fuelled by the Internet, which allows people to easily search for different types of partners. This evolving and aggressive 21st century sexual behaviour propped by a versatile Internet and unbridled sexual appetites are a major challenge to accepting Christian faith.

Humans are increasingly becoming slaves of their own scientific and technological developments. The Internet and the social media provide a powerful interactive tool for creating, sharing and or exchanging information and ideas in virtual communities and networks. While certain groups have utilised the facilities positively to develop themselves or benefit others, people with evil motives have used them to destroy themselves and others.

While the Internet and social media are useful wheels of development, in the wrong hands, they are one of the deadliest weapons. Unfortunately, our children are not well protected from the ugly sexual misbehaviour that has permeated our society. It is not surprising that cases of sexual abuse of children by other children are on the increase. A group of boys raped a very young girl in Cambridge (UK). Another newspaper article narrated how a young boy sexually assaulted a young girl. In both cases, the boys claimed to practice what they watched on TV in their bedrooms. Activities previously labelled as unacceptable are gaining popularity in certain sectors of society.

The Internet has become so sophisticated that illicit substances can be advertised and sold under the radar of law enforcement agents. An article by Steve Boggan in the UK Daily Mail (23 November 2013) reported a special investigation of the 'Dark Net', a cyber world where secrecy is guaranteed, and everything goes. This Web, which is independent of the World Wide Web, provides a hidden marketplace where drug dealers, gun runners, assassins, paedophile pornographers can peddle their products with almost no chance of being caught.

Illicit merchandize, including LSD, cocaine, heroin, and ecstasy are advertised on this Net as elaborately as products on Amazon. Messages have several layers of encryption to the extent that it is almost impossible to establish the identities of people on either end of the chain or to see what they are talking about, selling, swapping, or sharing. Interestingly, political activists have used this Net to share information in countries with oppressive regimes. This demonstrates science and technology could compromise national security.

Several European countries have beautifully decorated Church buildings with amazing window and interior designs. Many of them are either empty or are often frequented by the older generation. Declining Church attendance reveals different priorities and preoccupations of the current generation. Studies suggest that many young people spend most of the time watching TV programmes, on social media, watching films, and attending different social events.

In the past, strong family relationships rooted in the Christian faith meant that families regularly had time to read the Bible, pray and eat together. Parents took their children to Church. However, postmodernity has emphasized human rights and government policies, which give children the right to choose whatever faith pleases them. Parents cannot actively guide children in choosing their faith.

Some events and multimedia programmes demonise Christianity as a faith that deprives people of their choices, and discourages independence of thought, creativity, and rationality. Conversely, young people who attend Church find traditional praise and worship distasteful and not compliant with the current socio-cultural revolution. They prefer a mode of worship that embodies vast technological and socioeconomic changes that have characterized modern society.

Some young people have adopted different lifestyles and priorities from those of the older generation. They have a liberal approach to life including dressing, language, dancing and to worshipping God, compared with some conservative elderly Christians who strictly observe traditional liturgy. But, some of the liberal practices are compromising the Christian doctrines and values.

There are times when I reflect on our attitude and approach to worship because of my previous experience of strange behaviour to appease people in authority. A visit by the General Superintendent (GS) of an established evangelical Church to one of the local Churches illustrates the point. As a mark of respect for the GS, Church leaders advised their flock to observe a formal dress code. They emphasized that inappropriately dressed congregants would be excluded from the coverage zone of the cameras.

Why did people choose a more decent dress code when the GS visited? Is it because we don't physically see God in our service? I earnestly believe that the God believers worshipped when the GS visited the city is the same God they always worship in local assemblies. I am always amazed to see how people dress when they are invited to events such as interviews, meetings with prominent leaders, weddings, graduations, and meetings with national leaders and celebrities. But we rarely dress for God.

Society has schooled some Christians to believe that there are special events where we are expected to dress immaculately, but Church services are regular meetings and people should be allowed to dress as they wish. Is it the frequency of our meetings with God in the temple that cultivates the belief that we can dress anyhow, and God is still happy? Do we have scriptural references for our approach to modern dressing in the house of God?

Multimillion dollar schemes to disable Christianity

Apart from wolves in sheep's skin operating stealthily in the Church, the worldly bodies or institutions, used by the spirit working in the sons of disobedience, are devising deadly schemes to undermine Christianity. Some products of the film and music industries are promoting Satanism in and outside the Church. Some publications suggest that many people have come across materials that show prominent artists who have expressed their hatred for Jesus Christ through blasphemous statements, their declaration to fight the fascism of Christianity and to match on to hell, and their resolve to teach people to be their own gods, and rituals to burn, eat or shred the Bible.

Artists have also composed and sang songs that are satanic and have enticed their audiences to vow to go to hell and ensure that the Church is not allowed to interfere with their journey to their destiny. As scientific knowledge and technology increase, the world systems are arming themselves to their teeth to destroy the Church at any cost. The Church and individual Christians are targets of multimillion-pound institutions that are ready to invest as much as they can to divert people from their mandate and destiny. The battle can only increase in its intensity.

International statistics of the world's religions show that the population of Christians is steadily growing, but it is facing a lot of resistance in some countries. There are governments passing laws that either limit freedom of worship or force the Church to conduct its business based on rules, which constrain profession of Christianity. Many institutions are taking advantage of these national laws to victimize Christians. According to a story that featured in the Daily Mail of November 23, 2013 (UK), parents of eight-year-old children at Littleton Green Community School in Huntingdon, Staffordshire (UK), were ordered to send their children to a workshop on Islam or have them labeled as racist for the rest of their tenure of study in the school. The school authorities stated that it was a statutory requirement for primary school children to experience and learn about other cultures. The national governments and other institutions are putting pressure on Christians to compromise their communication and practice of faith.

The strategy to undermine Christian values

Satan has infiltrated the world systems to undermine what God has provided for his children. For centuries Judeo-Christian values have shaped the culture of people in the west. It is not surprising that policies, regulations, and various institutional structures have been shaped by these values. The Bible was a significant component of school assemblies, contents of school and university curricula. It defined ethics in science and other human operational systems. Not anymore.

The Devil knows that if the Bible and prayer remain a significant feature in the lives of people, his agenda to destroy God's creation will fail. His strategy is to project Christianity and its values as enemies of progress, discriminatory, and intolerant. Some governments have come up with language, actions and policies that are excessively calculated not to offend any particular group in society. These measures advance multiculturalism through carefully crafted language, affirmative action, and school and university curriculum reviews. Behind the scenes the Devil is rejoicing because of what he sees as bursting the cannon that has shaped societal values for ages. While the move is said not to offend or disadvantage any particular group, what it does is to push Christianity to the periphery, allowing other faiths to occupy the central ground.

What has happened to the values we so dearly held to that guided our culture? As we liberalize our system, we are allowing strong anti-Christian faiths to shape our thinking and way of life. The lie of the enemy is that those that deny the existence of God do not practice any faith. There is no single human being who does not have a belief system. For example, scientists who are also atheist write textbooks to present science as the only source of knowledge and further argue that anything that cannot be explained by science must never be accepted. In the name of creating a society that accommodates different groups, Christian values are savagely attacked, while elevating other faiths.

Domineering corporate culture

In some countries, the fast-growing corporate state that concentrates power in the hands of a few and wields unchecked authority against the Church is increasingly becoming a prominent feature in the 21st Century. Some major corporations have budgets that by far exceed budgets of some nations put together and they strongly influence the policies and strategies of nations in which they are located.

When large corporations promote technologies that raise ethical issues, many people look to Christian leaders for answers. Contentious issues such as cloning, fracking, fetal tissue research, genetic engineering, reproductive technologies, and three-way parentage have divided the society and Christian leaders are expected to give their views. Does the Bible offer guidance on these issues? However, decision makers scarcely consider Christian principles and values. Large corporations that have invested in these technologies have very strong marketing strategies, which at times override logic and godly counsel. In contrast, policy makers primarily consider the contribution of corporation tax to the economy, while ethical issues are treated as secondary.

Worldwide growth of Islam

Islam is the second largest faith group with a membership estimated at about 1.6 billion, but its growth has increased Christian persecution. Fundamentalist groups have widened their operational areas to include places originally free from their influence. Their activities are increasing in Africa, Asia and the Middle East, and some parts of Europe and America. As they spread their tentacles, some of the key targets are Christians who are beheaded, raped, starved, tortured, and forced to denounce their faith. Where Christians flee, they are deprived of their decent life through emigration and loss of livelihood systems.

The 21st century Church faces serious challenges from the fast changing social and cultural beliefs and values influenced externally by secular worldviews that strive to push it out of the public sphere, and internally by theologians and Christians propagating false and liberal teachings.

CHAPTER 10
Wolves in sheep's skin

The Christian Church has grown substantially since its beginning in the first century A.D., with much of that growth coming through conversion into the Church. According to the Centre for the Study of Global Christianity at Gordon Conwell Theological Seminary, the population of Christians exceeded 2.6 billion of the worldwide population of 8 billion in 2023. Representing nearly one-third of the worldwide population, Christianity is the largest religion in the world. But Christianity has declined in some countries, especially in the western world. Some institutions predict that it may experience net losses in terms of religious conversion.

The western world, mostly characterised by modern secular education, has witnessed the greatest shift from historically almost exclusively Christian countries to secular, globalised, multicultural and multifaith societies. In his book chapter, *The haemorrhage of faith 1939-97: the crisis of the Church connection*, Callum Brown describes an unprecedented religious crisis that emerged in the twentieth century in Scotland and other the western societies. He argues that *it is a crisis of religious practice, a crisis of people's connections with Churches, and a crisis of diffusive Christianity. In extremely large numbers, the people have stopped going to Church, stopped becoming Church members, and no longer recognise a substantive religious influence in their social lives*. He attributes this depressing decline in Church membership in the late twentieth century to the success of the industrial, urban, and capitalist society in the eighteenth and nineteenth centuries. This Church haemorrhage is continuing in the 21st century. Analyses of these crises pinpoint the political, socioeconomic, legal and philosophical forces external to the Church as a substantive explanation for the decline in her numerical strength.

While predictions of Church growth or net losses in religious conversion may have a grain of truth, the reasons given for these statistics do not fully explain the unfolding picture of the Church. The history of Christ's Church is inseparable from the history of Satan's attempts to destroy her. While difficult challenges have arisen from outside the Church, the most dangerous have always been those from within. The Church is losing many of her adherents to 'wolves in sheep's skin', people within the Church who use acts of kindness to disguise their malicious intent to lead the saints astray. While converts are entering the Church through the front door, saints are led out using the backdoor. These wolves are subtly destroying the faith of saints and driving them away from the presence of the Lord through cunning deceit. If we have wolves in the Church, how can we contend for the faith which was purchased through the blood of Jesus Christ and His forgiveness of our sins?

Understanding how the Devil is haemorrhaging the Church through 'wolves in sheep's skins' is key to finding ways of addressing the crisis. Who are these 'wolves in sheep's clothing'? How do they attack Christians in the Church? Why do they target Christians? When are saints vulnerable to wolf attacks? How can we identify the wolves? And how can we thrive amidst ravening wolves in the Church? Answering these questions will help us to walk steadfastly with God in a 21st century Church.

What does 'wolf in sheep's skin' mean?

The cautionary advice, *Don't trust the salespeople at the store; they are all wolves in sheep's clothing!* has been with us for many centuries. The phrase, wolves in sheep's clothing, is a metaphoric description of someone who outwardly looks harmless but is inwardly full of hate, evil and deceit. It is an idiom of Biblical origin used to describe those people who play a role contrary to their real character with whom contact is dangerous. This phrase originates in the Sermon Jesus preached on the Mount: *Beware of false prophets, who come to you in sheep's clothing, but inwardly they are ravening wolves* (Matt. 7:15 KJV). In the writings of the Church Fathers, centuries after the Sermon on the mount, a Latin proverb emerged which translates, *under a sheep's skin often hides a wolfish mind*. It refers to people who harbour malicious intent under the guise of kindness.

The wolves in sheep's clothing are like a rapist who offers an innocent woman a spiked drink with the intent of having non-consensual sex with her. What appears to be an act of kindness turns out to be a bait that renders the victim vulnerable to sexual exploitation. Such evil-minded people have existed in our society for several centuries as evidenced by several fables describing this predatory behaviour. In the 15th century, an Italian professor Laurentius Abstemius illustrated the behaviour of wolves in sheep's clothing using a fable. In his words, *A wolf, dressed in a sheep's skin, blended himself in with the flock of sheep and every day killed one of the sheep. When the shepherd noticed this was happening, he identified the wolf and hanged him on a very tall tree. On other shepherds asking him why he had hanged a sheep, the shepherd answered: The skin is that of a sheep, but the activities were those of a wolf.* His commentary on the story is consistent with the Biblical interpretation: never judge people by their outward appearance but by their works, because many in sheep's clothing do the work of wolves.

People who disguise their malicious intent to prey on their victims are found in every sector of our society including families, workplaces, marketplaces, and the Church. In the Bible, the phrase 'wolves in sheep's clothing' refers to false professors of faith. It provides accounts of false prophets and teachers as exemplars of these evil people. These heretics were a constant problem in the Old Testament, but their influence is even greater in our societies today. Warning the Israelites through Moses, the LORD described a false prophet as one who presumes to speak in His name anything He has not commanded him to say, or a prophet who speaks in the name of other gods (Deut. 18:20). They prophesy lies, false visions, idolatries, and delusions of their minds. They use the name of the LORD to disguise their malevolent activities.

While rebuilding the wall of Jerusalem, Nehemiah and other children of Israel encountered several false prophets. Prophet Shemaiah instructed Nehemiah to hide in the temple because men would seek to kill him by night.

But Nehemiah rejected the prophecy because the false prophet wanted him to sin and discredit himself and his God (Neh. 6:10-15). Then, the false prophet Noadiah and his cohort connived to prophetically intimidate Nehemiah to prevent him and the other children of Israel from completing the reconstruction of the wall of Jerusalem. Other false prophets also deceptively prophesied to the Israelites that no sword or famine would touch the land of Israel, but the LORD had not spoken (Jer.14:15). These camouflaged antichrists can perform signs and wonders to entice Christians to follow other gods instead of the LORD our God. Just as they were troublesome in the Old Testament, false teachers have also plagued the New Testament Church.

The Church has consistently encountered false teachings and prophecies. Writing to the Corinthian saints, Paul expressed his fear that their minds might be led astray from their sincere and pure devotion to Christ just as the serpent cunningly deceived Eve (2 Cor. 11:3). The Apostle John warned the saints that the spirit of antichrist was already in the world to entice believers to abandon their faith in Christ. The Apostle Peter also warned about "false teachers," much like false prophets, who will *secretly introduce destructive heresies* (2 Peter 2:1). As the disciples of Jesus Christ preached the Gospel, false teachers also spread false doctrines. Jesus likened these people to the enemy who planted tares among wheat at night while the farmer was asleep.

The Christian Church in Colossae had false teachers who propagated doctrinal errors arising from mixing Judaistic teachings with oriental and philosophic teachings. Warning the saints, Paul wrote: *Beware lest anyone cheat you through philosophy and empty deceit, according to the tradition of men, according to the basic principles of the world, and not according to Christ* (Col. 2:8 KJV). The false teachers mixed elements of astrology, magic, and Judaism to produce a doctrine that regarded Jesus as a mere angelic being. The false teaching, characterised by Jewish mysticism, encouraged the Colossian Christians to practice circumcision, observe the Jewish regulations about food and drink, and to keep laws about regular worship such as major festivals and the sabbath. These Jewish mystics shared the belief that it was possible for humans to ascend from earth into heaven, and to see God's throne and the angels in heaven. Christians were condemned by opponents because they did not practice ascent into heaven, and they did not worship angels which mystics saw during ascent. These mystics also claimed they had special revelation from God about mysteries unknown to everyone else. The beliefs of the mystics made them arrogant, and they no longer worshipped Christ. The greatest challenge we face today is that these false professors of faith are so skilful at twisting Scriptures and smuggling in false doctrines along the Biblical truth of the gospel.

The 'wolves in sheep's clothing' are false apostles, deceitful workmen, disguising themselves as apostles of Christ. These are false brothers who have secretly slipped in to spy out the freedom we have in Jesus Christ to bring us into slavery to sin (Gal. 2:4). They are children of the devil, and their desire is to do the will of their father who was a murderer from the beginning and does not stand in truth (John 8:44). Such heretics are dangerous as they disguise their malicious intentions. They profess to know God but deny Him by their works. Their aim is to deceive the elect of the LORD. We meet and talk with these people in our Church gatherings. False teachers take on many forms and are custom-crafted to times, cultures, and contexts. Paul, warning the saints at Ephesus said, *see then that you walk circumspectly, not as fools but as wise, redeeming the time, because the days are evil* (Eph. 5:15).

False teachers and heretical doctrines have become an increasingly serious problem in the 21st century Church. We are living in epic times when Christians are becoming increasingly vulnerable in the Church infiltrated by heretics. We need to recognize these false apostles who are working hard to subtly lead believers astray.

How do wolves in sheep's skin attack the saints?

When we sense danger, our instinct is to avoid it. The Devil knows we are too clever to accept a false doctrine that is presented in its raw state. So, he is devious, sly, and manipulative in his wolfish attack of unsuspecting Christians. The false teachers display different personalities that are explained below.

The masquerades

False teachers masquerade as godly ministers. They cover and colour their dangerous principles and soul-impostures with clever language, appearances, and plausible pretences, with high notions and golden expressions. Paul, writing to the Corinthian Church, said, *These people are false apostles. They have fooled you by disguising themselves as apostles of Christ. But I am not surprised! Even Satan can disguise himself as an angel of light. So, it is no wonder that his servants can also do it by pretending to be godly ministers*" (2 Cor. 11:13-15 NLT). Just as soldiers fighting in the forest camouflage themselves perfectly among the trees and shrubs to deceive their enemy, false apostles blend themselves perfectly among unsuspecting saints. They seem to preach the undiluted Word of God, pray fervently, lead deep dives into the Word of God, teach Sunday School, or even oversee denominations. Such people may hold senior Church leadership positions to mask their malice and earn the trust of their victims. They seem to be genuinely keen to help us to grow in our faith. Their friendly demeanour makes us to drop our guards and reveal our spiritual vulnerabilities to them. When this hedge of protection is breached, the serpent bites.

The heretics

The heretics secretly bring in false doctrines along Biblical truth. The Apostle Peter wrote, "*But there were also false prophets in Israel, just as there will be false teachers among you. They will cleverly teach their destructive heresies about God and even turn against their masters who bought them*" (2 Pet. 1:1 NLT). The heretics teach what blatantly contradicts an essential teaching of the Christian faith. They shrewdly play with words to either add to, twist, or remove from, the Scripture to smuggle in error into the Christian doctrine. They leverage their eloquence, position of trust and purported knowledge of the Scriptures to corrupt the sound Christian doctrine, even denying the foundational truth of the Gospel of Christ. They usually corrupt a believers' theology by exploiting their limited knowledge of Scriptures.

The heretics are normally influential figures and natural leaders teaching just enough truth to disguise their deadly heresies. Through their false teaching, they even deny the Christian faith and celebrate falsehood, leading the saints astray. Just as Arius of the third century reframed the doctrine of the Trinity, several Biblical scholars, Churchmen, and theologians have notably rejected the virgin birth of Jesus Christ. Mark Borg, an American New Testament scholar, and theologian, viewed the birth stories of Jesus Christ as metaphorical narratives, and stated, *I do not think the virginal conception is historical, and I do not think there was a special star or wise men or shepherds or birth in a stable in Bethlehem.* Such teachings contradict the core elements of Christian doctrine. Mormons believe that Christ's Church was restored through Joseph Smith and is guided by living prophets and apostles. We must carefully test every teaching in the Church to ensure it agrees with the Word of God.

The Baalites

False prophets may prophesy in the name of foreign deities. The LORD, through the prophet Jeremiah, said, "*I saw that prophets of Samaria were terribly evil, for they prophesied by Baal and led people of Israel into sin. Now I see that the prophets of Jerusalem are even worse! They commit adultery and they love dishonesty. They encourage those that are doing evil instead of turning them away from their sins. The prophets are as wicked as those of Sodom and Gomorrah once were*" (Jer. 23:13-14 NLT). The Baalites falsely prophesied in the name of an idol, Baal, the god of fertility, weather, seasons, war and sailors. They pretended they had their instructions and revelations from Baal, a non-entity. In our Churches today false prophets prophesy in the names of different idols including gods of money and material things, sex, fame, status, technology, science, and other things. False prophets of Jerusalem lured the Israelites into idolatry by their immorality, dishonesty and by encouraging the wicked in their wickedness. Such false professors of faith lead people astray.

The Sectarian

Sectarians direct Christians to certain parts of the Bible to the exclusion of the fundamental Christian doctrine. They tend to focus on either the Old Testament only, New Testament only or certain portions of the Bible. Some prophets avoid certain passages of the Bible. Such teachings deprive Christians of the solid foundation in Christ and hence they are easily tossed around by heresies. Paul, instructing his son Timothy emphasized that, *All Scripture is given by inspiration of God and is profitable for doctrine, for reproof, for correction: That the man of God may be perfect, thoroughly furnished unto all good works* (2 Tim. 16-17 KJV). Every part of the Bible originates from God and is beneficial to His children. The Scripture is profitable for doctrine because it teaches us what is true about God, man, the world we live in, and the world to come. It reproves and corrects us when it authoritatively exposes our false doctrine or our wrong conduct and embeds us in sound doctrine and in righteousness. When we embrace and practise all Scripture, we become perfect and thoroughly equipped for all good works, including resisting the sectarians.

The Hucksters

Hucksters exploit the sheep under their care. They distort the gospel to leverage the commonwealth of believers for personal gain. Through the Prophet Micah, the Lord said, "*As for the prophets who lead my people astray, they proclaim 'peace' if they have something to eat but prepare to wage war against anyone who refuses to feed them.*" (Micah 3:5 ESV). The hucksters are only interested in the Christian faith to the extent that it feeds their insatiable appetite for money, power, fame, and other worldly pleasures. The gospel is taken as a means of personal enrichment. The hucksters are at peace with Christians who agree fill their wallets but are ready to confront those who refuse to give them what they want. These people will use any means to get what they want from vulnerable Christians. They use their leadership positions to benefit from the wealth of saints. They cunningly deceive the hearts of the naïve to satisfy their financial and material desires through smooth talk and flattery (Rom. 16:18). The Apostle Peter warned saints that *in their greed, they will make up clever lies to get hold of your money* (2 Pet. 2:3 NLT). These false professors of faith are peddlers of God's Word (2 Cor. 2:17), who take godliness as a means of gain (1 Tim. 6:5).

Rebuking the leaders and rulers of Israel, the LORD said, "*Should you not embrace justice, you who hate good and love evil; who tear the skin from my people and the flesh from their bones; who eat my people's flesh, strip off their skin and break their bones in pieces; who chop them up like meat for the pan, like flesh for the pot?*" The LORD poetically describes the spiritual savagery of these false shepherds who shrewdly shred the Christian belief system of their victims and defraud them of their financial and material possessions. Jude describes these people as *blemishes at your love feasts, eating with you without the slightest qualm; shepherds who feed only for themselves* (Jude 12). *Like Balaam, they deceive people for money* (Jude 11 NLT). Simon Magus (the sorcerer), popularly known as the 'Great Power of God' (Acts 8:9-24), after becoming a Christian, offered to purchase from the Apostles Peter and John the supernatural power of transmitting the Holy Spirit, thus giving rise to the term simony as the buying or selling of sacred things or ecclesiastical office. The 21st century Church is seeing an increase in the number of such false apostles who are peddling the gospel of Jesus Christ. These people prey on the vulnerable and gullible to finance their extravagant lifestyles, the same kind of greed that motivated false prophecy and teaching in the early Church.

Hucksters leverage the craving for wealth and fame to deceive unsuspecting Christians. The desire to speedily acquire wealth and to live a celebrity lifestyle has lured Christians into accepting false claims that believing in Jesus Christ guarantees material and financial wealth. It is true that God prospers His children and gives them good success if they obey His commandments. Instructing Joshua, God said, *this Book of Law shall not depart from your mouth, but you shall meditate upon it day and night, that you may observe to do according* to all that is written in it. For then you will make your way prosperous, and then you will have good success (Josh 1:8, NKJV). He promised Joshua and the Israelites prosperity and good success on condition that they always kept and meditated on the Book of the Law and obeyed everything in it. But wealth, prestige, position, and power in this world do not by themselves constitute prosperity and good success; they are additions or by-products of abundant life: *Seek ye first the Kingdom of God, and His righteousness, and all these things shall be added unto you* (Matt. 6:33 KJV). If prosperity and success were to be defined in terms of economic, academic, and social status, most the prophets, apostles, Church Fathers, Jesus Christ, and modern-day Christians would have been disqualified. But false teachers focus on material things and social status in society as the key indicators of success and prosperity, rather than achieving God's plan and purpose.

The Schismatics

False teachers seek to divide the body of Jesus Christ. They use heresies to disrupt or try to destroy the Church. The schismatic cunningly drive wedges between Christians, Church leaders and families. Paul cautioned the Church in Rome to watch out for those who caused divisions and put obstacles in the way that are contrary to the teaching they learned (Rom. 16:17). The schismatics have *an unhealthy craving for controversy and for quarrels about words, which produce envy, dissension, slander, evil suspicions, and constant friction among people who are depraved in mind and deprived of the truth...* (1 Tim. 6:3-5). When they teach heresies or tell lies, some of the saints accept and spread them, some are indifferent, while others strongly oppose them, depending on their levels of spiritual maturity, the quality of pastoral care, the strength of Church fellowship groups, and the teachings on the true Christian doctrine. The Schismatics defy the Holy Spirit whose fruit yields enduring love and whose special work is holding believers together in the bond of peace (Gal. 5:22, Eph. 4:3). They strive more to win over men to their opinions, than to build them in their faith. Paul cautioned the Church in Rome to watch out for people who caused divisions and upset people's faith by teaching things contrary to the doctrine that they had been taught (Rom. 16:17). He admonished Titus to avoid foolish controversies and quarrels about the law (Titus 3:9); *As for a person who stirs up division, after warning him once and then twice, have nothing more to do with him, knowing that such a person is warped and sinful; he is self-condemned* (Titus 3:10–11). People who consistently cause divisions in the body of Christ should be avoided if they ignore correction or reproof by saints. Schismatics are worldly, defy the Spirit, and are relentlessly pursuing their own ungodly passions (Jude 18–19). If they are not controlled, they breed apostasy, tarnish the name of the Lord and increase the resistance to the Gospel of Christ.

The sensualists

False apostles seduce immature Christians to indulge in sexual sin through their impressive-sounding talk. The Apostle Peter, grieved by the false teachings, said, *"For when they speak great swelling words of vanity, they lure through the lusts of the flesh, through wantonness, those that were clean escaped from them who live in error* (2 Peter 2:18 KJV). The young converts in the early Church could not resist these false teachings because they appealed to the lustful desires of their sinful nature. The sensualists entice vulnerable people who have just escaped from the culture of living in sin by promising them freedom from earthly and eternal consequences of sin, while they themselves were slaves of moral apostasy. These sensualists seemed to teach that a Christian believer can indulge in sexual sin without remorse, while keeping all the benefits of a saint. In a post–war sexual revolution in western culture, people still follow their own sinful desires (Jude 16). The sensualist's urge and lust still motivate many to deny Biblical truth about God's design for sex and marriage and to justify human abortion. The immature Christians who are led astray after exposure to such false teachings are worse off than they were before they came to Christ.

In the book of Revelation, the Son of God reveals to the Apostle John the heresies that false teachers were spreading in the Churches. He instructed John to write a letter to every angel representing each of the affected Churches, specifying the false teachings and their effects, and the benefit of holding fast to the truth. The Nicolaitans in the Church in Pergamos taught the doctrine of Balaam, which instructed adherents to sin by eating food offered to idols and by committing sexual immorality. The Church in Smyrna was infiltrated by blasphemous teachers, who claimed to be Jews but were of the Synagogue of Satan. Similarly, the Church in Philadelphia harboured the agents of the Synagogue of Satan who propagated lies. About the Church in Thyatira, the Son of God said, *Nevertheless, I have a few things against you, because you allow the woman Jezebel, who calls herself a prophetess, to teach and seduce My servants to commit sexual immorality and eat things sacrificed to idols* (Rev. 2:20 NKJV). An influential self-proclaimed prophetess in the fellowship was advocating easy compromise with the immoral, idolatrous pagan world. Watch out for sensualists.

Abusers

There is an increase in the number of false teachers in Christian community today who are enticing new converts to the Christian faith to return to their sexually immoral lives. An abuser unapologetically uses his leadership position to exploit other people to feed his sexual lust although he may also desire power. Under the guise of caring for the vulnerable members of Christ's Church, he works his way into their lives, confidence, homes, and their beds. Abusers may propagate a corrupted doctrine that perverts the grace of God. Warning the saints against such teachings, Jude said, *some ungodly people have wormed into your Churches teaching that God's marvellous grace allows us to live immoral lives* (Jude 4 NLT). These false teachers pervert the grace of our God as licence for immorality. They encourage Christian believers to sin more boldly because grace has abounded, and still abounds, so wonderfully.

According to Dr Austin Lingerfelt, the Apostle Peter prophesied of distorted grace teachings more than 2000 years ago. He cites one of the most famous grace teachers, who argues that 'once you become a follower of Christ, all your past, present and future sins are covered, and you never need again to confess or repent.' This teaching has led some Christians astray and deprived them of their gift of continued repentance to be holy. Apart from sex cults and other depraved perversions that affected the early Church, sex scandals have also rocked the 21st century Christian Church. The individual leaders were either accused of, admitted to, or found guilty of, heinous sexual crimes with individuals in or out of the Church, ultimately disgracing their families, congregations, and God. The abusers who choose to consolidate their power are domineering and abusing people on their way to prominence although their activities are coated with love and humility.

The Accusers

The false teachers make false accusations against saints, Church leaders and God. They are known for casting dirt, scorn, and reproach upon the persons, names, and credits of Christ's most faithful ambassadors. Korah, Dathan, and Abiram accused Moses and Aaron of taking too much upon themselves, considering that the whole congregation was holy (Num. 16:3). Accusing Paul of mischief, the false apostles said, *For we have found this man a plague, one who stirs up riots among all the Jews throughout the world and is a ringleader of the sect of the Nazarenes* (Acts 24:5 ESV). Tertullus, a Jewish lawyer appointed by the Sanhedrin to lead the prosecution of Paul when he appeared before the Roman Governor Felix, falsely branded Paul as a danger to the peace of the Roman Empire. He described him as a pestilent fellow causing public nuisance with an edge of treasonous intent. It is true that a week before his trial, Paul stirred a riot in the province of Asia when he was accused of preaching against the Jews everywhere, telling people to disobey Jewish laws, and defiling the holy place by bringing a gentile to the temple. The Jews mobilised themselves and beat Paul, who was later rescued by soldiers.

In Ephesus, idol makers almost rioted because of Paul's message of forgiveness and healing which became so popular that many magicians and Aternis-worshippers turned to Christ. With only one riot in Governor Felix's jurisdiction, the claim that Paul was stirring riots among all Jews throughout the world (Roman Empire) was an exaggeration of the reality. Satan falsely accuses Christians before God, but he also accuses God before man.

When Jesus healed the demon-possessed man, the Pharisees falsely accused Him of performing miracles through Satan's power. They said *this fellow does not cast out demons except by Beelzebub, the ruler of demons* (Matt. 12:24). Unwilling to let go of their unrighteousness, they accused Jesus of being Satan's servant. Satan also falsely accused God of withholding the fruit of the tree of knowledge of good and evil from Eve (Gen. 3:4 NIV). The Devil presented himself as a caring being who was fighting for Adam and Eve to gain the knowledge of good and evil. The Devil knew he did not tell them that disobeying God would attract His wrath. There are numerous false accusers of brethren in the Church today whose aim is to disgrace faithful disciples of Christ.

A false accusation is a deadly weapon that the accuser uses to drive a wedge between God and His children. Just as the Devil falsely accuses God and His children, Satan's servants also spread lies about God and His children. Warren Wiersbe asserts that Satan is the counterfeiter. . . . He has a false gospel (Gal. 1:6-9), preached by false ministers (2 Cor. 11:13-12), producing false Christians (2 Cor. 11:26). . . . Satan plants his counterfeits wherever God plants true believers (Matt. 13:38). Do not be surprised when people in the Church accuse you of offences you never committed.

The Charlatans

The Charlatans claim to be gifted by God to speak fresh revelation outside of Scripture. The prophetic word could be new, an authoritative word of perdition, teaching, encouragement, or rebuke. The false apostles falsely claim the gift of prophecy, or divine inspiration, or to speak for God, or to make such claims for evil ends. They are commissioned by the Devil to mislead and destabilise Christ's

Church. The Apostle John said, *Beloved, do not believe every spirit, but test the spirits to see whether they are from God, for many false prophets have gone out into the world* (1 John 4:1). Sometimes we find ourselves in difficult situations which tempt us to seek solutions from different sources and false prophets appear as servants of God ready to help us. Every Christian must test every spirit to determine whether the prophecy originates from the Holy Spirit. The prophecy must not contradict the Word of God.

The false prophets have featured throughout the history of the Church. In the second century, Montanus was labelled a heretic because of his belief in new prophetic revelations. John Smith, a nineteenth century religious leader and co-founder of Mormonism, claimed to have received *The Book of Mormons* from the Angel Moroni. Christians must test every spirit to determine if it originates from God.

The Tickler

Ticklers customize their teachings to what the hearers crave to hear. These false apostles are ear-ticklers. Paul said, *for the time is coming when people will not endure sound teaching, but having itching ears they will accumulate for themselves teachers to suit their own passions and will turn away from listening to the truth and wander off into myths* (2 Tim. 4:3-4). Ticklers preach more to please the ear than to profit the heart. They are motivated by popularity and the praise from their audience. These people care less for God's commission to preach the gospel of Christ but focus on everything the itching ears of the people are keen to hear. They play to an audience that will not endure sound teaching to obtain maximum approval. Ticklers are like evil chirurgeons that skin over the wound, but never heal it. Ahab, Herod, Nero and Alexander were victims of flattery.

The ticklers respond to people with depraved itching ears who seek to assemble false teachers who can craft teachings to suit their own passions. The false apostles maintain their following in the Church by teaching only the parts of the Bible that appeal to the passions of their audience. By turning away from the truth, the victims have wandered off into myths. People with itching ears define boundaries for acceptable teachings, filtering out anyone teaching the Biblical truth. The preachers speak less about, or avoid, the truth about sin, hell, judgement, accountability before our God and other difficult Biblical truths. Instead, they focus on topics such as happiness, heaven, or blessings. They easily gloss over the great and weighty things of both of law and gospel and stand most upon things that are of the least significance and concernment to the souls of saints. The modern Church has ticklers who preach false doctrines and responds to post-modern, hedonistic, and relativistic values of predominantly millennials and generation z.

The Speculator

The speculators stretch the interpretation of Biblical texts to satisfy their obsession for novelty, originality, and speculation. They offer views and theories on profound ethical, physical, metaphysical, logical questions, as new and innovative ways of understanding the Bible. The speculators, driven by the desire to discover new things outside the old Biblical truth, derive their reputation from originality. We must not be distracted by strange, new ideas (Heb. 13:8-9). Jesus Christ has always existed as a person from eternity past, with no beginning and no end. He is eternally established in heaven and human beings operate within the created realm of eternity. The desire to generate original truth outside that revealed by the Holy Spirit leads to speculation. Christians are warned not to be attracted to strange, new ideas. The quest for originality in obscure parts of the Bible trivialises the bulk and weighty content of the Truth. Considering that the speculator aims at destroying the Christian faith, the result can only be leading the victims astray.

There are false teachers in the Church who seek kill or destroy the saints and derail God' plan for His creation. They can manifest a single or a combination of traits associated with false teachings and false prophetic words. If we understand these characteristics, we can recognize them, shun their teachings, and avoid the risk of apostasy.

Why does a wolf attack sheep?

The Devil's mission is to steal, kill and destroy God's masterpiece of creation. Jesus said, *the thief does not come except to steal, and to kill, and to destroy. I have come that they may have life, and that they may have it more abundantly* (John 10:10). The Lord revealed Satan's primary goal in everything he does. Regardless of how good his activities seem he has six objectives which are underpinned by a deep-seated hatred for God and His children. According to Stephen Nielsen, Satan wants to be God, to destroy God in the person of Christ, to hinder all the works of God, to make us wilfully obey and worship him, to exercise power over us and control us, and to afflict and destroy us. Every Christian is by default engaged in fierce battles against principalities, powers, rulers of the darkness of this world, and against wickedness in higher places. The false teachers in the Church seek to implement Satan's plan.

The hatred that Satan harbours for God and his children can be traced back to his evil ambition to make himself equal to God and to usurp His honour. Out of pride, Satan wants to be God (Isa. 14:14 KJV). He set his will against the will of God. Losing this battle in heaven, Satan, and his cohort of fallen angels were cast to the earth which he believes is firmly under his control. He absolutely hates God and the humans, who are made in the image and likeness of God.

Throughout history Satan has tried to destroy God by killing Jesus Christ. In the Old Testament, he tried several times to destroy the bloodline of Jesus Christ. The Apostle John also said, *when the dragon saw that he was cast unto the earth, he persecuted the woman which brought the man child* (Rev. 12:13 KJV). Satan plotted through King Herod to kill Jesus but failed miserably: *And the dragon was wroth with the woman and went to make war with the remnant of her seed, which keep the commandments of God, and have the testimony of Jesus Christ* (Rev, 12:17 KJV). He tried again to kill Him on the cross, but Jesus Christ defeated death because he resurrected landing a fatal blow to Satan's bid to derail God's plan for redemption of His creation. But we have overcome him by the blood of the Lamb, and by the word of our testimony (Rev. 12:11).

Satan is still determined to upset God's plan for His creation and to exterminate as many of God's children as he can (Rev. 12:17). In his article, 'What the Bible says about Satan's goal', Richard T. Ritenbaugh says *'Ever since God created the first man and woman in the Garden of Eden, Satan has been interested in nothing else but the eradication of humanity from his "proper domain" (Jude 6). He sees mankind, made after the God-kind (Gen. 1:26-27) with the potential of being born again into the God Family (John 3:3-8; Rev. 14:1-5; 20:4-6), as interlopers, squatters and vagrants in his realm. He is painfully aware that God intends humanity to replace him and his demons as rulers of this planet, and he is fighting like a cornered rat to retain his place and power.'* He strives to deceive, destroy, and kill as many human beings as he can. While causing physical, financial, emotional, and mental suffering is a key component of his toolkit for frustrating God's plan for humanity, spiritual death is his primary goal.

If Satan had the power to execute his will, he would rather exterminate all the humans from the earth. In the Garden of Eden, he sought to destroy humans by severing their link to God, their source of life and daily provisions. The Devil was convinced he had succeeded in snuffing the life out of God' prized creation but he was shocked to realize that God foreordained His Son to pay for our freedom from sin with His blood and to forgive our sins. Satan knows that Jesus has defeated him. He also knows that he has already been judged and stands condemned, but He is determined to wreak havoc in the Church. Every Christian is an obvious target of the Devil, and he works hard with his children to hinder God's work by leading the whole world astray (Rev. 12:9). He attacks Christians to compromise their prayer lives and fasting, fellowship, spiritual growth, Bible studies, community outreach and evangelism. We must be vigilant to escape his deadly traps.

Satan deploys his apostles in the Church to covertly influence the children of

God to abandon their Father and wilfully obey and worship him. The false teachers secretly introduce distorted doctrines to get us to question and doubt the integrity of God, while presenting the Devil as the better option. Accepting these teachings feeds into his desire to exercise power and control over us. Satan derives pleasure in controlling us, in making us his subjects and in afflicting us. His aim is to rip us apart just as the lion tears apart its prey without mercy (Hos. 13:8, Psa. 22:3, 1 Pet. 5:8).

The increased frequency and intensity of ferocious wolf attacks in the Church is a fulfilment of Jesus' prophetic message on mount of Olives when the disciples asked him to tell them what would signal His second coming. He said many prophets shall rise and shall deceive many (Matt.24:). We must watch out for false teachers who seek to ensnare and destroy the faith and testimony of the saints.

When are children of God vulnerable to wolf attacks?

Wolves do not attack sheep at random. They look out for an opportunity when they can kill them with minimum effort and limited or no interference from the shepherd or other sheep. There are conditions that favour the spread of false teachings in the Church. We can encourage false teachers to deceive us when we resist sound doctrines, align ourselves with teachers who feed our lusts and false beliefs, and when we turn away from the truth. Timothy prophesied that *the time will come when they* (saints) *will not endure sound doctrine; but after their own lusts they heap to themselves teachers, having itching ears; and they shall turn their ears from the truth* (2 Tim. 4:3-4). When people resist the sound doctrine and hunger after messages that feed their fleshly desires, they wilfully gather and engage false teachers. This gives the false teachers the opportunity to slip in false teachings.

As Christians, when our minds focus on the flesh, we lose our affinity for the undiluted Word of God. Believers seeking to satisfy fleshly desires may embrace the gods of this world including ungodly entertainment, pleasure, fame, money and material possessions, power, and sex. The false apostles take advantage of these worldly desires to psychologically manipulate and harm believers using false teachings for self-gratification. Warning the Church in Rome, Paul said that *the mind that is set on the flesh is hostile to God, for it does not submit to God's law; indeed, it cannot* (Rom. 8:7 ESV). The deceivers exploit a mind that is hostile to God to lead saints astray.

Christians are vulnerable when the Church leadership is immature, ill prepared and poorly trained for ministry. Even when the saints are eager to study the Word and the Church is prepared to exercise discipline, false teachings can still thrive if the leadership is pastorally weak. The quality of pastoral training and ministry will determine their ability to recognise false teachings. The heretics can be suppressed by a diligent Church leadership. But lapses in pastoral care enable heretics to lead believers astray. Paul urged Church leaders to look after themselves and the flock entrusted to their care by the Holy Spirit. He knew that after his departure fierce wolves would come in among them, not sparing the flock (Acts 20:28-30). In his letter to Timothy, Paul said, *as I urged you when I was going to Macedonia, remain at Ephesus so that you may charge certain persons not to teach any different doctrine, nor to devote themselves to myths and endless genealogies, which promote speculations rather than the stewardship from God that is by faith* (1 Tim. 1:3-4 ESV). He urged Timothy to restrain false teachers from promoting speculations instead teaching people the stewardship of God that comes by faith. The Church leaders who are unschooled in historical theory may not recognise the reincarnated ancient false teachings and their attempt to explain away problems and contradictions in their teachings. We must know the truth to detect falsity.

A major recipe for nurturing heresies in the body of Christ is inadequate understanding and deployment of the five-fold ministry. Writing to the Church in Ephesus, Paul said, *Christ gave these gifts to the Church: the apostles, prophets, evangelists, pastors, and the teachers. Their role is to equip God's people to do his work and build up the Church, the body of Christ, until we come to such unity in our faith and knowledge of God's son that we will be mature and full grown in the Lord, measuring up to the full stature of Christ* (Eph. 4:11-13). These gifted leaders are anointed to oversee ministry areas to grow until the unity in our faith and knowledge is achieved. However, false teachers can thrive if the Church leadership disregards the five-fold ministry model due to inadequate understanding of its structure and functions, abuse of power, and the self-appointment of people to positions of influence and authority without submitting to the Holy Spirit.

Even under the watchful eye of a good shepherd, false teachers can still discretely teach heresy in the Church. In the parable of wheat and tares, the farmer planted good seed during the day but the enemy interplanted the crop with weeds at night. A mature pastoral team may be vigilant at overseeing activities at a large scale but may neglect what goes on in Church groups where false teachers may be sowing seeds of dissention. As the Church grows, the Church structures may not develop at the same pace. This could expose saints to inadequately supervised teachings.

False teachings can grow out of ungodly ambition, ignorance, and conceit. Satan can use overzealous and ambitious teachers to propagate false doctrines, myths, or unproductive genealogies to draw people away from the presence of God. The enemy uses teachers, who lack proper understanding of what they teach, to distort the Scriptures. Paul cautioned Timothy about false teachers who "*wandered away into vain discussion, desiring to be teachers of the law, without understanding either what they are saying or the things about which they make confident assertions*" (1 Tim. 1:6–7). These could be genuine servants of God who labour to share the gospel to the best of their understanding but end up teaching a distorted gospel of Christ. If the Church leadership fails to screen the teachers who feed the flock, false doctrines may creep in. The Apostle John wrote: *Nevertheless, I have a few things against you, because you allow the woman Jezebel, who calls herself a prophetess, to teach and seduce My servants to commit sexual immorality and eat things sacrificed to idols* (Rev. 2:20 NKJV). Some believers circulated a video on social media of a guest speaker, who argued in a Church Bible discussion that Jesus Christ is not the only way to God. But the saints openly dismissed the false teaching while the Resident Pastor sat there and listened. The Church leadership has a pastoral mandate to test all the teachings to safeguard the flock against heresies rooted in ungodly ambition, ignorance and conceit.

Institutional failures can create a medium for nurturing corrupted doctrines in the Church. The Church largely depends on three operational areas to function: preaching of the Word of God through the fivefold ministry; the right administration of the sacraments; and the exercise of discipline, which undergirds the other functions of the Church. When the organs of the Church are corrupted or ineffective, false prophecies and teachings thrive. Speaking through the prophet Jeremiah, the LORD said, *the prophets prophesy falsely, and the priests bear rule by their means; and my people love to have it so; and what will you do in the end thereof* (Jer. 5:31 KJV). Ideally, when prophets prophesy falsely, the priests are required to filter all the messages to protect Christians against falsehood. The believers are vulnerable when the priests rule by their own authority and keep God out of their priestly functions. They even rule based on false prophecies. The situation is further complicated by God's people who love the heretic teachings when the Church institutions support such teachings. Such Church leaders turn a blind eye to heresy because the teachers are popular or have 'mega or successful ministries', or simply to avoid conflict in the Church. We may find ourselves in a Church where the spiritually dysfunctional institutions and the saints promote heresy.

We are vulnerable to heresy when we put up with every teaching or prophecy without testing it against the Word of God. False teachers prey on spiritual immaturity of the believers. The spread of false teaching in the Church is partly explained by the general lack of Bible knowledge and discernment among the people. The minds of such believers may easily be led astray by beliefs in a different Jesus, a different spirit, and a different gospel (2 Cor. 11:3-4; Gal. 1:6-

7). Paul was concerned that the Church at Corinth was vulnerable to false teachings when he said: *I fear that somehow you will be led away from pure and simple devotion to Christ, just as Eve was deceived by the serpent. You seem to believe whatever anyone tells you, even if they preach about a different Jesus from the one we preach or a different spirit from the one you received, or a different kind of gospel from the one you believed* (2 Cor. 11:1-4 NLT). In a world courted by a dreadful enemy we cannot afford to gullibly embrace any teaching or prophecy without testing it for consistency with the Word of God.

The Church may brood false teachers because they are dissatisfied with the status quo. Not every teacher is satisfied with describing various historical interpretations or presenting historically Biblical truth in a clear and convincing fashion. The quest to find new and innovative ways to understand and interpret the Bible has led some Christians into uncharted territories. We must be careful when teachers are driven by the need to blaze a path where no one has gone before, teaching the Bible in a way that is not dependent on any predecessor. The desire to organize the Bible and its prophecy into a single definitive system led John Nelson Darby to develop the dispensational theory based on the concept that God has acted in different ways in dealing with his chosen people throughout human history. His teachings led to deviations from historical understanding of the Church, the sacraments, and the original sin. This false teaching was destructive to the listeners.

We can raise false teachers because of the quest for solutions to long-standing biblical issues. These individuals are driven by the desire to solve definitively a thorny Biblical issue that has pre-occupied theologians for centuries. Such curiosity has entertained untested ideas and interpretations of the Bible which have landed them in Satan's territory. The Jesuit scholar Luis de Molina thought that he had discovered a way to reconcile the age-old conflict between theologians about free will and predestination in the new teaching of "middle knowledge" resulting in a strange theory of open theism. It is rare to find a completely new teaching that has completely eluded the Church fathers, apostles, prophets, and scholars over centuries. We must apply educated scepticism when people try to convince us of a great new insight into the Bible that has never been heard before and when they claim to have received an unprecedented revelation leading to some new teaching.

We are likely to distort the Word of God when we overreact to error in interpretation of the Scriptures. Attempts to passionately defend the Church doctrine has occasionally led to heresy. Studying how Jesus Christ is both human and divine led Nestorius and his followers to a false teaching that there was a sharp division between the humanity and divinity of Christ, presenting Him as two distinct persons. To bridge the divide between the two distinct persons of Christ, Eutyches and his followers taught that Christ has only one nature, that the divine swallows up or absorbs the human nature of Jesus, such that he is left with but one – the anthropic nature. This teaching essentially denied the humanity of Christ. The overzealous teachers replaced one false teaching by another. When teachers claim to correct errors in Biblical interpretation, we need to carefully test the new interpretation to avoid embracing an alternative heresy.

A heretic may be created when a teacher wants to avoid criticism. When teachers are overcautious to avoid breaking ranks with the norms, especially if the teachings are likely to attract criticisms from the surrounding culture such as science. Such people do not like to be thought of as ignorant, uncultured, or uneducated. This may defy a fundamental part of what it means to be a Christian, believing that what God says in His Word is true even if everyone around you disagrees. The Bible tells us that *let God be true though everyone were a liar* (Rom. 3:4). When teachers in the Church believe that their teachings may not be effective to the listeners unless they are presented in a way that is acceptable to the culture, they are bound to distort the Word of God. There are several topical subjects in the Bible that create problems for teachers. There is a tendency to avoid the Biblical doctrine of creation (Gen. 1-2; Col. 1); the theory of evolution; and the departure from the Biblical truth about atonement and Christ's sacrifice, sexuality and marriage, abortion and suffering. The heretics mislead believers to treat all forms of suffering as stemming from unbelief and living in sin. They teach believers to pray against all forms of suffering including that which is necessary for growing our Christian faith. We must be cautious of those teachers who twist the gospel to accommodate the latest cultural thinking.

Scepticism in our modern society is a perfect medium for propagation of Satan's strategy of deceiving the whole world into believing that he doesn't exist (Rev. 12:9). He has succeeded in convincing the world that if people cannot see it, they should not believe it. This false belief gives Satan enough space to virtually manoeuvre unnoticed. Richard T. Ritenbaugh warns that 'Satan deceives people to attribute his malicious works to "natural causes," "unfortunate accidents," "coincidences," "delusions," "mental illnesses," "misunderstandings," even "progress." Thus, the valueless educational methods of today are considered by the intelligentsia to be an evolutionary step forward for mankind. But the truth is that Satan has merely handed Western civilization a time bomb calibrated to render millions of people spiritually deaf to God's call.'

As Christians we must be aware of the diverse conditions that give rise to false teachings and false prophecies in the Church. These conditions provide a favourable camouflage for Satan and his followers to develop and propagate heresies among Christians. The conditions are produced by the Church and the saints, and the manipulation by the enemy. Unless the Church as an institution and the saints understand these conditions and resist their development, Satan will continue to lead the people astray.

What are the effects of false teachers in the Church?

Although the extent of damage that Satan and his agents cause in the Church is difficult to quantify, it is huge. The magnitude of the destruction in the Church is always underestimated because it is masked by the subtlety of the consequences, unquantified spiritual and emotional damage, and destruction that is falsely attributed to natural disasters, mental health, delusion, coincidences, and other unknown factors. Despite these confounding factors, we can detect several effects of false teachings.

When discerning saints are exposed to false teachings, they are likely to detect and discard the heresy. Unfortunately, some saints fall for the false teaching and the consequences are dire for the faith. The enemy knows that if his actions are violent, sudden, and fatal, he may give away his position and undermine his strategy to destroy or derail God's plan for His creation. His strategy is to gradually, but steadily, starve and suffocate the faith of a believer. The process of dismembering a saint from the body of Christ is so subtle that the victim is led away from the presence of God while believing he is doing the will of God. Seeds of deceit arouse curiosity in a saint as the thoughts are led astray from sincere and pure devotion to Christ. The desire to delve deeper into heresy gives the devil a firm position to challenge the truth that underpins our faith. In this state, we begin to question the Biblical truth and entertain doubt. As the enemy fuels our doubt, the urge to resist the truth grows. The result is disobedience and eventual complete apostasy from God.

Over the past four decades several Christians in my family, school, workplace, and the Church have walked away from the faith. The heretics cause people to err and to totally lose the faith. They seduce the elect and lead them into by-paths and blind thickets of error, blasphemy, and wickedness, where they are lost forever. The distorted gospel alienates Christ. In his book, *The Great Spiritual Migration*, Brian McLaren wrote, "*What happened to Christianity? What happened to Jesus and his beautiful message? We feel as if our founder has been kidnapped and held hostage by extremists. His captors parade him in front of cameras to say, under duress, things he obviously doesn't believe. As their blank-faced puppet, he often comes across as anti-poor, anti-environment, anti-gay, anti-intellectual, anti-immigrant, and anti-science (not to mention pro-torture, pro-inequality, pro-violence, pro-death penalty, and pro-war). That's not the Jesus of the Gospels! That's not the Jesus who won our hearts!*" When the enemy distorts the gospel through false teachings, people see a different Jesus who discriminates against some people and other works of God's creation as if some sins are weightier than others. But the gospel of Christ is an open invitation to all sinners giving everyone an equal opportunity to access His saving grace. Jesus paid the highest price for the redemption of every soul with His blood and has forgiven every sin. Accepting people of all backgrounds in the Church does not imply that we condone the lifestyles of everyone God brings to the body. Every disciplined child of God learns how to 'eat the fish and spit out the bones.' We love everyone created in the image of God although we may not accept their lifestyles.

Satan labours might and main, by false teachers, to deceive, delude, and for ever undo the precious souls of men and women. Apart from making God's people to err, false apostles lick and suck the blood of innocent souls. They destroy and scatter the sheep of God's pasture (Jer. 23:1-2) and seduce the saints to turn to a different gospel and to desert Christ who called them by His grace. The people exposed to such false teachings can blaspheme the way of the truth and are greedily exploited with false words (2 Pet. 1-3). The Apostle Peter warned that *in their greed they* (false apostles) *will make clever lies to get hold of your money* (2 Pet. 2:3 NLT). Paul also explained that *such persons do not serve our Lord Christ, but their own appetites, and by smooth talk and flattery they deceive the hearts of the naïve* (Rom. 16:18 ESV). The false apostles intentionally leverage the needs of Christians to satisfy their own desires. They prey on vulnerable people craving for miraculous interventions in their situations. Such people are ready to do anything to receive a prophetic word and special prayers. In the process, false ministers promise things that the God will never do.

The Devil strives to shift believers' eyes from teachings that lead to spiritual abundance to those that feed fleshly desires. Some false teachers exploitatively charge members for prayers. They have taught their congregations that general prayers during a Church service can't address certain issues. Members who need a divine intervention in their situations were asked to pay a specified amount of money for every special prayer offered on individual basis. However, most of these congregants are frustrated because they seem not to have received their miracles. The victims of unanswered prayers are then accused of unbelief. Asking believers to pay for prayers to guarantee God's response to prayers demeans the grace, mercy, and love of God.

Some people have shipwrecked their faith by rejecting faith and good conscience. Examples of such people include Hymenaeus and Alexander, whom Paul handed over to Satan that they might learn not to blaspheme (1 Tim. 1:18-20). As Christians, we need to avoid the schemes of the enemy because God will judge the false teachers and the victims of their teachings.

Walking away from God's presence for any reason, including false prophecies, attracts the wrath of God and will result in saints losing their saintly prizes. The Apostle John said, *watch out, so that you do not lose the prize for which we have been working so hard. Be diligent so that you will receive your full reward. For if you wander beyond the teaching of Christ, you will not have fellowship with God* (2 John 1:8-9 NLT). False teachers can undo the redemptive work of God, the fruit of the Spirit and the eternal life of a saint. The heresies can, among other things, lead to apostasy, blasphemy, maligning the name of the Lord, and losing the prize we have laboured for. We need to avoid false teachings to remain steadfast in our walk with the Lord.

How do we recognize false teachings and false prophecies?

The Church is an ideal place to listen to God-centred, Christ-exalting, Bible-saturated and Holy Spirit-dependent servants of God who genuinely serve the Lord. Such sound teachings and prophecies could edify the saints. However, there is no perfect Church that is devoid of heretic operatives regardless of how righteous or holy the assembly looks. This condition, coupled with Biblical illiteracy and spiritual laziness, has driven many people away from the presence of God. In His sermon on the Mount, Jesus taught how few people take the narrow and difficult road to discern the truth and explained why we should care about this.

False teachings and prophecies may be difficult to detect because they may not be totally wrong. The enemy blends false teachings with some truth to make the whole message sound authentic. If we do not dedicate hours, mind energy, and eyeballs to study God's Word, we will struggle to recognize false teachings in the Church. Every saint needs to watch out for the false apostles and their ideologies by acquiring tools and techniques for testing the teachings and prophecies, and the behaviour, of the apostles. There are several ways of testing the teachers and teachings, and prophets and prophecies, for consistency with Scripture.

Test the fruit of the life of every teacher or prophet

We must always test the fruit of the life of every teacher or prophet bringing the Word in the Church against the Word of God. Does the teacher or prophet exhibit the behavioural qualities that edify the body of Christ and glorify God? Apostles in the Church do not have marks on their foreheads to show us whether they are genuine or false teachers. The onus is upon a believer to test the behavioural fruit of such people. A false teacher may teach with charisma and conviction, pray fervently, perform miracles, and influence major decisions of the Church. Such people may be gifted, skilful and insightful in their teachings. They may appear to have the hallmarks of great Bible teachers any Christian should listen to. Despite these great virtues, the inner being of a false apostle is that of a ravenous wolf seeking to destroy the believer. Jesus said, *beware of false teachers which come to you in sheep's clothing, but inwardly they are ravening wolves. Ye shall know them by their fruits* (Matt. 7:15-16 KJV). The external appearance of an animal or plant may not necessarily reflect its inner nature. What we see in the teachers and prophets, and what we hear when they teach and prophesy may not depict their inner nature. False apostles put on an appearance of innocence, brotherhood, and dedication to shepherding God's flock. They seem to walk in, and to be led by, the Holy Spirit but they are as deceptive and dangerous as wolves are to sheep.

A genuine apostle bears the fruit of the Spirit which expresses love, joy, peace, longsuffering, gentleness, goodness, faith, meekness, and temperance (Gal. 5:22-23). The behavioural fruit of a teacher should be tested against this fruit.

Paul placed a huge premium on the principle of holiness and righteousness in his own life-giving credibility to the gospel he preached. Writing to the Church at Thessalonica, he said, *for our gospel did not come to you in word only, but also in power, and in the Holy Spirit and in much assurance, as you know what kind of men, we were among you for your sake.* He literally said, you know what men we have proved to be, so judge us by our lives as we preach the gospel. There are several behavioural features that characterise false teachers. They abuse Church resources and break the national laws and regulations. The Church has come under scrutiny because of abuse of the charity status by heretics. While the Church income is exempt from tax in many countries, some governments have observed irregularities in Church financial accounting systems prompting special investigations of financial misconduct.

While some Ministers of Religion have genuinely acquired wealth through their business ventures, others have exploited the Church for personal gain. I watched to a very disturbing television interview involving a woman whose mother died from cancer. When the daughter examined her financial records, she realized that the mother gave her savings to the Church because she was taught that by doing so, she would be healed of her cancer, but she still died. Distortion and commercialization of the gospel for personal financial gain is a big challenge facing the Church today. False apostles may also claim their teaching is new because of a special knowledge received on our behalf. God speaks to us through other believers but when someone claims unsolicited special knowledge on our behalf, especially if the prophet claims he alone can access that knowledge from God, it raises a red flag. Watch out for such teachers or prophets.

While the external appearance of false teachers may be deceptive, their inward nature will always be revealed by the fruit of their lives. If we carefully examine the teachers, we can identify those who distort and contradict the Scripture and claim to have special knowledge or revelation for believers. Apart from following their sensuality and lacking moral restraint (2 Peter 2:2), they entice the saints with sensual passions of the flesh (2 Pet. 2:18-19). Some of these teachers exploit believers (2 Peter 2:1-3) and make money the message rather than preaching the gospel of Jesus Christ. They teach a different doctrine. The body of Christ also harbours false apostles who devote themselves to myths and endless genealogies which promote speculations (1 Tim. 1:3-4). Such people tend to rebel against the Church leadership, create divisions in the body of Christ and they even offer an alternative worldview of the Bible. *They teach vain philosophy and empty deceit, according to human tradition, and according to the elemental spirits of the world, and not according to Christ* (Col. 2:8). The Bible refers to such false teachers as slaves of corruption (2 Pet 2:18-19) who are spiritually destructive, egocentric, and unproductive, bringing upon themselves swift destruction (2 Pet. 2:1). They destroy and scatter the sheep of God's pasture and lead them astray. The motive of the enemy is to ensnare and destroy the faith and the testimony of saints.

False teachers strive to draw away disciples after them (Acts 20:28-30) by teaching a different doctrine that contradicts the teachings of the Lord Jesus Christ and prophecies that align with godliness. They are puffed up with conceit and lack understanding. Such people have an unhealthy craving for controversy and for quarrels about words, which produce envy, dissension, slander, evil suspicions, and constant friction among people who are depraved in mind and deprived of the truth, taking godliness as a means of gain (1 Tim. 6:3-5).

A key strategy of false apostles is to pervert the grace of God into sensuality, using grace as a permit for indulging in immorality. They also display a conflicting behaviour. Their signs and wonders are accompanied by the invitation to serve other gods. The law of Moses states that, *if a prophet or a dreamer of dreams arises among you and gives you a sign or a wonder, and the sign or wonder that he tells you comes to pass, and if he says, 'Let us go after other gods,' which you have not known, 'and let us serve them,' you shall not listen to the words of that prophet or that dreamer of dreams. For the Lord your God is testing you, to know whether you love the Lord your God with all your heart and with all your soul*

(Deut. 13:1-3 ESV); *They profess to know God, but they deny him by their works. They are detestable, disobedient, unfit for any good work* (Titus 1:16). The false apostles perform signs and wonders to authenticate their heretic messages which are tagged with a hidden invitation to go after other gods. We are cautioned not to be carried away by the miracles but to identify and reject the invitation of these detestable, destructive, disobedient, and unfit apostles who deny Jesus Christ through their false teachings. More importantly, we need to assess these works carefully to pass any test the Lord administers through these teachings.

Test the source of the message

Christians recognize the Bible as God' authoritative Word to humanity and every sound doctrine and prophetic word must originate from this treasure trove of the truth. False teachings are based on stories heretics have made up (2 Pet. 2:16). While referring to the Bible, false apostles usually rely on their creativity, visions, emotions, speculations, and peculiar revelations when developing their teachings. Be wary of people who claim to base their teachings and prophecies on sources other than the Bible for God's messages. Selected belief systems exemplify teachings from multiple sources. While affirming the Bible, Mormons affirm the inspiration of the *Book of Mormons, Doctrine and Covenants*, and the *Pearl of Great Price* based on the premise that the Bible is incomplete and not inerrant. They also believe that they can receive authoritative interpretations and new authoritative revelations through their elaborate hierarchy of Church leadership. The Jehovah's witnesses reject the Christian Doctrine of Trinity, inherent immortality of the soul and hellfire, which they consider as unscriptural doctrines. They also prefer to use their own Bible translation, the *New World Translation of the Holy Scriptures*. As Christians the Bible is the authoritative source of our teachings.

Cults attract people through emotional appeals and use of so-called sacred text. When false teachers compose their messages from these diverse sources, the Scripture-coated false teachings may sound authentic. People will notice if the message is way off, but they won't notice as much if the message contains just enough truth to appear as truth while being false. The best safeguard against Christian apostasy is studying, and getting saturated, with the Word of God. We need to know the truth to recognize unauthentic sources of teachings.

Test the substance of the message

True teachers centre their messages on Jesus Christ while false teachers position Him at the margins of their teachings. Movement away from the centrality of Christ is subtle. A false apostle may even deny the sovereign Lord. Warning the saints about false teachers, the Apostle Peter said, *they will secretly introduce destructive heresies, even denying the sovereign Lord who bought them* (2 Pet. 2:2 NIV). Such teachers speak about how other people can help change our lives, but if we listen carefully to what they are saying, we will notice that Jesus Christ is not essential to their message. Always test the teachings for consistency with fundamental Christian doctrines including creation, the fall, salvation through Jesus Christ, the divinity and humanity of Jesus Christ, and Trinity of God, among others. The substance of their message is distorted and contradicts Scripture on these doctrines, reflects their special authoritative interpretation and revelation knowledge on behalf of saints, and substantially relies on extrabiblical sources, focusing mainly on non-Christocentric sources of knowledge. They tend to reject the authority of the Bible or the exclusivity of salvation in Christ. But these heresies are usually meshed with Biblical truth.

Some false teachers exploit the flock for personal gain. It is not wrong for the Church to preach and teach about generosity, sacrificial giving, and tithing. Neither is it wrong to financially support Church ministers. If done properly, giving is an act of worship, and it supports God's work. God demonstrated this act by giving His only begotten Son as a price for our freedom from sin through His blood. The Bible specifies what, when, why and how to give according to God's will. It teaches us that we must: bring a gift in proportion to the way the Lord our God has blessed us (Deut. 16:17; Luke 21:1-4); give what we have decided in our hearts, not reluctantly or under compulsion but to give freely as we have freely received (Matt. 10:8); give to the hungry and or thirsty enemy (Prov. 25:21); share with those in need (Luk 3:11; Matt. 25:35-40) and to give generously (2 Cor. 9:6; Deut. 15:10; Psa. 37:21). There are several benefits of such giving: a gift opens the way and ushers the giver into the presence of the great (Prov. 18:16); those who give to the poor lend to the Lord and lack nothing, for the Lord rewards them for their generosity (Prov. 19:17; Prov. 28:27); a generous person will prosper, for whoever refreshes others will also be refreshed (Prov. 11:25); God will supply and increase a saint's seed store and enlarge his harvest of righteousness (2 Cor. 9:10); generosity results in thanksgiving to God (2 Cor 10:11); and tithes and offerings ensure there is enough food in the temple and fling open the windows of heaven to release abundant blessings. However, false teachers pervert the principles and practices of godly giving to divert resources of the Church to their personal accounts. They subtly piggyback on this sacred act to exploit the saints for personal gain. We need to carefully distinguish between genuine teachings about money and the love of money, which breach the principles of good stewardship of God's resources.

Test the results of teacher's behaviour and the teachings

Always test the results of the teachings, the prophecies and the behaviour of the teachers and prophets in the body of Christ to ensure they are consistent with Scripture. After the apostles have ministered, where does the message ultimately lead us? Does the message edify us or lead us astray? There are several outcomes of false teachings and false prophecies. When a prophecy does not materialise in space and time, the Lord has not spoken. *When a prophet speaks in the name of the Lord, if the thing does not happen or come to pass, that is the thing which the Lord has not spoken; the prophet has spoken it presumptuously; you shall not be afraid of him* (Deut. 18:22 NKJV). God's prophetic word is cause-driven, audience-specific and designed to be fulfilled. If its fulfilment is conditional upon a recipient doing something, it should happen once the condition is met.

When a false prophet speaks presumptuously, nothing happens. The Lord instructs that such workers of iniquity should not be given the honour due to the office of a prophet. Unfortunately, the victims of heretic teachings are usually blamed for lacking faith. Test the behavioural fruit of the apostle to ascertain whether God has spoken.

False apostles leave their intended beneficiaries distraught, apostate, blasphemous, atheistic, gnostic, proud, openly rebellious against constituted authority, sexually immoral, and or immoderately desirous of acquiring money or wealth, depending on the nature of teaching or prophecy. These effects may develop over time, progressively alienating the victims from their faith as heresies take root. Detecting these effects largely depends on the size of the Church, the level of commitment of the saint to the Church activities, the level of spiritual maturity, sensitivity to the Holy Spirit and the organizational culture. In a large Church where believers have limited interactions with others, several of these effects of heretic teachings happen without people realising, unless they are close to the victim. We need to be deeply connected to the body of believers to detect signals of the effects of heresies in the Church. False teachers take advantage of people who are either lonely or loosely connected to the Church.

Test the appeal of the message

The true teachers appeal to what the Holy Spirit directs them to teach from the Scripture. The Apostle Peter said, *we have the word of the prophets made more certain and you will do well to pay attention to it* (2 Pet. 1:19). The false teacher appeals to the fallen human nature. *By appealing to the lustful desires of sinful human nature, they entice people who are just escaping from those who live in error* (2 Pet. 2:18). They exhibit works of the flesh including adultery, fornication, lewdness, idolatry, sorcery, hatred, contentions, jealousies, outbursts of wrath, selfish ambitions, dissentions, heresies, envy, murder, drunkenness revelries and the like (Gal. 5:19-20). The true teacher focuses on what God has said in His Word, while the false teacher is interested in what people want to hear or what will appeal to their flesh. The false apostles will distort the Scripture to control the behaviour of others. Their motivation is often power. Some false teachers will pervert Scripture to live as they want and participate in otherwise immoral behaviour for selfish motives. By so doing, the way of the truth is maligned, and the name of the Lord is blasphemed.

Test the impact of the teachings on the life of the Church

False teachers create and entrench divisions in the Church. There are different forms of Christianity within the Church. The Pluralism Project at Harvard University identified three major versions of Christianity: Evangelicalism representing a diverse group of Christians who often prioritize spiritual rebirth, proselytizing, and spiritual piety; Fundamentalism which is characterized most notably by Biblical literalism; and Pentecostalism which refers to Christian denominations which prioritize the Holy Spirit and whose worship services may include speaking in tongues, faith healings, and other charismatic expressions. These groups have held different positions on science, environment, intellectualism, Trinitarianism, abortion, homosexuality, the divinity and humanity of Jesus Christ, exclusivity of salvation through Jesus Christ, among others. False teachers take advantage of diverse views to promote a pluralistic view that all religions lead to salvation of souls. They try to convince people that Christians who believe that Jesus Christ is the only way to the Lord our God are hateful, narrow-minded and a threat to peace.

The theological debates that question the nature and character of God are feeding into the increasing animosity against God, especially in the western world. Some theological scholars are questioning God's perfect and exhaustive knowledge of the future. They argue that God does not have exhaustive knowledge of the future emphasizing God's limitation in dealing with humans. The heretics further teach that God has created intelligent humans with freedom of choice, and hence precludes the need for God to predetermine or foreknow moral choices of humanity. Such false teachings have led Christians astray.

There are debates on which Bible version Christians must use to ensure they engage with the original Word of God. Some Christians believe that the King James Version (KJV) is the only authentic version, which any genuine Christian must use as a pilgrim's manual. This is based on the belief that other translations do not carry the same authority as KJV because they dilute, distort, or change the original sense of the Word. Others believe that versions that consider manuscripts discovered after the publication of the KJV are more accurate than earlier versions. Some Bible teachers argue that other translations of the Bible are equally valid. This debate has fed into the Today's New International Version (TNIV) controversy. Although the proponents of this new translation describe it as a gender-neutral translation that communicates Scriptures with accuracy and clarity of English, some evangelical Christians are very sceptical about the translation. They also contend that it has potential to significantly split the evangelical movement. False teachers leverage these controversies to teach that the Bible contains errors and must not be believed in its entirety.

False teachers have divided the Church into two camps based on divergent views on gender roles in the Church. One group consists of evangelical egalitarians who argue that equality between sexes implies that there should be no functional distinctions between men and women. A spiritually qualified woman should be allowed to occupy any ministerial position in the body of Christ, such as pastor, teacher, elder or Bishop. The other group comprises complementarians, who believe that both sexes are equal in essence, but God-ordained functional differences should be maintained and therefore some positions should be for men only. The Devil is using this debate to cause divisions in the body of Christ.

False teachers are starving the body of Christ resulting in spiritual malnutrition or Biblical illiteracy. Such Ministers discourage believers from studying the Word of God. The laisez-affaire approach to the Bible has resulted in Churchgoing adults questioning some doctrinal aspects including the accuracy of the Bible, the existence of Satan, sinless nature of Jesus, the second coming of Jesus Christ, and the need for evangelism. It also leads to the belief that good works are one of the keys to persuading God to forgive our sins. Such Christians have low to medium commitment to Christianity. Christian malnutrition feeds into 'juvenilizing of culture and the Church.' As Christians observe their spiritual discipline, it is expected that their spiritual ideas, customs and social behaviour will reflect the life of Christ. However, the culture of many 21st century Christians is largely that of Christian babies because of the lack of discipline in our walk with God.

While the universal Church is growing through conversions, dechristianization due to heretic operatives in the Church is increasingly becoming a major challenge in the 21st century. The population of false teachers in the Church is increasing rapidly. The key to thriving in a Church with ferocious wolves is understanding who they are, how they operate, and mastering the tools and techniques for resisting them.

How can we thrive amid false teachings and prophecies?

If we belong to the body of Christ and participate in the life of the Church, we will be exposed to heretic teachings. Recognizing the risks of heresies by itself does not offer adequate safeguards against these destructive vices. We must build a robust multipronged defence against the ferocious wolves in the Church to run the full course of our Christian race on earth. The golden rule is that you must know the truth to detect falsehood. J.E.B. Spredemann said, *unless you know the truth, you are simply indoctrinated with error: "It's been said that only the educated are free, but I contend. Only those who are educated with TRUTH can be inherently free. Otherwise, you are simply indoctrinated with error.* There is no substitute for knowing the absolute truth in the detection of false teachers and their heresies. God gave Joshua the secret to prosperity and good success in his walk with Him: *This book of the law shall not depart out of thy mouth; but thou shalt meditate therein day and night, that thou mayest observe to do according to all that is written therein: for then thou shalt make thy way prosperous, and then thou shalt have good success* (Josh. 1:8 KJV). When we study and meditate on the Word of God, God gives specific knowledge and instructions to live according to His purpose and plan. This knowledge revealed to us through the Holy Spirit is the spiritual lens for detection of false teachings.

We must always test every spirit against the Word of God to see whether it is from God. Paul instructed the saints in Thessalonica to test everything and hold fast to what is good (1 Thess. 5:21). It is not an act of insubordination to test every message the teachers and prophets bring to us for consistency with Scripture. True teachers must teach believers to examine their messages for consistency with Scripture. Warning the saints, the Apostle John said, *beloved, do not believe every spirit, but test the spirits to see whether they are from God, for many false prophets have gone out into the world* (1 John 4:1 ESV). The Acts of Apostles also state that the *Jews (Bereans) were more noble than those in Thessalonica; they received the word with all eagerness, examining the Scriptures daily to see if these things were so* (Acts 17:11). Christians who desire to fend off false teachings and prophecies must study and know the Word and use that knowledge to sense-check every message they receive from servants in the Church to ensure it originates from God. We must reject any message that disagrees with the Scripture regardless of who brought it. Just as animals rely on sensory cues to know a predator is around, we need to develop our physical and spiritual cues to know when we encounter false teachers. The cost of corrupting our faith with heresy could be massive including apostasy, loss of the prize you have laboured for and eternal damnation.

Christians must resist and expose false teachings and unfruitful works of darkness. Paul instructed the Church at Ephesus not to take part in the unfruitful works of darkness, but instead expose them (Eph. 5:11). If a Christian detects false teachings in the Church, they must bring them to the attention of the Church leadership. The Apostle John stressed that, if anyone comes to you and does not bring the doctrine of Christ, do not receive him into your house or give him any greeting, for whoever greets him takes part in his wicked works (2 John

1:10-11). The Apostle implies that we are not rude, unfriendly, or unwelcoming when we refuse to entertain or greet false teachers in our homes, otherwise we will be taking part in their sin. We must deal firmly with heretics, rebuking them and never tolerating their heresy.

The Church must identify and discipline the false teachers to protect the flock. Church leaders who shepherd the flock have a duty of care to protect it against the ravenous wolves. Writing to Titus about heretics, Paul said, *they must be silenced, since they are upsetting whole families by teaching for shameful gain what they ought not to teach. One of the Cretans, a prophet of their own, said, "Cretans are always liars, evil beasts, lazy gluttons." This testimony is true. Therefore, rebuke them sharply, that they may be sound in the faith, not devoting themselves to Jewish myths and the commands of people who turn away from the truth. ...* (Titus 1:10-16). Not all false teachers are irredeemable. Once detected, the Church must silence and rebuke the heretics sharply to restore them to sound faith and to protect the flock. Paul urged Titus to stay in Ephesus to command people to stop teaching false doctrines and devoting themselves to myths and endless genealogies (Tit. 1:3-4). Paul also cautioned Timothy that in the last days, there will be difficult times and people *will act as if they are religious, but they will reject the power that could make them godly. You must stay away from people like that* (2 Tim. 3:5 NLT). It is not cowardice to stay away from potential sources of spiritual catastrophes. As a precautionary measure, avoid people who teach false doctrines and cause believers to err. Never consider yourself strong enough to withstand the venom of such people, lest you fall.

We cannot win the war against heretics without the leadership of the Holy Spirit and full use of the armour of God. The major weapon for disarming and resisting false teachers and their teachings is knowing the truth through the tutorage of the Holy Spirit who is resident in us. If we observe the discipline of prayerfully and meditatively studying the Scripture, He will teach us the truth we need to detect and deflate the false teachings. The Apostle John wrote: *I write these things to you about those who are trying to deceive you. But the anointing that you received from him abides in you, and you have no need that anyone should teach you. But as his anointing teaches you about everything, and is true, and is no lie—just as it has taught you, abide in him* (1 John 2:26-27 ESV). Spirit-filled Christians carry the anointing that teaches the whole truth that is needed to detect and resist heretic teachings and prophecies. The greatest author and teacher of the Word abides in us and gives us access to the wondrous truth embedded in Scripture. Be careful of the enemy's strategy to distract us from studying and living out the Word of God under the guidance of the Holy Spirit.

We need to protect the treasure trove of faith and good conscience in our jars of clay. Paul instructed Timothy to guard the deposit entrusted to him and to avoid the irreverent babble and contradictions of what was falsely called knowledge, for by professing it some swerved from the faith (1 Tim. 6:20-21). A Christian can labour to access pure milk or meat from the Word through the Holy Spirit but if the repository of the knowledge is porous to other knowledge sources, it could easily be corrupted and hence the need to guard the deposit. A secure deposit of knowledge depends on setting guard rails for our physical and spiritual sensors and ensuring the gates keep out false teachings and prophecies.

Encounters with heretics are part of the evil schemes we experience everyday no matter how peaceful and serene a day seems. The real war against false teachers is spiritual. Fighting this war requires us to be fully trained and equipped with spiritual weaponry. Paul urged the saints in Ephesus to put on the full armour of God to withstand the devil's schemes (Eph. 6:11). An intact armour comprises the belt of truth, the breastplate of righteousness, the gospel of peace, the shield of faith, helmet of salvation and the sword of the Spirit (Eph. 6:11-18). This is coupled with different types of prayer and requests. The armour of God is unique defence tool with multiple and delicate parts that are interwoven to provide maximum protection against a well-equipped fighting enemy force. For the armour to effectively protect a saint, it must be intact, with a full set of components that are fully functional and in a superb condition. A Christian must always wear this full armour because we are always at the battle front with ravenous wolves whose aim is to destroy us and anything that God has created or to derail God' plan for creation. The full armour of God is the epitome of our weaponry for our battle front.

Wolves in sheep's skins are a real danger in the 21st century Church. Their stealthy activities in corrupting the gospel have cost the Church many souls. Every Christian must strive to understand who these wolves are, what they do and their impact on a believer's faith, why they attack believers, and how to detect and resist them. Every believer has access to the weaponry for fending off wolfly attacks. Walking with God involves detecting and defeating ravenous wolves.

PART 4
Is walking with God in the 21st century an illusion?

Some people have argued that Christianity, which has dictated societal norms for centuries has been debunked and is no longer relevant today. The scientific, technological, socioeconomic, cultural, and theological developments have allegedly rendered this worldview irrelevant. The Church is facing unrivalled hostility from enemies within and enemies without. Is walking with God in this century a realistic expectation or an illusion?

CHAPTER 11

Unmasking the god of this world

As the Church operates in an increasingly hostile environment, there is a temptation to resort to conventional approaches to adapting to the conditions. If the Church legally functions in a country where the laws of the land are respected, the national security system should provide adequate protection to ensure Christians can practice their faith without the fear of persecution. Where institutional structures are inadequate, corrupted, or are part of the national apparatus for persecuting the Church, Christians have either fled, changed their identity, petitioned legislators, operated undercover, fought back, campaigned against persecution, or endured the hardships. These are helpful, but very superficial solutions to the issues facing Christians today. Considering that the Church is the world's most persecuted faith group, its increasingly intense and diverse challenges are scarcely understood.

The challenges facing Christians today are symptoms of a hidden problem. We need to fully understand the underlying cause of the increasingly antichristian atmosphere of our age. The truth is that Satan, working behind the scenes, is the driving force behind this evil and perverse fascination with persecution of Christians. What the Devil is doing in secret manifests as scientific, technical, sociocultural, theological, ideological, and philosophical resistance to Christianity.

We need to unmask the god of this world to understand how he afflicts Christians today. Satan is the prince of evil spirits, the adversary, or the inveterate enemy of God and of Jesus Christ, and the deceiver, who masquerades as the angel of light. His objective is to steal, to kill and to destroy God's creation. He can work through people and systems to achieve his objectives. He can also take possession of human bodies and afflict them.

The Devil is strategic and secretive in his operations. In August 2015, my wife and I watched a TV episode entitled, 'Monsters inside me' in which the narrator Justin Peed and the Biologist Dan Riskin explained how and why tapeworm cysts in pork or tapeworm eggs in contaminated food or drinks could lead to loss of sight. Dan explained how a cyst can survive in a human body for several years before it harms a person. When a human being ingests a cyst, the immune system of the body fights it and restrains its activities, but it can hide in the body for almost 25 years until conditions are favourable for it to attack the host. At this stage the cyst can migrate to the eye, which then produces substances that cause permanent loss of sight. The devil, like the tapeworm, uses different strategies to attack his victims, some of which are explained in this section.

The Devil is an alien species that has colonised human species

The Devil is an invasive or alien species that colonises humans and the earth they were given to rule. He is strategic in his manoeuvres to invade and rule over God's earthly creation. Tapeworms, 'invasive species' in a human body, have developed traits that enable them to survive in, and to injure, kill or destroy the host. They infect people as their definitive host. For us to understand how dangerous invasive species are, we need to examine their characteristics.

Experts in animal health have reported that invasive species are able to quickly colonise a new environment because: they stealthily invade the host or new environment; they have the ability to produce many highly dispersing offspring within a short period of time, which grow and mature very quickly; they easily adapt to new conditions; they are hard to kill and have no predators in their new environment; and these species have the ability to alter the system.

The invasive species develop ways of dealing with the resistance or blocking the defence system of the new environment. They are very aggressive and strategic when selecting their location and sites of action, and they use their host to launch fresh attacks in other areas. These unique features mean that the worms can live in the body of the victim provided the host is alive. The aim of the tapeworm or an invasive species is to fulfil its own purpose. It is not interested in the welfare of the host. The species also forcibly use the system of the victim to satisfy its own needs. How do characteristics of invasive species manifest in Satan's assault on Christians?

Satan has usurped the power of man to rule the earth and has become the god of this world. Satan overstepped his boundaries and lost his position in heaven. Lucifer and cohort of angels forfeited their heavenly citizenship, and he was stripped of his beauty, position, and rights to heaven. They were cast to the earth where they became alien species because God has given the earth to humans. (Gen. 1:26; Psa. 115:16). God, who entrusted the governance of the earth to humanity, has unmatched intelligence and wisdom, which are powerfully expressed through creation and its functions. But He delegated the authority to rule the earth to man.

Any species God has created has traits which enable it to live and function in specific environment. God created man and all other living things on earth to have physical bodies, while heavenly beings are spiritual creatures. Even the Son of God had a physical body to blend with earthly beings. By contrast, Satan and his minions are aliens or invasive species on earth, different from us, and not created for this earth. Satan is a spiritual parasite who uses human beings to achieve his own goal of rebelling against the authority of God.

Genesis 1:26 describes the nature and function of people who God created. God the Father, God the Son, and God the Holy Spirit created a human species that bore His image and likeness or that reflected His qualities. How do we describe God? God is, among other things, loving, kind, peaceful, light, patient, good, merciful, righteous, holy, long suffering, wise, humble, meek, caring, faithful, sociable, intelligent, creative, and purposeful. Man, created in the image of God, had mirror images of these qualities as God's representative on earth.

The nature and character of God in man enables him to commune with

God, to know Him, to hear His voice, to understand what He says, to think like Him, and to carry out his purpose. Man needs these qualities to rule over God's creation. Since Satan was not created to rule over the earth, he lacks these qualities of stewardship. This alien species accounts for the dysfunctional nature of the corrupted earth and everything in it. No wonder the devil uses the image of God in people to rule the world. Satan can never achieve anything without the cooperation of humans. If we resist him, he will flee and abort his schemes. As a Christian you have the power to block the evil plans of the Devil on earth.

The primary function of humans to govern the earth. A healthy creation praises, worships, and glorifies God. Humans are expected to care for the creation to effectively worship Him. God expects Christians to proactively lead everyone in caring for the earth. This must be an integral component of the great commission. Through disobedience, humans and the rest of creation were cursed, and we abdicated our rule over creation. The gospel should reconcile both the human and the non-human creation to the Lord our God and enable us to regain our rule over creation. The alien species, the Devil, has strategically blinded many Christians to neglect their primary function of ruling over God's earthly creation.

When God created humans in His image, He blessed them. He gave them the ability to express their full potential (Gen. 1:28). God blessed man to: be fruitful - to bear offspring to perpetuate his own species, engage his intellectual faculties to generate novel ideas, work with his hands, be creative and constructive with his words, and express the fruit of the Spirit; multiply – the fruit containing seed(s) must grow, develop and be nurtured to produce several dispersing offspring; and to spread the seed over the entire earth and to ensure controlled distribution of God's creation on land, and in the air and the sea. God also provided humans with food and gave them everything they needed to rule over earthly creation.

When our ancestors disobeyed God, He did not withdraw the ability of man to multiply and replenish the earth and subdue it. The invasive spirit of Satan controlled the human spirit causing man to reproduce and multiply, replenish, and subdue the earth outside God's plan. The corrupted human seed has reproduced after its kind. Satan behaves like a virus, which does not have the ability to reproduce and multiply on its own. It invades and uses the cells of other living things to reproduce and multiply. The Devil is alien to the earth and does not have the ability to function on this earth without the cooperation of humans. He has reproduced invasive species through us.

Humans were good before Satan invaded them

Before a person ingests the tapeworm cysts or eggs, he is healthy, functional, and productive, and enjoys a normal life. As soon as the parasites enter the body, he is infected. Similarly, before Adam and Eve ate the fruit from the tree of knowledge of good and evil in the Garden, they were sinless. They were happy and had a good relationship with God and other earthly creatures. God knew He had made a very good human species.

Although humans did not attend any equivalent of our kindergarten, primary or tertiary education institution, their knowledge and skills were outstanding. Think of it, God brought each animal He had created to Adam for naming, and He approved every name Adam assigned to each species of the animal kingdom. Did God simply accept every name Adam gave to animals to please him? No, Adam was the first taxonomist on earth to accurately assign names to animals and his helpmate based on their characteristic features.

After God, the Chief Orthopaedic, surgically removed a rib from man under general anaesthesia, He made another being from it. When Adam woke up from his sleep, God presented another human being to him, and his classification and naming skills were accurate and precise. He recognized her as a bone of his bone and a flesh of his flesh. He called her woman because he knew she was taken out of his body.

Where did Adam learn these naming skills? He was able to do these things because of the image of God. If you are made in His image, you have the potential to be good - much desired for your sake or fit for purpose. All these unique human qualities demonstrate that we were specially created to rule over God's earthly creation. In the original governance structure of heaven and earth, Satan had no position, but he was determined to oppose God's sovereign rule.

The Devil works under cover and stealthily invades the host

People do not know when they ingest the tapeworm cysts or when they eat food or take drinks contaminated with tapeworm eggs or cysts. A key strategy of the Devil is to operate under cover, like a stealthy plane on a bombing mission. Invisible to radar, you only know it is in the vicinity when you see the damage. The biggest challenge to human beings, both Christians and non-Christians, is to be consistently conscious of Satan's presence around us because he does not have a physical body. Even atheists would behave differently if they saw a physical Satan with horns and a pitchfork as he is often portrayed in some books. We easily forget that the Devil is a spiritual being always lurking around us.

The Psalmist, David, prayed for God's protection when he realised that his enemies were surrounding him intending to throw him to the ground (Psa. 17:11). In the spiritual realm, the Devil and his cohorts are consistently looking for an opportunity to attack us. If God, for a moment, opened our spiritual eyes to see the multitude of demons in our space, we would understand why it is important to walk with God consistently and to put on the full armour of God.

Watch out for Satan and his agents in your career, ministry, family, school, business, Church, and other spheres of your life. He revealed his strategy when he presented himself with sons of God before the God (Job 1). When asked to consider God's servant, Job, he confessed he could not attack him because God had created a hedge around him, and his family and possessions. The danger is that we cannot assess his might and hence tend to underestimate his strength and power.

Imagine how you would respond if you visualised Paul's description of our battle with Satan. *For we struggle not against flesh and blood, but against principalities, against powers, against rulers of darkness of this world, and against spiritual wickedness in higher places* (Eph. 6:12, NKJV). Christians are engaged in a fierce face-to-face, hand-to-hand and foot-to-foot close quarter combat with the Devil and his demons in the spiritual realm because Jesus Christ is our personal Lord and Saviour. Because we are more familiar with physical reality, we tend to underestimate spiritual powers that operate behind the scenes with people as physical extensions of the invisible Devil. The real enemy lurking behind these people is Satan himself, with whom we are wrestling.

Paul stresses that our warfare is against an elaborate hierarchy of angelic powers employing schemes a thousand times more vicious than the flesh (Eph. 6:12,). He outlines four types of evil spiritual powers: principalities – principal rulers or chieftains capable of controlling affairs of nations; powers – angelic beings assigned specific powers over souls and minds; rulers of darkness of this world – angelic rulers that preside over regions of the earth or human minds that are dark, depraved, ignorant and sinful, and which lie outside the safety of the wider covenant of the gospel; spiritual wickedness in heavenly places, which refers to spiritual hosts of wickedness, including evil spirits in the atmosphere, and they are the most frequently encountered enemy. The Devil's structured fighting force has the capacity to take on any earthly being or army, and unless the Lord intervenes the results can be catastrophic.

The rank and file of Satan's dedicated army is designed to fight at different scales ranging from small scale (an individual) to the most sophisticated body of Christ. If the Devil was courageous enough to fight God's army in heaven, he is determined to fight any battle to counter everything that God has ordained for humanity and the earth. While remaining invisible, Satan holds control that can be scarcely felt, but is absolutely domineering.

If the Devil has such a sophisticated military system using multiple strategies, why don't Christians sit up and take the battle to the enemy? If we only understood that the Devil has invested heavily in this battle of life, our approach to life would change. The warfare is real and intense, and the Devil is beefing up his arsenal. Just think, the sky hosts evil spirits, and the enemy can use people around us as tools for attacking us. An invisible army is always surrounding us, waiting for an opportunity to strike.

The Devil uses good people or things to conceal his true identity and intentions

The Devil hides poisonous substances in objects or conditions that appear to be harmless. People often ingest tapeworm cysts or eggs through nice cuts of pork which look good and irresistible. Humans do not normally eat food known to contain substances that are likely to cause diseases. If you find yourself in the wild and come across apparently very clean water, you may be tempted to drink it, but if you find a muddy water hole frequented by wild animals, there is a high probability that you will avoid it, unless there are no alternatives. The Devil knows that if he wrapped his poison in obviously contaminated material, you would probably not come near it. Satan disguises himself as an attractive person to gain your trust before he attacks.

As the Chief worshipper of the Most High God, Lucifer knew the qualities of his Master, which qualified Him as the Almighty God, the Creator of the heavens and earth. Observing how all creation worshipped and honoured Him, Satan knew that if he also displayed these divine attributes, creation would accord Him the same dignity that God enjoyed. Unfortunately, Satan was not created with the same features as Almighty God. His only option was to acquire some features, which resembled those of God. Of course they were counterfeits.

The Devil knows that God is light (1 John 1:5). After speaking the heaven and the earth into existence, God said *Let there be light. And God saw the light and it was good* (Gen. 1:3-4, NKJV). The LORD covers Himself with light as with a garment and it is His domain because He lives and works in light. Created in the image of God, man was light. Christians are the light of the world and their light must shine before men/women so that the world may see the good works of believers and glorify our Father in heaven (Matt. 5:14, 16, NKJV). Christians ought to walk with God and to have fellowship with Him in light. Hence, all transactions between God and His creation take place in light. How does the Devil interact with God and His people when he is not light?

The Devil is not happy that God and His children are light and conduct their business in light, while he lost his attribute as a bright morning star. The only way the Devil can interact with God's creation is to transform himself into an angel of light. This self-transformation impersonates the loyal angels of light in heaven.

Are you surprised that when *the sons of God went to present themselves before the Lord, Satan was also among them* (Job 1:6, NKJV). How could he have done this except to present himself as an angel of light? This is a camouflage that the Devil uses to deceive and corrupt the world. It is a strategy he uses to conduct business with God's creation without creating suspicion, especially when we lack spiritual discernment.

Paul concludes that there is one thing in common between the Devil and his ministers. They hide their identity: *And no wonder! Satan himself transforms himself into an angel of light. Therefore, it is no great thing if his ministers also transform themselves into ministers of righteousness whose end will be according to their works* (2 Cor. 11:14-15, NKJV). Light and righteousness are admirable qualities of God and His disciples. The Devil and his ministers covet these attributes as a cover for their covert activities. Unfortunately, he uses this false identity to deceive unsuspecting Christians.

Have you ever tried to catch fish? If you are an experienced fisherman or angler, you know that if you throw a bare hook into a river, the chances that you will catch any fish are slim. If you bait a hook, you are likely to catch fish. The Devil uses the same strategy to trap his victims. Many vulnerable Christians are destroyed inside the Church because they have trusted the agents of Satan deeply embedded in the body of Christ. Bishops, apostles, pastors, teachers, evangelists, elders, deacons, prophets, and other Church workers hold positions of trust and Church members look up to them for godly counsel. However, the Devil uses some of these Church leaders to attack the saints.

Some people pretend to be godly to lure their targets into Satan's web and victims may never realise until they are hurt, destroyed, or killed. How many souls have been destroyed because of false teachings and prophecies? How many children and vulnerable young adults have been abused in the house of God? How many marriages have broken up due to infidelity involving Church leaders? How many robberies have been organised by 'Church leaders'? How many dirty deals have been sealed in the house of God? How many false marriages have been held in the Church?

The Devil attacks Christians through *false apostles, deceitful workers, transforming themselves as apostles of Christ* (2 Cor. 11:13, NKJV). They pose as believers who are good and trustworthy and yet are vipers in human bodies. Some believers in Corinth boasted that their work was as good as that of Paul and his co-workers to win trust of believers so that they could smuggle in false doctrines. Paul cut off every opportunity for them to do so. The Devil exploits the trust, confidence, reputation, power, and honour that believers command in Christendom and in the secular world to disguise his deadly attacks on Christians.

There are wolves in Sheep's clothing and Christians are taught to test every spirit to ensure they don't fall prey to deception. *Dear friends, do not believe every spirit, but test the spirits to see whether they are from God, because many false prophets have gone out into the world* (1 John 4:1, NIV). It doesn't matter how anointed a preacher, teacher or bishop is, test their spirit to see whether it has come from God. Many Christians are deceived because they are made to believe that testing the spirit of the man or woman of God is disrespectful and is a sign of unbelief.

Even the Son of God had to test every spirit to see if it was from the Father.

When Jesus informed His disciples about his imminent death and resurrection, *Peter took Him aside and began to rebuke Him, saying, "Far be it from You, Lord; this shall not happen to You! But He turned and said to Peter, "Get behind Me, Satan! You are an offense to Me, for you are not mindful of the things of God, but the things of men* (Matthew 16:22-23). As an inner circle disciple of Christ, Peter seemed to be gravely concerned by the cruel death that Jesus was to encounter, and hence expressed his wish that his Master be spared the ordeal. Any disciple who genuinely loves his master would strive to defend him as Peter did. So why was Jesus' response to Peter's rebuke so oppositional? Was He upset because His disciple rebuked Him? Was it an issue of insubordination? Did Peter suddenly turn into Satan? Far from it!

Jesus Christ tested the spirit in Peter and knew that it was not from God. The spirit behind Peter's utterances was foreign. No wonder He took exception to the statements Peter made: they were not his own; they contradicted God's plan to sacrifice His Son to redeem fallen humanity and hence were offensive; the words focused on human concerns; and Satan spoke through Peter to conceal his identity and his intention to abort God's plan to save humanity. Therefore, rather than addressing Peter, Jesus attacked the real source of his words, Satan. This is a very big lesson for us. We should learn to see through words and actions to uncover and rebuke the real source of trouble, Satan who works behind human fronts.

Unless Christians identify the real source of the problem, there is a high probability that the course of action they take to deal with it will be ineffective. The devil shoots arrows from a thicket. How have you handled Satan's covert actions in your life? This trick is responsible for many sins and disasters in our lives. Let us suppose you were the husband of a woman who was brought to Jesus because she was caught committing adultery. How would you have reacted? Would you have addressed Satan who steered the woman into adultery, or would you have condemned her?

Remember, every human being has been created in the image of God and can do good works provided the Devil does not hijack him or her to carry out his plan of disobedience. What would you do if you discovered that a colleague at your place of work has bad-mouthed you to your Line Manager? How would you respond if your mother- or father-in-law spoke rudely to you? What would you do if someone abused your child? What would you do to a person who stole from you or destroyed your property? What would you do if thieves murdered your son or a close family member? What would you do if your child openly abused you? Although I cannot read your mind, the response to each of these questions may vary from forgiving the person to a physical confrontation. However, let us always remember that negative things people say or do against us originate from Satan. Like Jesus Christ, always address Satan in the man or woman. But we need to learn how to distinguish between the person created in the image of God and the alien spirit expressing himself through him or her.

Satan waits for his victims at their favourite locations

Satan hides at locations you visit frequently. The Devil is intelligent and has a very sophisticated surveillance system to profile the lifestyle of an individual, monitor his every move, and to watch out for opportunities to attack. David likens his enemies to *a lion that is hungry of his prey, and as it were a young lion lurking in secret places* (Psa. 17:12, NKJV). The Devil is like a hungry and fierce lion crouching in cover ready to pounce on its prey. I came across a very captivating article by Vanessa Janion about the hunting habits of lions which illustrates the strategy of the Devil.

Vanessa Janion explained that lions have two hunting methods: the grandmother's footsteps, when the lion stalks from cover to cover, with a final burst of speed at the end when it is close enough to its prey; and waiting in cover where its prey often drinks or feeds. The second method utilises two strategies. First the lions are good at hiding and are phenomenally patient. Second, many species of prey are mentally slow and rarely learn from previous mistakes. Vanessa cited the work of George Schaler who studied lions in Serengeti National Park and his findings were astonishing.

Schaler watched a group of Thomson's gazelle crossing a patch of thick bush on their way to a water hole. As the animals entered a thick area of bush, bristling with lions, one gazelle didn't make it to the water source because the lions instantly grabbed and ate it. Barely two hours later, the same group of gazelles, having apparently forgotten the fate of one of its companions tried twice to use the same route to the water source. George made another interesting observation; prey species are more comfortable feeding while staring at a visible lion than when they cannot see their predator. What can lions teach us about the wiles of the Devil?

First, lions have more than one hunting method to match different hunting conditions. Similarly, the Devil and his ministers have devised multiple strategies to cast down a Christian in different conditions. He stalks Christians in their different environments, including workplaces, schools and universities, pubs, business premises, meetings and conferences, holiday spots, ministry, families, the internet, entertainment halls and in the Church. He devises different strategies to suit diverse environments. Every area of life has satanic traps and Christians usually stumble because of failure to recognize the presence of Satan working behind the scenes. We must be sensitive to the diverse schemes of the enemy who is determined to strike any time we drop our security guards.

Second, lions devise strategies that play to their strengths, while capitalizing on the weaknesses of their prey. Lions can hide, wait patiently, and pounce on their unsuspecting prey. However, the Thomson's gazelles have a short memory and cannot learn from the previous encounters with lions. The Devil understands his weaknesses. He knows that he cannot win any battle against God and Christians who: abide in Christ; are surrounded by the hedge that God has created around them and their families and possessions; have put on the full armour of God; are indwelt by the Godhead; and those that dwell in the shadow of the Almighty God. The Devil also knows that he cannot tell the truth and he is not as powerful as the Lord our God. He cannot withstand the Word, the blood of Jesus, prayer, and the power of God in a believer, which raised Jesus

Christ from the dead and sat Him at the right hand of God the Father. This is the arsenal of a believer.

If we remain in Christ, Satan cannot cast us down. However, he believes in his professorship of lies, which has earned him the title, 'Father of lies' and the 'Deceiver of the World', the strongest attribute of his ministry. Other strengths include patience, invisibility, ability to disguise himself, and to invade and manipulate human beings to fulfil his purpose. The Devil knows that believers are susceptible to the lust of the flesh, lust of the eye and pride of life. When the Devil dangles things that appeal to our eyes and flesh, and that puff our ego, we easily break God's hedge and the serpent bites. We often commit the same sin repeatedly and regret only after we have sinned.

The Devil understands that Christians tend to stray from God's presence when they are subjected to certain conditions, and he patiently stalks us until they are favourable for him to attack us. Satan's hunting strategies are driven by his urge to derail God's plan for humanity, the earth, and everything in it. Good hiding instincts and phenomenal patience enable the Devil and his cohorts to stalk or wait for long periods until an opportunity arises to bring down Christians. The Devil is intelligent and understands our qualities, and the peaks and troughs of our lives. Always beware of the invisible enemy in your surroundings.

Ability to produce many highly dispersing offspring within a short period of time

The Devil knows that one of the most effective ways of overwhelming his enemy is to send large numbers of his well-drilled and skilled soldiers to invade multitudes of his unsuspecting victims. A tapeworm-infected person can excrete as many as 300,000 eggs in a day, each containing an infective embryo. This strategy of producing many eggs within a short period of time increases survival rates of the worm's offspring and its ability to multiply and infect thousands of its victims. Multiplication of living things is natural attribute that the Devil uses to invade and dominate his victims.

Satan borrows heavily from God's principle of biological multiplication and dominion. When God created humans, He blessed them to be fruitful and increase in number, fill the earth, and subdue it (Gen. 1:28; 13:16; 16:10). The Devil knew that: God created humans with the ability produce many offspring, novel ideas, good works, and desired results; reproduce individuals with desired attributes; replenish or fill the earth; and have control or steward all creation. God wanted His creatures with very good attributes to reproduce, multiply and steward the earth to glorify Him. The Devil like the tapeworm, corrupts this God-given life-sustaining process to propagate his schemes to prevent God's plan and purpose for man and the earth.

The Devil can produce many highly dispersing offspring through physical reproduction of corrupted seed, which exhibits three traits: loss of righteousness; loss of communion with God; and corruption of human faculties. Adam and all his descendants were contaminated with sin. The Devil feeds corrupted seeds with corrupted word (preaching, prophesy, etc.), activities and intellectual ideas based on false doctrines or lies.

The Devil's schemes produce offspring, which grow and mature very quickly. In the 21st century, scientific, technological, sociocultural, philosophical, and other catalysts promote increased growth rate of corrupted seeds. What took the older generations several decades to build can be achieved in a few years. We have children or a generation that is living far beyond its biological age because of enhanced access to technology and knowledge.

Ability to easily adapt to new conditions

The Devil has an outstanding ability to adapt to new conditions. When he was cast down to earth, he had to quickly adapt and develop ways of coping with earthly creatures and conditions. As an alien species, the Devil is good at transforming himself to work effectively in a new environment.

The Nile Perch, an alien fish species, which can grow to a length of 1.8-2.0 metres and weigh around 240kg, was introduced in Lake Victoria in the 1950s. Its outstanding ability to adapt to this new environment caught the local people by surprise. This fish species: ate a wide range of foods; grew very quickly; had a very high reproductive rate; was extremely mobile; was a habitat generalist found almost everywhere in the lake; lived long; and proved invasive outside its range.

The Nile Perch competed for food with local fish species and starved them, resulting in extinction of at least 200 local fish species. It also fed on several local fish species to become the greatest predator of fishes in the lake. The ability to quickly adapt to, and colonise, the new environment enabled this fish species to outcompete and dominate local fish species.

Another species in Lake Victoria, the water hyacinth, is a plant that originated from Latin America. The lake was polluted with raw sewerage, industrial effluent, and eroded soil, which significantly increased nutrients. These conditions degraded the welfare of living things in the lake. But this invasive plant adapted to the local water temperature and chemical conditions of the lake.

The Nile Perch and water hyacinth demonstrate how alien species or organisms can adapt to a new environment and suppress or kill the local living things. Christians need to be aware that Satan is intelligent and creative to adapt to our environments that are new to him. The Devil knows how to court an unbeliever, new Christians, upcoming scientists, newly wedded Christians, newly ordained pastors, fresh undergraduate students, new employees, new Christian entrepreneurs, or Christians in courtship. As Christians, our environment is dynamic, but the Devil also evolves his strategies to fit our current situation. Just as companies invest huge amounts of money in marketing research to ensure their products meet dynamic needs of customers, the Devil constantly provides Christians with the state of the art 'alternatives' to God's provisions for us.

The enemy is hard to control and has no predators in its new environment

The Devil is hard to control and worse still to kill because he has no predators on earth. God and He alone can terminate the life of the Devil. But God has sovereignly set time to judge and send him to his eternal place. While we cannot control or kill the Devil, when we submit ourselves to God, we can resist him and he will flee from us (Jam. 4:7). We do this using the word of God, prayer, the blood of Jesus and the full armor of God to withstand his wiles. Unfortunately, some Christians have been bruised or even destroyed because they have used wrong weapons to wrestle with the Devil.

Some Christians believe that they can kill the Devil through fiery prayers. But he laughs because he knows that he will not die as such prayers contradict God's verdict. Can we also learn from invasive species and parasites? When the larvae enter the blood stream of humans and eventually settle in their tissues, the immune system does not recognize them. They can live in the body for many years without causing any symptoms and victims don't know they have them. When the Devil invades a person, the demons may live in a person without manifesting for years until the Word and Spirit of God torment them.

Through deception the Devil usurped power and authority of humans to rule this world. He assumed control over all created things on earth. The Devil employs the world systems to advance his kingdom and ensure that people do not regain control over the earth. As Christians, we can only resist our enemy if we abide in the true vine and put on the full armor of God.

Ability to alter the system or the environment

The Devil is shrewd in the way he invades and controls world systems and humans. One of the most effective ways to disarm his victims is to alter their systems and or environment. Let us use the water hyacinth and fish in Lake Victoria to show how an invasive species either degrades or destroys the habitat and native species before it establishes itself in the new environment.

The water hyacinth destroys life in water because it uses up oxygen and prevents rotting of plant materials, reduces nutrients for young fish in water, provides a new place for snails harbouring bilharzia parasites to breed, increases diseases and the number of toxic substances for both fish and humans, and it provides an excellent breeding area for mosquitoes and other insects. This plant drastically alters the water environment making it extremely difficult for native living things to survive, while it colonises the area.

Similarly, the Nile Perch competed for food with local fishes and changed competition within local fish groups and completely changed the social behaviour and economic activities of people in the area. It also changed Lake Victoria from a highly complex ecosystem to a stressed ecosystem with a simple food web, modified the nutrient supply for fishes, and eliminated native fishes. This fish species also changed the products and services of the lake, altered the structure of habitat and the composition of organisms at the bottom of the lake, and increased the incidence of diseases. The invasive fish reduced the number and abundance of other fishes, resulting in massive growth of algae.

The two invasive species have four major things in common: they changed the lake environment; they either reduced the number of or killed many fish species; they monopolised the use of resources in the lake; and they took over or controlled the lake habitat. The Devil operates on similar principles as he steals, kills, and destroys God's creation to assert himself as the ruler of the world.

In heaven, the Devil led a rebellion against the authority of God to rule in heaven and he altered or disturbed the serenity of heaven. However, he could not wrestle power from God and hence he was cast to the earth. Not giving up his fight against God, he replicated his strategy of rebellion against God through humanity on earth.

The Devil altered the environment in the Garden of Eden when he tricked humans to eat the forbidden fruit: their eyes were opened and they realised they needed to cover their nakedness; they could no longer speak freely to God; man, woman, the serpent, and the ground were cursed, and their conditions changed; the communion between God, man, and non-human creation was destroyed; governance over the earth changed hands from man to Satan; and humans died.

Altering the habitat is a cunning strategy of the enemy to incapacitate us because our features cannot operate well in this degraded environment, which suits Satan. The conditions for human habitation in the Garden were breached and their disobedience undermined their status. The atmosphere of rebellion and corrupted governance structure left humans exposed.

The Devil alters our environment by sowing seeds of lust of the flesh, lust of the eye and pride of life. In business, he can tempt us to evade tax or cheat on measurements. Such activities remove our business from God and hands it over to the enemy, deprives the individual of God's blessings, and allows the devourer to plunder resources.

In a healthy marriage, the devil can plant a seed of infidelity, which results in mistrust, strained communication, poor sexual relationships, and strained family altar. In a community of believers, the Devil alters the environment to reduce our commitment to the Word, fellowship, prayer and fasting, sharing of meals, sharing with the poor, caring for creation, and practising our vocations.

Christians need to understand an individual belongs to either the Kingdom of God or the Kingdom of Satan. We are either under the Law of God or the law of sin and death. The Devil's strategy is to transform your habitat from the Kingdom of God to the Kingdom of Satan by altering your marriage, ministry, business, family, and career conditions. Satan alters our environment to disconnect us from God and assert himself as our ruler.

Satan develops ways of dealing with the resistance or the defence system of the new environment

Satan understands that Christians who abide in Christ are strong and powerful and have put on the indestructible full armour of God to withstand his strategy (Ephes. 6:10-18). He can never touch believers unless they choose not to put on the armour, put on a cracked armour through sin, or if God permits him to tempt us.

The Devil knows that he cannot force God to compromise His armour that believers have put on or deny them access to divine strength and power to withstand his strategies. The easiest way to access and attack a believer is to tempt him/her to either take off the whole armour or put on an incomplete armour. In the Garden of Eden, the Devil tempted humans to eat the forbidden fruit and they lost their righteousness and communion with God, and they were corrupted. They broke the law and compromised the hedge around them.

In the spiritual realm, God has built a hedge around believers, their families and properties, and the Devil and his angels pace around looking for a breach in the barrier. Satan carefully examines God's armour, and his aim is to lure Christians into cracking it before he can strike. He also looks for conditions that render believers vulnerable to his attacks.

Unchecked spiritual, mental, physical, and emotional fatigue and stress due to life's battles and works of our calling predispose us to enemy attacks. Equally crippling are vices classified as lust of the eyes (money, possessions, or other material things), lust of the flesh (inflamed sensual pleasures), and pride of life (boasting, arrogance, pride in self). These will keep us away from the Word, prayer, fellowship, and shared meals, compromising the quality of the armour of God.

Satan has a sophisticated war strategy to kill and destroy or steal from believers. He targets the vital parts of a believer (the heart, the mind, the body, the soul), which are strategic to his walk with God. The Father of liars distorts the word of God and cuts the believer's communication with Him. He whips up situations, which breed anxiety and rob us of God's peace that guards our hearts and minds against the venom of the Devil.

The good news is that God understands that we cannot withstand the might of the Devil unless He fights our battle. Knowing our deficiencies and issues of life that could numb our God-consciousness, and the Devil's weaponry and strategy, God has provided us with a complete armour which totally and decisively destroys the enemy's war strategy, if used it correctly.

Before the Devil declared war on believers, God profiled his strategy and weaponry. He then made the armour for believers with great capacity to intercept and destroy all arrows from the enemy's camp. Unless the Lord builds your defence system, every effort to resist the Devil is worthless. In our world, nations build interceptor missiles to shoot down any missile from their enemies. Yet not every missile is shot down. God's interceptor missiles bring down all of Satan's missiles if believers remain in Christ.

Paul instructs us to put on the full armour of God several reasons. First, every Christian needs the armour to stand the wiles of the Devil and any other armour is ineffective and leaves you totally exposed. People tend to acquire human-made armours including wealth, networks of friends, education, family, charms, science, technology, and career. These were not designed to counter the Devil's schemes, but he tries to convince us they were. But if the Devil has a hand in building these armours, who tells you he will give one that will withstand his own weapon? If he designs the weapon, he knows its strengths and weaknesses.

Second, Paul instructs believers to be proactive and personally responsible for putting on their armour. Unless we do it, nobody will do it for us. We often make the mistake of depending on others to put the armour on us. When we allow our Bibles to gather dust on our shelves, while totally depending on other Christians to teach us, the armour is ineffective. We miss the opportunity to study the Word and receive personal instructions from God through meditation.

Believers who totally depend on others for the Word risk being misled; they cannot test the authenticity of what they are taught. This is very dangerous, especially in a world full of false teachers and prophets. The Bible encourages us to test every spirit to ensure it comes from God. Some Christians struggle to pray and anytime they face challenges they depend on others to pray for them and not with them.

Believers may fail to put on the armour of God due to laziness, cluttered spiritual lives, issues of life or deception. Imagine a world-class football player buys a designer football boot to enhance his performance on the pitch. Instead of using it during training sessions and in competitive matches, the player displays his pair of boots in the display cabinet of his memorabilia. Every day, as he walks past the cabinet, he admires the beauty and sophistry of his boots. Will this player achieve the objective for buying such an expensive and specialist pair of boots? I have also watched tag matches of two wrestling teams of two. When a wrestler in the ring needs assistance, he must stretch out his hand and touch that of his teammate outside the ring. But there are extremely agonizing cases when the wrestler pinned down in the ring fails to establish contact with the teammate and the pair ends up losing the fight. The Devil uses this tactic to prevent a Christian from either putting on the full armour of God or reaching out for help from God.

Paul stresses the importance of putting on a complete armour of God, which has all the components that are intact and fully functional. All the parts of the armour are interwoven and must always be used together if the armour is to be effective in battle. Unfortunately, many Christians wear armours with some missing components. Soldiers from the battlefront understand how a defective armour could cost one's life. A single missing component may be all the enemy needs to cast you down. After studying the behaviour of his enemies, David said, *They have been following me, and now they are all around me. They watch me, waiting to throw me to the ground. Like hungry lions they want to kill and eat me* (Psa. 17:11). The enemy is always stalking us, waiting for an opportunity to throw us down. His motive is clear, to steal, kill and destroy. With such a vicious enemy ready to attack, a defective armour could spell disaster.

If God was to provide us with infrared goggles to watch how thieves pace around the perimeter of our fenced property to find a hole to gain access into the property they intend to burgle, we would really appreciate Paul's warning to be always alert. Can you imagine that a simple lie is all the enemy needs to breach your armour? We are instructed to consistently wear the belt of truth, which holds several parts of the soldier's military attire together.

When a Christian lies, the belt of truth is compromised and the effectiveness of all the gadgets strapped to it is affected. But what happens when a Christian does not study the Word of God? We forfeit God's instructions and guidance. The LORD said, *This Book of law shall not depart from your mouth, but you shall meditate in it day and night, that you may observe to do all that is written in it* (Jos. 1:8, NKJV). This is God's secret code to prosperity and good success as we walk with Him. The Word cleans us, guides us, reveals His will and plan, and keeps us in step with God.

Meditation can be likened to rumination in animals with a four-chambered stomach like sheep, cattle, and goats, among others. When such animals graze, they break down the grass into small particles in their mouths and swallow the food, which eventually up in the first chamber of the stomach where it is digested, and some nutrients are absorbed. However, larger feed particles that cannot be digested in the chamber are sent back to the mouth, re-chewed and re-swallowed for further digestion in the second and other chambers of the stomach to release more nutrients to the animal. The principle is that the food is broken down to release nutrients through repeated chewing in the mouth and digestion in the stomach.

Christians are expected to study the Word and break it down carefully through meditation. This process involves analysing the Word with the help of the Holy Spirit while asking questions: What was the context in which the Word was written? What does the scripture mean? Why did the author write that Scripture? When and for whom was the scripture written? How does the Word apply to our current situation? What specific instruction does the Word require me to do? What are the things it is asking me not to do?

When the Holy Spirit takes us through this analysis of Scripture, He reveals God's will and issues instructions to guide our way of life. He helps us to understand who God is, what he likes and dislikes, the purpose for our existence, and the instructions for Christian living. However, during meditation, there will be parts of Scripture that remain chunky and require further breaking down. Like a cow, we need to chew it again to access further pieces of truth in the Word. Because the Word of God is rich with truth, meditation must continue day and night. The more we meditate on the Word of God, the sharper and more elaborate the instructions are and the stronger our faith becomes. The Devil and his cohorts know the Word and their trick is to distort it and mislead Christians. Unless we know the truth, we can never detect a lie. A Christian who does not study the Word of God and meditate on it creates a hole in the armour of God, which the Devil exploits to cast him down. The Devil will do everything possible to stop Christians from studying the Word and meditating on it. How many times have we opened the Bible, quickly read the portion of Scripture and before long we are on our way? We need to regularly set aside time to study the Word and mediate on it and allow the Holy Spirit to speak to us.

A key component of the armour of God, is the sword of the Spirit, which is the Word of God. A sword is a special combat weapon that can be used to fight an opponent who also has one. With this weapon, we can defend ourselves and/or attack the enemy depending on our circumstances. God has given us the sword of the Spirit as part of our armour. However, the sword of the Spirit comes with a big responsibility. We must study the Word of God and meditate on it because the products of meditation are what the Holy Spirit uses as His sword when we fight our battles. This implies that a life that has few products of meditation limits resources the Holy Spirit works with as He helps us to fights our battles.

If we do not study the Word, the sword is not as strong or as sharp as it should be. This is not a reflection of the deficiency of the Holy Spirit because it is our responsibility to put on the full armour of God. The Holy Spirit will not use the Word that you have not studied and meditated on. God said, success and prosperity would come from doing all that is contained in the Word. The content of the Word can only be accessed through meditation. God reveals His will through meditation.

The quality of the armour of God is determined by the accuracy and precision of the truth, the measure of faith, the degree of freedom of the Holy Spirit while at work in us, the consistency and constitution of our righteousness, the richness of the Word of God in us, our salvation and the degree of sanctification, and the richness of our prayers. As we walk with the Lord, the quality of the armour also depends on our desire to tell the good news about peace. Inadequate meditation on God's Word compromises the quality of the substance used to make the armour, and hence increasing our vulnerability to spiritual attacks. A good armour of God will withstand everything the Devil throws at us. But its quality depends on how we use the resources God provides.

The Devil is aggressive

The Devil is laser-focused on one thing, to steal, to kill, and to destroy what belongs to God. Peter warned Christians to be sober and vigilant because our adversary roams around like a roaring lion, seeking someone to devour. The Devil is our adversary, and he is not confined to an area like a lion in a zoo. If he had restricted operational areas, we could easily avoid him.

The behaviour of a predatory hunting lion qualifies it as the king of the jungle. Many wildlife experts and local people who have encountered or studied lions agree that they are probably the most dangerous and aggressive animals in the wilderness and very few animals are comfortable to have them in their vicinity. Peter's choice of the lion to depict the Devil's aggressive behaviour was based on his understanding of the behavioural patterns of the Devil and the lion.

Species that invade new territories are very aggressive. The Nile Perch illustrates the aggressive behaviour of invasive species. The Devil deceptively and forcefully dispossesses saints of their belongings. Christians often behave as if what the Bible says about the aggressive behaviour of the Devil is fairy-tale. But the Bible has several accounts of Satanic attacks on saints.

We don't fully grasp the brutality of the Devil because he is invisible and works mostly through his agents and acts of violence are usually associated with his cohorts rather than the source of such heinous acts. How often do people seriously attribute a road accident, juvenile delinquency, marital unfaithfulness, fraud, racism, pornography, robberies, persecution of Christians, pick pocketing, and other evil acts to the Devil?

In a society that has lost the fear of God these vices are blamed on people physically involved in the crime who are contracted to do it, while the architect of the crime, the Devil, watches from a distance. Paul warned the Ephesians that Christians do not wrestle against flesh and blood, but spiritual entities. Then, why do we try to wrestle with humans rather than the Devil himself?

From Genesis to Revelation, the fingerprints of the Devil are evident on every sinful act. Think about it. Who displaced man from the Garden of Eden? Who killed Abel? Who threw Joseph in the well? Who seduced Joseph to sleep with Potiphar's wife? Who threw Daniel in the den of lions? Who threw Shadreck, Meshack, and Abednego in the furnace? Who was behind the fall of Samson, David, and Saul? Who persecuted the disciples of Jesus Christ? Who imprisoned Paul? Who stoned Stephen to death? Who was behind Judas' betrayal of Jesus Christ? Who is behind the evil things we do?

Satan developed his trait of violence in heaven and when he was cast to the earth, he resolved to destroy anything that God has created. Creation still stands because God holds all things together and the Devil cannot destroy them unless the Lord permits him. The story of Job clearly shows how violent the Devil is if he is allowed to touch God's people. He killed all his children and livestock, and inflicted Job with terrible wounds. Jesus Christ knew how aggressive the Devil is when He said, *And from the days of John the Baptist until now the kingdom of heaven suffers violence, and the violent take it by force* (Matt. 11:12, NKJV). The days of John the Baptist marked the beginning of advancing the Kingdom of God through preaching the message of repentance. Before this, the prophets and the law prophesied about the coming of Jesus Christ. The Kingdom of God expands at the expense of the kingdom of Satan.

The Devil knows that Jesus Christ has drawn the battle lines and the battle is fierce. Like a cornered rat, he is determined to deal ruthlessly with anyone associated with Christ. The Devil sees a believer as a dangerous enemy he must exterminate at any cost. Even if we choose to avoid the battle, the Devil still sees you as his worst enemy. It would be unwise for a Christian to assume that the Devil will be peaceful when he is trapped in the battle zone.

An invasive species uses its host to launch fresh attacks in other areas

The Devil does not legally have property or an inheritance whether on earth or in heaven. What he claims to be his is what he forcibly grabs from God's creation. Like invasive species that invade a host, Satan uses his victims to advance his kingdom. Do you remember how a tapeworm anchored in a person's gut produces hundreds of thousands of infective eggs that are excreted through human stool to infect thousands of new victims? This resembles what Satan has done and continues to do on earth.

The Devil knows that humans are God's representatives on earth with delegated authority to share in God's rule over the earth and its inhabitants. Satan needed intelligent people he could easily manipulate to hand over the governance of the earth to him and to work for him. The Devil uses the human intellectual power to colonise what God entrusted to our care. God created intelligent beings to use their gifts to serve and honour Him, but they handed over their mantle to rule the earth to the Devil. Satan uses talented musicians, sportsmen/women, media experts, businessmen, financial experts, artists, academics, teachers, writers, craftsmen, theologians and engineers to try and undermine God's authority.

In the Church, the Devil uses gifted preachers, worship leaders, and other leaders to adulterate the gospel. He would like to use our gifts to fulfil his desires. Corrupting human minds and hearts is just part of the job, but the Devil's aim is to spread his ideas or works through these imprisoned minds. He does not educate the scientists nor train the musician, but he uses their skills to advance his kingdom.

The Devil's aim is to destroy the seed

The Devil's strategy is to corrupt the human seed to produce generations of corrupted offspring. He knows that the seed carries hereditary material, which is passed on to the next generation. His aim is to alter the content of the seed, which is inherited by its descendants. Introducing wrong genetic information in the seed guarantees perpetuating wrong characteristics in subsequent generations.

In the agricultural sector, there are companies and research institutions, which study and breed seeds to combine desirable qualities into crop varieties and animal breeds. Agriculturists can cross animal breeds and crop varieties to gain desired plant and animal characteristics and products. I learned how to multiply the genetic material of superior milking cows through artificial insemination and embryo transfer. Using this technology, a superior milking cow could produce, with the help of surrogate cows, 6-8 superior calves in a year instead of one calf. Females bred using this technology have potential for growing into superior cows capable of producing as much milk as their mother.

Plant and animal breeders spend time to produce and multiply superior seed, and farmers who want to produce good yields always go for this seed. These breeders ensure that seeds are pure and all the traits are transmitted to the next generation. Imagine what would happen if at any stage of breeding, a saboteur introduces an undesirable gene in the seeds. The bad gene would be passed on to all descendants. That is exactly what Satan did to the human seed in the Garden.

Adam and Eve carried the seed for establishing nations on the earth. God commanded them to be fruitful and multiply, fill the earth and subdue it, and to have dominion over His earthly creation. He also made very good plants, animals, fishes and birds with the ability to multiply and fill their environment. God's intention was, and has been, to fill the earth with superior living things through the superior seeds. Corrupting the human seed meant corrupting all the nations they were commanded to give birth to and other creatures of God.

When God confirmed his covenant with Abram, He said, *I am almighty God: walk before me and be blameless. And I will make a covenant between Me and you, and will multiply you exceedingly* (Gen. 17:1-2, NKJV). God does not multiply bad seed. He picks potentially good seed, improves it and then multiplies it. When God appeared to Abram, he introduced Himself as Almighty God. This tells you that He was not dealing with a case that was humanly possible. Both, 99-year-old Abram and 89-year-old Sarai were well beyond their childbearing age. Medical consultants of our time would have totally ruled them out as potential parents – carriers of superior seed. This was no longer a case of biological possibility, but supernatural enhancement.

Abram and Sarai needed the Holy Spirit to supernaturally activate their reproductive systems and renew their strength. They would not only have a miracle child, but God would multiply them exceedingly. God would clear the way for Abraham, Isaac, Jacob and several subsequent generations and the project would only succeed if God consistently blessed them and dealt with all unusual situations that would surface later.

God commanded Abram to walk before Him and be blameless. Before God could fulfil his covenant and multiply Abram exceedingly, Abram's condition needed to please God. God wanted to multiply good quality seed. Just as our animal and plant breeders will only multiply superior germplasm, Abram needed to be the quality of seed that God would gladly multiply.

While the seed is important for multiplying superior genetic material, it can also be used to destroy other seeds. Scientists who want to biologically control certain plant and animal populations release sterile males to mate with native females resulting in a female that cannot breed. If enough sterile males are released over a sufficient period of time, pest populations are either eliminated or suppressed. This technique has eliminated the screwworm fly and Mediterranean fruit fly in USA and Latin America. This underlines the importance of a seed in reproduction and the Devil knows that humans know how to manipulate species.

The Devil understands that what goes into the seed determines the fate of all generations bred from it. The Devil knew that if he corrupted Adam and Evil, all their descendants would inherit the fallen nature. Any forward-looking nation invests in young people because once they embrace an idea it will be passed on to other generations. In Egypt, when they realised Children of Israel were multiplying very quickly, they instructed Hebrew midwives to kill Hebrew baby boys at birth. The Devil targets children because they are softer targets than adults. Children and youth are easily attracted to evil attractions - wrong music, movies, books and games, which can hook them to evil things.

The Devil attacks the altar in a family

Every family needs an altar to ensure that we build a very strong basic unit for building a strong local Church and a stable society. A normal altar brings together parents and their children to study the Word, worship God and pray. A family that grows in faith and maintains strong family bond has regular sessions with God. The Devil knows that family Bible study and worship is best guarantee to raise Christian children with good moral standards and that will not drift away from God when they grow up, especially through the teen years. It is a family that has a witness for Christ in the community, and that takes Church seriously and enjoys going to all the services.

A Christian home that has quality daily devotions makes a good Bible school where the children can be grounded in the truth that enables them to face the humanistic, evolutionary philosophy of our modern society. A key strategy of the devil is to destroy the altar through unfruitful busyness, laziness, family feuds, wayward children, idolatry, and marital unfaithfulness.

The Devil tries to preoccupy Christians with worldly commitments that distract them from family devotions. How difficult has it been for you to maintain the discipline of gathering at the family altar every morning to have fellowship with our God? The Devil also tempts Christians to have irregular family devotions and he whispers uncountable reasons to justify skipping the altar. What the Devil does is to subtly lure you out of the presence of God where a Christian enjoys superior protection. He fully understands that God desires that we consistently walk before Him and remain holy.

The Devil attacks marriage

Our cultural battles over marriage and the family are symptoms of something deeper and more destructive than our natural senses can perceive. The assault on marriage - between one man and one woman, open to life, intended for life and the foundation of a stable family - is staged in the courts of law, the legislative chambers and in our culture. Satan knows that God created marriage as a beautiful living picture of Christ and the Church. He will do everything to drag it in the mud.

Keith Fournier stresses that the conjugal embrace, uniting spouses, spawns new life, broadening the circle of love with children. The cleaving of male and female in marriage is a representative of the image of God and it mirrors the love of the Holy Trinity. Marriage is also a profound mystery of which the wedding is the figure; metaphor of God's love for Israel (Hos. 2:19, 20, NKJV) throughout the Old Testament; an expression of God's self-giving love through integrated human persons, body soul and spirit; and a representation of God's covenant relationship with his people. However, we have an enemy who is against the Christian genre of marriage. In Jesus Christ, marriage is elevated to a mystery that reveals Christ's love for His Bride, the Church (Ephes. 5:32, NKJV).

Satan hates God and he hates marriage because it is a portrayal of the gospel (Eph. 5:32, KJV). To tear down marriage is to undo God's design built into creation from the very beginning. Apart from attacking God's relationship with man, Satan attacked the first marriage in the Garden of Eden. The old serpent, the deceiver of the world, deceived Eve and destroyed the harmony of the first married couple and subsequent marriages subjecting them to slavery in the kingdom of darkness. Like wasp maggots in a fig fruit, Satan's attack on internal mechanics of the marriage destroys the family unit. I was astounded to learn from sociologists that almost 85% of children that exhibit social disorders come from either fatherless homes or homes of parents that are not married. According to Professor David Popene, a sociologist, as society shifts from marriage to cohabitation, family instability increases. The devil's strategy is to breakdown heterosexual marriages.

Satan wants to distract Christian spouses from each other and from their impact for Jesus using one of the spouses, extended family, friends, and others for his purposes. He strives to lure spouses to develop a pattern of obeying their worldly desires instead of God's direction; to underestimate how susceptible they are to temptation; to weaken their trust for each other; and to deceive them with the forbidden fruit of lust.

The Devil instills in Christian spouses marital fears including insecurity (financial, domestic, relational), rejection, abuse (control, verbal, physical, mental), and failure. He creates pride and stirs division between spouses by fueling irritations, conflicts, disagreements, miscommunications, conflicting values, and unforgiveness. Worse still, the Devil seduces a spouse to find pleasure, relationship, and intimacy elsewhere through different vices including pornography, adultery, workaholism, and family commitments. Engaging in any of these activities undermines the integrity of marriage. Satan attacks marriages to destroy the beauty of the covenant between husband and wife to distort the image of God's love for us. If the Devil can destroy marriage, he destroys the mystery of a loving God who is in an unbreakable covenant relationship with us.

Satan understands that a functional marriage is not only determined by what happens when a man and woman enter a covenant relationship on their wedding day, but also what precedes the vows at the altar. From the day a man and woman start dating, the Devil stalks them to plant a seed that will eventually manifest in their marriage and family. The Devil challenges abstinence from premarital sex. He whispers in the ears of dating Christians that premarital sex is an expression of love for each other; after all, it is a matter of time and they would become husband and wife.

Another lie our adversary propagates is that courtship is a trial phase when those involved should share everything, including sex, to ascertain whether they are suited for each other. He works hard to convince the man or woman that being sexually intimate will also help you to detect sexual problems and deal with them before they walk to the altar. He goes further to assure the dating Christians that abstinence from premarital sex is not possible in the 21st century. He whispers in their ears that premarital sex between dating Christians was clearly justified because it is not like a man and a prostitute meeting on the street.

In many cases, Satan deceives the marriage aspirants into believing that the caution never to meet in private or secluded places by themselves underrates their faith and spiritual maturity. He works hard to convince us that we are mature Christians who can resist the urge to indulge in premarital sex even if you found yourselves locked up in the room with a person of opposite sex. The enemy may also undermine the Christian doctrine about marriage by introducing rights and privileges, which antagonize biblical principles of marriage.

Satan tries to convince Christians that the Church is dogmatic and tramples on the rights and freedoms of its members. After all, most of the Christian teachings were not meant for this generation. If anything, the Church tries to place yokes on the necks of its members. Satan tries to deceive people into believing that there are weightier things to worry about than what most of the premarital counseling focuses on. Through Satan's deception, many Christians present themselves before the altar with their dating, engagement, and courting marked with sexual impurity. When this happens, the Devil has succeeded in sowing a seed that will eventually erode the foundation of the marriage. If you fell victim to this, ask God to forgive you.

The Devil knows that the quality of Christian life of an individual is determined by an individual's personal relationship with God, the stability of the family altar a marriage aspirant is coming from, and the commitment to a sound local Church one attends. What the Devil tries to do is to deflect the attention of the marriage aspirants from their fellowship with God, question some of the foundational truths about marriage, exclude some of the key people in decision-making on vital areas that may require external godly counseling, or label people trying to advise as imposters wanting to live their lives through them.

Satan tempts believers into believing that they know better than anyone else and therefore are more qualified to manage their lives with minimum guidance from the Church and family. The strategy of the Devil is to ensure that these courting Christians have as many uninformed areas as possible, which he can then fill with his lies. Once the foundation is shaky, before the couple settles in marriage, the Devil will have caused so much damage that the couple either choose to divorce, separate, or go through a traumatizing phase of re-adjusting or restoration of their marriage.

A husband's love for his wife represents Christ's love for the Church. This guarantees God's intention that marriages should never be broken. Satan knows that permanent marriages demonstrate the permanency of God's love for humanity, which the devil passionately hates. Satan has therefore taken what God created for good and has twisted it beyond recognition. Just as he deceived Adam and Eve in the Garden, Satan wants to trick us into believing that God does not really love us or have our best interests at heart. Once he has convinced man that this is the case, it is easier for man to neglect exercising the God-given responsibility to love the wife.

The strategy of the Devil is to plant seeds of hatred that will deflate the love a man has for the wife. There are several ways the Devil can prevent a man from loving his wife. The Devil starves man of spiritual nourishment by keeping him away from the Word of God, which teaches him to love his wife. The Devil deprives man of the Biblical truth and keeps him in a state ignorance about his duty to love his wife. The Devil may also expose man to weird worldly teachings. He then capitalizes on his spiritual immaturity and his walk in the flesh rather than in the Spirit. As I grew up my people in the village taught me that expressing love to your wife is a sign of weakness because a man was not meant for one wife. If anything, a woman must fight for a man. This is a lie from the pit of hell.

Satan entices men into believing that women should never be trusted or loved because humanity was corrupted through their disobedience. The Devil whispers that, if Eve had not accepted to eat the fruit from the tree of knowledge of good and evil the humans wouldn't have found themselves in this predicament. The Devil tries to convince men that women need to be closely monitored and controlled otherwise they would continue to betray humanity. The Devil deceives men to treat women as slaves or servants.

The Devil preoccupies men with different activities in life so that marriage becomes the least of his concerns. The husband has little or no time for the wife. Our adversary tempts man to express his love outside his marriage by bringing in his life other women. He blinds man to the godly relationship he is meant to enjoy with his wife. The Devil may also deceive man that having a sexual relationship outside marriage is an endorsement of his elegance and masculinity, and that he is marketable.

The Devil and our culture deceive husbands into thinking that love is all about feelings. In some of the marriage counseling sessions, some Christian men have told me that they no longer have feelings for their wives and that was enough for them to contemplate divorcing their wives. The Devil sows a seed of doubt in the mind of a husband about the wife's love for him. Have you ever heard a husband asking, 'Does my wife really love me? How do I love someone who may not love me?' The Devil dismisses the fact that a husband ought to love his wife just as Christ loves the Church and laid down His life for her (Eph. 5:26).

We are living in an era where the Biblical model of marriage (Gen. 2:24; Eph. 5:31) is challenged and treated as one of the models rather than the model. What the Devil has done is to dismiss the Bible as the instructional manual for humanity. This has created space for the Devil to populate it with alternative models of marriage. When these alternative models are rationally justified as credible practices, society accepts them as plausible models rivaling the Biblical model of marriage. This is compounded by the fact that our society is gripped with the unhelpful ideology that truth is relative. The Devil uses this lie to convince people that the Biblical instruction that marriage is a God-ordained union between one man and one woman is not universally applicable to humans. People have several credible marriage options other than heterosexual marriage and they should be allowed to pursue their options. Since you know what the Devil's strategy for human families is, gird yourself to fight for your family through Christ.

The Devil attacks the family

Many advocates of a stable society have argued that there are three key cultural systems that strongly shape our societies: family, religion, and the education system. A family lays the foundation of an individual's life on earth and in eternity. Solomon said, *Train up a child in the way he should go: and when he is old, he will not depart from it* (Prov. 22:6 KJV). God designed a family, comprising a husband, wife and offspring as a perfect unit for expression of His love, community, glory, stewardship, purpose and will. The family is key to fulfilling the creational mandate of humanity to rule (steward, keep and take care of) God's earthly creation. To achieve this, God blessed man to be fruitful, multiply, fill the earth and subdue it, and to have dominion over all creation. He wanted a God-fearing family to keep and care for His creation to glorify and worship Him.

The Devil hates your family because it comprises people created in the image of God, people created to rule over God's creation and people who are blessed to fulfil the plan and purpose of God. When you exalt, honor, and worship the sovereign God you fuel the rivalry between God and Satan, and stir up his fury. The human family was a priority target of the enemy even before the fall because it would: glorify God; perpetuate the image of God; reproduce God's representatives on earth; keep and take care of creation to display God's power and glory, and His invisible attributes; and the family was destined for eternity.

The human family was so important in the fulfilment of God's plan and purpose for the earth that the Devil was determined to totally remove it from the presence of God. So, the Serpent's strategy to deceive the woman in the Garden of Eden was not an accident. It was a calculated move to drive a wedge between God and our ancestors; this misfired for both humanity and the Serpent. After the fall, the first family attracted curses that compromised its relationship with God.

The Devil hates the human family even more because of the curse placed upon him when he deceived the woman in the Garden of Eden. God said, *I will make you and a woman to hate each other; her offspring and yours will always be enemies. Her offspring will crush your head and you will bite their heel* (Gen. 3:15 GNV). God invoked an irrevocable hatred between a woman and the Serpent, preventing any peaceful communion between them.

The Devil seeks to steal, kill, or destroy anyone and anything linked to a woman. He also knows that the offspring of the woman has been empowered to crush the head of his offspring. Jesus Christ has crushed the head of the offspring of the Serpent. A Christian, who abides in the true vine, Jesus Christ, has also crushed the head of the offspring of the Serpent. Our adversary can afflict us with diseases, marital problems, financial difficulties, death or other trials and temptations, but we are more than conquerors through Christ who strengthens us. We should always remember that our enemy has no ceasefire in his battle strategy. He will fight our families until he is finally judged by the Lord.

God increased the trouble of the woman in pregnancy and her pain in giving birth, while the Serpent is enraged by the curse of having to craw on its belly and eating dust for as long as it lives. Man was told he would have to work hard throughout his life to produce enough food from the cursed, weedy, and thorny ground. Apart from evicting the couple from the Garden, where they had access to the tree of life and fruit trees, the first family experienced tough life, including sibling rivalry which culminated in the death of Abel. The Devil humiliated the first couple, who realized their nakedness and had to hide from God. This is not what beings created in the image of God had imagined would happen if they ate the fruit from the tree of knowledge of good and evil. But the Devil is still causing trouble for families today.

The Devil targets human families because he knows they are nurseries for the Church and nations. Understanding how crafty and destructive our enemy is, the LORD instructed Jewish parents to teach their children the laws: *You shall teach them diligently to your children, and shall talk of them when you sit in your house, when you walk by the way, when you lie down, and when you rise up. You shall bind them as a sign on your hand, and they shall be as frontlets between your eyes. You shall write them on the doorposts of your house and on your gates* (Deut. 6:7-9 NKJV). The Jewish families were instructed to teach their children the laws in and outside their homes through talking about it and by writing them on objects, wrist bracelets and frontlets between eyes. The children were consistently reminded of the law to ensure it shaped their hearts and minds. The family also reinforces what the children are taught in the Church, at school and in the marketplace. The Devil understands the role of the family is the nurturing of children and helping them to become good citizens.

The family is the basic building block of a stable society, the foundation of thriving communities and the hatchery of servants of God. Satan hates the family because he hates God and seeks to destroy the plan for His children. Our adversary is constantly engaged in warfare against the family to destroy what God has prepared for it to reflect the communion of the Trinity. Satan, the father of lies, is using individuals and organizations to persuade society to believe that the days of the Biblical family model of "a father and a mother, bound to each other by covenantal marriage, raising children bound to them by biology— is a stubborn relic, a national symbol that is somewhat unrealistic." He is working hard to convince society that the traditional nuclear family is no longer realistic in a 21st century. You should not be surprised when you see members of your family at war with each other. This is a result of a long-term strategy of the enemy to corrupt family and society beliefs and values.

The Devil knows that most societies, especially in the west, built their systems on the solid foundation of strong Christian values, which recognized a family as a medium for socialization and integration of people in the Church and wider society to reflect His glory. Any country that recognizes this strategic role of a family in building a progressive society seeks to protect and support families.

Human families thrive in a society that strongly supports family life, especially where a strong link exists between the state and the Church. A nation that formulates policies and passes laws that support families and their Christian faith thrives: *Blessed is a nation whose God is the* L*ORD* (Psa. 33:12). The Devil is working behind the scenes to influence countries to promote ideologies and philosophies that disparage family values.

While some governments claim to recognize the validity and equality of all faiths, this move has pushed Christianity out of the public and replaced it with other faiths, eroding the structures that support Christian family life. With the Bible removed from schools and other public places, he has developed a world system that works hard to destroy the traditional family and to promote programs that portray a heterosexual marriage as a hindrance to realization of human rights and freedoms. Every Christian family should be reading the changing conditions in different countries which are becoming increasingly hostile to their values.

Laws have been repealed to the extent that divorce has been made easy, tax laws, and government welfare system in some countries penalize families. The changing societal values and belief systems is a direct attack on the sanctity of the family. From the foundation of the earth God loved families, Jesus was born and nurtured in a family, and He still loves and blesses families. There are seven areas the enemy targets in a family setting: premarital behavior of people in courtship; the Biblical model of marriage (Gen. 2:24; Eph. 5:31, KJV); the conduct of Christian spouses (Eph. 5:3, KJV); headship of man and submission of the wife (Eph. 5:22, KJV); husband's love for his wife (Eph. 5:25, KJV); children honoring parents (Ex. 20:12; Eph. 6:1-3, KJV) and how parents relate to their children (Eph. 6:4, KJV).

The family is under siege because Satan works hard to distort two mandates of spouses in marriage, headship and submission. John Piper, in his book, *This Momentary Marriage*, defines headship as "the divine calling of a husband to take a primary responsibility for Christ-like servant leadership, protection and provision in the house." He also referred to submission as 'the divine calling of a wife to honor and affirm the husband's leadership and help to carry it through according to her gifts.' Similarly, in his *Letters and Papers from Prison*, Dietrich Bonhoeffers writes about the husband that, 'As the head, he is responsible for the wife, for their marriage, and for their home. The devil has invested heavily to distort these two mandates.

The Devil through culture, special interest groups and government agencies has challenged the God-given responsibilities of spouses in a Christian marriage. A major justification for this contention is that the Scriptures are not applicable in the 21st century where women work and even earn more money than their husbands. The Devil therefore deceives people that men heading or controlling families portrays a selfish and self-serving attitude, which must be always fought. It is not uncommon to see men cede responsibility for guiding the family to the wife because of cultural power relationships. In such cases, the husband dares not talk because he is no longer respected as the head of the wife. In contrast, Satan manipulates some husbands to abuse their wives. In such cases, the Devil has succeeded in persuading husbands and wives to abandon God's model for marriage.

Children are major targets of the enemy. There are several Biblical references that explain the Devil's rage against children. The Devil hates children because they originate from his enemy, God. In Genesis 1:28 (NKJV), Moses says, *Then God blessed them, and said, "Be fruitful and multiply; fill the earth and subdue it;*

have dominion over the fish of the sea, over birds of the air, and over every living thing that moves on the earth. Satan passionately hates children because they: represent the seed of the being created in the image of God, are genetic material for multiplication of men and women; are a mechanism for filling and controlling the earth; and they are a way of achieving the critical mass of people to rule over the earth. This emphasizes the fact that children are a major part of God's plan for ruling the earth.

The Devil cannot stand the fact that Children are a heritage from the Lord, offspring, and a reward from him (Psa. 127:3, NIV). This is God's expression of his love for humanity in an environment where there is harmony in relationships between God and man, God and non-human creation, and human and non-human creation. Children are an expression of a harmonious relationship in God's community and this enrages the Devil.

Since Jesus Christ is the Seed of the woman who has bruised the heard of the serpent, the Devil hates children who share a similar origin. Despite Satan bruising the heel of the Seed of the woman, he emerged as a loser in the unevenly contested battle.

The virgin birth of Jesus Christ, who would eventually annul Satan's position as the god of the earth, vexed him. So, he worked through Herod to try and kill the Child, Jesus Christ, but failed. The Devil feels helpless because he could not prevent the birth, death, and resurrection of Jesus Christ; this has resulted in numerous births in the kingdom of God. In John's gospel, Jesus Christ said, *For God so loved the world that He gave His only begotten Son, that whoever believes in Him should not perish but have everlasting life* (John 3:16, NKJV). This was, and still is, bad news for the Devil because he has no control over children who are being born in the Kingdom of God in large numbers daily.

The Apostle John writes in Revelation 12:17 (NIV), *And the dragon was enraged with the woman, and he went to make war with the rest of her offspring, who keep the commandments of God and have the testimony of Jesus Christ.* After realizing that he could not stop the redemptive plan of God, the Devil has decided to make war with children of God who keep the commandments of God and testify of the saving grace of our Lord Jesus Christ. No wonder the devil is so furious and roaming around to prey on God's children.

The Devil has not been successful in his attempt to destroy the children of God, but he is still determined to fight to the end. He attacks our children at different levels. He tried to destroy the offspring of humanity by targeting Adam and Eve in the Garden of Eden. Satan also closes the wombs of women; destroys unborn children through miscarriages and abortions; and causes deaths at childbirth and thereafter. He uses his agents to carry out these missions. He tried hard to kill Moses, Jesus Christ, and many children in families to stop the plan of God. The battle has been raging as the Devil engages the Church and individual Christians in running battles. He is targeting the children in our families.

One area where the Devil has been waging fierce battles is in relationships between parents and children. Paul instructing children said, "*Children, obey your parents in the Lord, for this is right. Honor your father and mother.*" This is the first commandment with the promise: "*that it may be well with you and you may live long on the earth* (Eph. 6:1-3, NIV). God expects children to accept the authority He has given to their parents for two reasons: that it may be well with them, and that they may live long. However, the Devil has tried to undermine parental authority in the home by instigating children to resist instructions from their parents.

Satan seeks to render parents incapable of exercising their authority over their children by feeding them with messages of insubordination. He achieves this by employing the media, literature, music, theatre, societal values and norms, television programs to promote values that undermine Christian family values. Some of these materials portray parents as control freaks, father figures that are foolish, naïve, old schooled, and out of touch with contemporary culture.

I was amazed when I stumbled across an article that cited a song that incites children to resist parental authority. The relics of Billy Joel's song read, 'My Life' blatantly addresses parents: 'I don't want you to tell me it is time to come home. I don't care what you say anymore. This is my life. Go ahead with your life, leave me alone.' The Devil subtly turns the hearts of children against their parents.

Satan whispers to children that submission and obedience are not mandatory because parental authority undermines their freedom and rights. Satan's objective is to destroy the relationship between parents and children so that parents are denied the opportunity of training their children in the ways of the Lord. He does that using the card of false independence of children. He knows that once the children defy the authority of their parents, he can easily step in to teach them beliefs and values of his kingdom.

Satan may also use parents to oppress or abuse their respectful and obedient children to erect a dividing wall between them. Paul cautions fathers not to wind up their children, when he wrote to the Ephesian Church: *And you, fathers, do not provoke your children to wrath, but bring them up in the training and admonition of the Lord* (Eph. 6:4, NKJV). The Devil may incite a father to use his parental authority to abuse children or to treat them in a way that upsets them. Satan has at times succeeded in persuading fathers to either shout or molest their children because someone upset them at their workplace. An innocent and helpless child is abused by an irresponsible parent.

As a young boy, there were moments when my father beat me because my stepmother maliciously accused me of having misbehaved. Even after realizing I was caned for no reason, he found it difficult to apologize to me. Although I was not old enough to challenge my father in my own way, I used to wonder why my dad could not allow me to explain before lashing me. But things changed when he turned to the Lord and divorced my stepmother (second wife).

Satan prevents parents from effectively bringing up their children in the ways of the Lord. He does this by keeping them extremely busy under the guise of career development and making money for the family, and by persuading the parents that the Church is more qualified to teach children adequately to live morally and spiritually upright lives. The Devil distracts parents from carrying out their God-given responsibility to hear the voice of God and teach their children to obey what God expects them to do.

In cases where the parents are available to teach their children, Satan corrupts the parents' understanding of the Word of God and they teach children distorted Christian faith claims. The Devil also destroys the environment in the home to make it virtually impossible for the children and parents to focus on the Word of God. He achieves this by creating conflicts between parents, and between parents and their children. The Devil can also influence children to rebel against their parents making it difficult to discuss the Word of God. Whenever, we experience any of the above conditions, the enemy is working hard to destroy the family. However, God who created man and ordained marriage and family life is faithful and mighty to preserve it. It doesn't matter what the Devil has done to your family, if you cry to God to restore it, He will.

The Devil targets the Church

After the fall of man, the Devil was convinced that the destiny of humans was shunted out of God's will and purpose forever, and he was determined to permanently keep man outside the ways of God. When he realized that God had a redemption plan for humanity, he was so upset and distraught that he vowed to fight any attempt to implement this plan.

The Devil employed chief priests, teachers, and elders to predict and prevent the birth of Christ. He used king Herod to trick the wise men into providing him with information about the royal birth in Bethlehem. Realizing that he was outsmarted by the wise men, the Devil used King Herod to slaughter all baby boys below the age of two years in Bethlehem with the hope of destroying baby Jesus in the multitude of slain baby boys.

Satan tracked the Messiah throughout his life before and during His ministry, but he could not destroy Him. He tempted Jesus just after his 40 days of fasting, to turn stones into bread, to throw himself from a pinnacle of the temple so His Father could send angels to catch him before He struck His foot on the ground, and to bow before him in exchange for his kingdom. But all his temptations never succeeded in destroying God's plan for redemption of humanity.

During the life and ministry of Jesus Christ on earth, the devil used kings, priests, and other people to try to either kill Jesus or simply stop him from doing what His Father sent Him to do. Do you remember that he also used Peter to try and talk Jesus out of His assignment to die for the world? Trying everything possible, he used Judas Iscariot, the kings, priests, and other people in Jerusalem to capture and kill Jesus Christ.

The Devil celebrated the death of Jesus because he was convinced God's redemption plan was in tatters. His plan was to humiliate and torture Jesus Christ, and to ensure that He was eliminated from the earth and never to rise again. Why not scare them and humiliate Peter by having a young girl quiz him about his association with Jesus? The Devil worked tirelessly through the Roman system to seal and guard the tomb of Jesus to disgrace God and the followers of Jesus Christ. What do you do when all efforts to a eliminate somebody don't work? Surely, it was time for the Devil to quit, but that would be out of his character. After the death of Jesus, he deceived the disciples to abandon their calling.

After witnessing the resurrection of Jesus Christ, the Devil realized that all his efforts to eliminate Him and prevent His resurrection were in flames. What next? Why not prevent the spreading of the news of His resurrection? That is exactly what the Devil did and still does. He persuaded people to deny the resurrection of Jesus Christ by propagating a lot of conspiracy theories. Even some of his disciples doubted his resurrection.

As Jesus finished His ministry on earth, the Devil realized that his strategy to stop Jesus Christ fulfilling His Father's plan was beyond His control, but he still had hope that after their big Brother ascending to heaven, he would deal ruthlessly with the disciples to discourage and prevent them from spreading the good news about the resurrection of Jesus Christ. To his surprise, the disciples received the power of the Holy Spirit to witness for Christ and started making disciples in all nations, baptizing them in the name of God the Father, the Son and the Holy Spirit, and teaching the converts what Jesus Christ taught them. Despite his vicious attacks on the disciples of Jesus, the Devil witnessed the birth of the Church and has since fought its growth.

What is the message to the Devil from our Lord? As Jesus Christ spoke to His disciples, the Devil was devastated to hear Him telling Peter that, *you are Peter, and on this rock I will build my Church, and the gates of Hades will not overcome it* (Matt.16:18, NIV). This was the most unpleasant truth that Satan had to soak in. While he was rejoicing that the defiant Son of God was returning to the Father leaving His work in the hands of apostles, little did he know that that Jesus Christ, through his life and teaching had equipped the disciples to continue doing the work He had started with the Holy Spirit.

As soon as the disciples were baptized in the Holy Spirit, they turned into beings that the Devil couldn't restrain. He was frustrated to learn that the disciples started gaining ground very quickly. Peter, who feebly denied Jesus Christ three times as He was being tried before His death and resurrection, was filled with the Holy Spirit and boldly and uncompromising preached the gospel of Christ resulting in about 3,000 converts. The Devil realized that the teachings and life of Christ, coupled with the Holy Spirit baptism, had produced a different breed of apostles capable of ruining his plan. He resolved to destroy the disciples to discourage them and instill fear in the people that witnessed the persecution of the followers of Christ.

As Satan meditated on Peter's role in building the Church, it dawned on him that the disciples of Christ were fully empowered to recover what he had stolen. This confused him. How possible was it that the disciples of Jesus Christ had so much power that they were able to plunder the kingdom of darkness long after

Jesus had ascended to heaven? The apostles were fully committed to preaching the gospel and seeing souls saved from their sinful nature through the death and resurrection of our Lord Jesus Christ.

Peter passionately and incisively reminded the Jews how the prophecy about the death and resurrection of their Messiah was fulfilled when they crucified and killed Jesus, and how the buried Messiah rose from the dead and ascended to heaven. The Devil witnessed a mass exodus of souls from his kingdom to the Kingdom of God. Satan couldn't believe that his followers asked Peter what they needed to do to follow Jesus Christ. To rub salt into his wounds the new disciples of Christ were baptized and committed themselves to the teachings of the apostles, the fellowship of believers, and breaking bread and praying together. The Devil realized that his master plan to humiliate Jesus Christ and establish himself as the king misfired and instead, he was publicly disgraced as he helplessly watched thousands of his followers abandon him.

Satan is still chasing after believers in the 21st century as they strive to carry out the great commission. He still believes that Christians can easily shift their focus from Christ to the unique attractions of this century because Jesus Christ ascended to heaven. The Devil knows that Jesus Christ assured His disciples that, even after ascending to heaven, He would not leave them destitute but pledged to be with them till the end of the world (Matt. 28:18). He also knew that Jesus promised to release God's power on the disciples. This would enable them to witness for Christ throughout the world.

What a painful time it was for the Devil to witness the fulfillment of all proclamations of our Lord. We can safely conclude that the Devil knows that Christians in the 21st century also have access to the same Holy Ghost power that disciples had and the same Jesus Christ lives in and through believers. However, he is still determined to deceive followers of Christ out of the Kingdom of God with the level of aggression and craftiness that Christians have never experienced before. Christians tend to forget that Satan has been wounded and he is roaming the world to steal, kill and destroy the followers of Jesus Christ.

We need to learn from the disciples of Christ who paid a huge price for deciding to stay with the Lord.

The enemy of the cross persecutes followers of the Lord Jesus Christ. The Lord talked highly about John the Baptist (Matt. 11:11, KJV). As an ordained messenger of God, John challenged people to prepare for the coming of the Messiah by turning away from sin and being baptized. Not only did John deliver the message with authority, but he was so bold that he even challenged Herod to repent of his sins. It is not surprising therefore that people flocked in hundreds to hear him and be baptized. However, Herod Antipas had John the Baptist arrested, chained, and imprisoned. The Devil worked through Herodias, the illegal wife of Herod and ex-wife of his brother Philip, to twist the hand of the king and John the Baptist was beheaded (Matt. 14:8-10) in about 29 AD.

Judas Iscariot, a very senior disciple of Jesus Christ and the treasurer of His apostolic team, was lured by the devil into betraying his Master. Luke said, *Then Satan entered Judas, surnamed Iscariot, who was numbered among the twelve. So he went his way and conferred with the Chief priests and captains, how he might betray Him to them* (Luke 22:3-4, NKJV). The Devil did not only enter and use Judas to betray Jesus Christ, but he also led Judas to commit suicide: "falling headlong, he burst open and all his entrails gushed out" (Acts 1:18, NKJV) in a field he bought using the wage of iniquity.

As King Herod stretched out his hand to harass Christians, he also killed James the brother of John with the sword shortly before the day of the Passover (Acts 12:1-2, NIV). Stephen was falsely accused of cursing Moses and God and was stoned to death by an angry mob after subjecting him to an unjust trial (Acts 7:57-59, NIV).

Although the Bible only records the deaths of the two of the twelve disciples of Jesus Christ (Judas Iscariot and James the brother of John), research and early historical records show that other apostles also died as martyrs. Condemned to die by crucifixion, Peter (the first traditional Bishop of Rome) felt so unworthy to be hanged the same way Jesus was and requested to be crucified with his head downwards during the persecutions of Emperor Nero. After preaching in Achaia and Scythia, Andrew was crucified in a spread-eagle position on an olive tree at Patras in Achaia. Bartholomew preached the gospel in India but was crucified in Armenia. While preaching the gospel to the Jews in Jerusalem, James the son of Alphaeus was stoned to death. Philip preached the gospel in Phrygia and was crucified in Hierapolis (eastern Turkey). Thomas was thrust through in the four members of his body with a pine spear. These disciples were killed for deciding to carry out the great commission.

What about the apostle Paul, the servant of our Lord Jesus Christ? Was it not Saul, later known as Paul who persecuted Christians (Acts 8:1, KJV)? Bible scholars say that Paul was persecuted on 30 different occasions. Among others, Paul: was abused when Demetrius and other advocates of the goddess Atermis stirred people in Ephesus to riot against gospel of Christ that he preached (Acts 19:23-34, KJV); Paul and Barnabas were whipped and thrown in the inner cell of the jail, with their feet shackled between blocks of wood after they cast out a demon in a servant woman who had an evil spirit that enabled her to predict the future (Acts 16:2-24, KJV).

Paul was also arrested in the temple, dragged out and beaten after Jews from the province of Asia stirred up the crowd against him (Acts 21:30-35, KJV). He was targeted by some Jews who vowed that they would not eat or drink until they had killed Paul (Acts 23:12-16, KJV), and ship-wrecked in Malta, he ended up in jail in Rome. Paul was finally crucified in Rome with apostle Peter. John, the brother of James, preached the Gospel in India, but was banished to the Isle of Patmos by Dominitian, the King, and died in old age.

In the Old Testament, Joseph, Daniel, the three Hebrew boys (Meshack, Shadreck and Abednego), and Job were among several servants of God who were persecuted for their faith. The Devil and his demons have tried to exterminate God's people for over millennia, but they have failed. Satan has persecuted believers and will continue to do so until the Jesus Christ permanently condemns him to the Lake of fire. We must be aware of the Devil's ploy to persecute the Church and we should be ready to face him with Christ in us.

The Devil targets universities and research institutions

A major strategy of the enemy is to poison the source of the river and anyone who drinks of its waters downstream would be destroyed. Any war strategist will warn his troops not to drink water from unknown sources at the battlefront. During my period of military training, I understood the importance of a water bottle during military operations. The devil understands the strategic position of universities and research institutions in shaping the thought and culture.

William Craig, in his article '*In Intellectual neutral*' provides a very useful analysis of the problem of the Church being filled with Christians who are idling in intellectual neutral. Such Christians focus on the Bible and consider any academic work as a distraction to their faith. Asking them to consider faith and science would be regarded as straying from their focus on faith. The devil relishes this position because he knows that when faith is challenged by science or other ideologies, the believer will not respond. This has forced some Christians to retreat to the closet of fundamentalism.

Universities and research institutions are oases of knowledge, but the challenge facing the Church is that the level of engagement with the research process has been minimal. As scientists and theologians develop research ideas, assumptions, hypotheses and study methodologies, there is very little interest from the Church. Most of the debate has centred on research findings, but at that stage it is difficult for Christians to intellectually engage with researchers. The Devil prefers to keep Christians out of the research process and hence disarm them. The inability of the Church to intellectually engage with contemporary issues deprives us of a vital apologetic tool and exposes us to ideologies we cannot reconcile with our faith.

Universities are arguably the single most important institution in the Western world where our future political leaders, journalists, lawyers, engineers, scientists, and business executives formulate or embrace the worldviews, which ultimately shape our thought and culture. It is against this background of thought and culture that the gospel is heard. The Devil will do anything to ensure development of a student's thought at the university is devoid of solid Christian truth.

The strategy of the enemy to exclude Christian truth claims in the formative stage of worldviews at the university takes several forms. He disguises the fact that there is an intellectual war raging in the universities and in professional journals, marketplace, and scholarly societies, which basically dismisses Christianity as irrational and obsolete, and millions of our future leaders have embraced this viewpoint.

The Devil has for a long time deceived the Church into downplaying the need to raise up Christian scholars to create a place at the university for Christian ideas. In such an environment, Christians cannot challenge the views of great secular and naturalistic or atheistic scholars. This further deprives students of a cultural milieu in which the gospel can be shared as an intellectually viable necessity for thinking men and women. We also need to be mindful of "Christian researchers" who dismiss or question core Christian doctrines. If a theologian questions the death and resurrection of Jesus Christ, know that such an individual is far from the truth.

The Devil propagates the lie that pastors and laymen in the body of Christ need not bother about intellectually engaging with issues. Craig believes our contemporary pastors have become our 'new disablers' because they are idling in intellectual neutral. The knock-on effect is that we have Churches that are filled with Christians who are also coasting in intellectual neutral.

Satan subtly tries to convince the Church that theological colleges should produce pastors and not scholars. This contrasts Wesley's vision of a pastor: 'a gentleman, skilled in scriptures and conversant with history, philosophy and science of his day.' Craig argues that theologians and pastors must be intellectually engaged if the Church is to make an impact in our culture. The Devil pushes secular views to the centre stage, while Christian views are pushed to the periphery.

Universities and research institutions are fertile breeding grounds for worldviews and the environment plays a major role in what becomes of a student after going through the system. These institutions stress the mantra that science is the adjudicator of all truth. This is a very delicate stage that requires students to be grounded in Christian faith, especially if the student believes he knows it all. This is the prime time for the Devil to display different competing ideologies with the aim of tagging the student with a non-Christian worldview.

The Devil's strategy concerning universities and research institutions clearly undermines the sacrifice that Jesus made on the cross. Paul, writing to Church at Ephesus said, *The Church you see is not peripheral to the world; the world is peripheral to the Church. The Church is Christ's body, in which He speaks and acts, by which He fills everything with His presence* (Eph. 1:22, MSG). The Devil tactfully entices the Church to abdicate its central role of fully contributing to the training of future leaders. God's desire is that Christian students and the university/research institutions speak and act on His behalf. Such potential leaders should represent God in these circles.

The Devil uses the media as his propaganda machine

The media is very effective in dissemination of information in space and time. It is so well structured that it can appeal to all ages, educational backgrounds, and political and religious persuasions. The Devil identifies key media channels, key figures, well-crafted Christian-unfriendly messages, and uses them to his advantage. There are numerous ways in which the enemy is using the media to attack the Church.

The Devil influences people working in the media industry to discriminate against or block dissemination of Christian messages. In November 2015, many leading cinemas in the UK refused to show a Church of England (CoE) 60-second advertisement of the Lord's Prayer because the Digital Media Agency

(DMA) banned it. Although the organization justified its decision by insisting it does not accept political or religious advertisements, several commentators didn't find anything unusual about the CoE advert. Some Christian programmes are censored or aired on channels with limited viewership.

The Christian entrepreneurs who apply for licences to establish radio or TV stations are subjected to very difficult conditions and have struggled to run these operations. Articles or messages that are considered as divisive in Christian circles, anti-Christian, or which criticise the Church leadership and the Church are more widely covered than those that speak positively about the Christian faith. TV Land produced an irreverent comedy entitled 'Impastor', which depicted a pastor as an adulterer, gay, drug dealer, and impersonator, and other atypical qualities of a clergy of his standing. The enemy rejoices when Christian leaders are portrayed negatively to the public because he can use bad media coverage to advance his own cause.

The Devil works hard to ensure that Christians do not get enough funding to afford commercial broadcasting licence fees. Many Christian TV stations do not have adequate financial resources to pay licence fees. Consequently, Christian programmers have resorted to non-commercial stations and have relied on viewer donations to cover their costs. This means that the programmes have a very limited audience and coverage. But the Kingdom of God is still growing.

The challenges facing Christians in the 21st century reflect the Devil's strategy to manipulate humanity behind the scenes. Understanding how he influences our spheres of life from his hidden platforms is crucial in developing a productive relationship with our God. Always analyse your daily activities through the lens of scriptures to defeat the enemy.

CHAPTER 12

Can I walk with God in the 21st century?

The 21st century has experienced unprecedented conditions that are hostile to Christianity. They include, among others, dechristianization of vital institutions in our societies, propagation of antichristian ideologies, persecution of the Church, proliferation of false teachers and false prophets, hedonism, a cultural revolution against Christianity propped by science, technology and negative media coverage, outlawing of Christianity and secularization of nations, and propagation of the narrative that the severity and high frequency of natural and human-induced disasters preclude the existence of a loving and omnipotent God. In some countries, owning a Bible, sharing the gospel, conversion to Christianity, and even mere suspicion that one is a Christian can attract a prison or death sentence.

Walking with God is a non-negotiable attribute of Christian living. But this has proved difficult in many situations, especially when faith is put to a strenuous test as is the case today. Jesus Christ said that His followers must *enter by the narrow gate; for wide is the gate and broad is the way that leads to destruction and there are many who go by it. Because narrow is the gate and difficult is the way that leads to life, and there are few who find it* (Matt.7:13-14). The Lord emphasized that the disciples of Christ must enter the narrow gate by stripping themselves of sins and by abiding in Christ despite the hostile environment in which we practice our faith. He also warned that, *"Not everyone who says to Me, 'Lord, Lord,' shall enter the kingdom of heaven, but he who does the will of My Father in heaven. Many will say to Me in that day, "Lord, Lord, have we not prophesied in Your name, cast out demons in Your name, and done many wonders in Your name?" And then I will declare to them, 'I never knew you; depart from Me, you who practice lawlessness"* (Matt. 7:21-23, NKJV). Many people genuinely believe to be His disciples and yet the Lord does not know them. Only those who know and do the will of His Father will enter the Kingdom of Heaven. These words, which our Lord spoke over 2023 years ago are still valid in this century and every Christian needs to consider what it means to be a disciple of Jesus.

Jesus Christ ministered to mixed multitudes, which consisted of observers who were curious to find out what this young Jew was saying and doing, cynics who looked for opportunities to criticize Him, people who came with needs and genuinely needed Jesus' intervention, would-be disciples who wanted to follow him, and His disciples. In the parable of the Sower (Matt. 13:1-9), Jesus also reveals metaphors of four categories of people based on the responses of their hearts to the seed: the wayside, rock, thorns, and fertile ground. He demonstrated that only a small fraction of his audience received the Word, applied it, and produced fruit. Has this picture changed in the history of the Church?

The Church has faced different challenges throughout her history, but the magnitude and severity of issues today are unprecedented. What is so unusual about the 21st century that should warrant special consideration in a Christian's ability to walk with God? What could constrain walking with God in a postmodern world? Is there a provision for a Christian to walk with God in this century?

What is so unusual about the 21st century in a Christian's decision to walk with God?

Our society today is shaped by a three-way worldview struggle in academic and popular culture: the belief in the existence of a supernatural God (ethical monotheism); the worldview which denies objectivity of reality, truth, value, and reason (postmodernism); and the view that hard sciences are the only source of knowledge, and they are vastly superior to non-scientific sources (scientific naturalism). The jostling of worldviews shapes our culture in which the Christianity is practiced. In the process of analysing prospects of walking with Christ, potential disciples of Christ must decide in full knowledge of all these pressures of the century.

The dawn of the 21st century ushered in new challenges for Christianity from within the Church, the marketplace or public sphere, and the Academia. Christianity exists in a milieu that determines how it is shared, perceived, and practiced. Every Church age has presented its own set of conditions (philosophies, theological postures, socio-cultural conditions), which have shaped the religious landscape in which the Christian faith is practiced. The 21st century presents its own conditions that influence people's response to the gospel and they are briefly described below.

The 21st century has witnessed a paradigm shift from modernity to postmodernity. Postmodern culture argues that there is no objective truth, the human mind cannot access the world or reality, and that we cannot know reality. This has implications for how God, creation, Jesus, and humanity are perceived. How does the Church present the gospel if it is not objectively true?

If words or text are perceived as human constructs without meaning of their own except what man has assigned to them, why should people bother about subjective views? What stops people from believing that the Bible is a collection of views of the authors, which may not be relevant to our place and space? Describing the Word of God, one of the philosophers wrote, *they are the everlasting oracles of life. They are to be questioned and consulted anew, with every age, approaching them with its own variety of ignorance and understanding, its own set of problems and its own inevitable problems. This implies that already given solutions cannot therefore serve us. The powers must be consulted directly, again and again. Our primary task is to learn, not so much what they have said, as how to approach them, evoke them. Fresh speech from them and understand that speech* (Zimmer 1993).

Zimmer suggests that every generation must approach the Word of God based on current social and cultural conditions, and hence solutions provided in the Bible are not applicable across generations. He insinuates that the powers must be consulted periodically for fresh solutions, obtaining fresh speech that must be understood within the context of the revelation. I have no objection to the fact that the context of the Word must be considered. However, to suggest that 'already given solutions cannot serve this age' is questionable. The solutions that the Bible provides are relevant regardless of the Church age.

The core of Zimmer's argument is dismissal of the objective truth and universal nature of the Word of God. He accuses Christians of the "objective truth syndrome", which allows them to detach from their community and reality, and to look at the Word with a general rather than personal lens. This means that Christians use the objective truth from the Bible in their witness to Christ rather than their Christian convictions and practice to evangelize. This is viewed as a disincentive to a Christian's testimony.

It is true that Christians must live out, symbolize, and conserve their faith claims but the notion that there is no objective truth, our human mind cannot access reality, and that we cannot know reality does not hold. The challenge is for Christians to live out Biblical principles and values in such a way that people see the nature and attributes of God in them.

As the world struggles with diversity, tolerance, and inclusiveness of socio-cultural systems, there is shifting of power across structures, which has a significant impact on the Church and how Christians practice their faith. Laws, policies, and procedures for regulating the conduct of individuals and organizations, bordering on political correctness, are affecting Christianity.

In trying to create a level playing field for various worldviews and to protect minorities and vulnerable groups, Christians are expected to embrace practices that contradict their teachings, convictions, and practices. The government, agencies, human rights groups, and other agencies seek to regulate how the children in Christian homes are brought up in relation to Christian values, how Christian hotels and Bed and Breakfast facilities serve their customers, the curricula of Christian schools, and how Churches conduct some of their programmes.

The process of mainstreaming diversity, tolerance and inclusiveness in the Church is not only contradicting Christian belief systems but is an attempt to erode Christian beliefs and values. Upholding Christian principles, values, and practices may breach government and company laws, policies, and regulations. Cases of litigation against Christian institutions, employee dismissals, and executions are on the increase. The rate at which laws antithetical to Christianity are passed makes Christianity look like an endangered species. Christians are persecuted for their faith.

There are several examples of the state regulation of the Church. In Cuba, 1,400 Assemblies of God Church buildings were seized and/or demolished by August 2016 and many Pastors were detained. The Hungarian Government passed a law in 2011 to cramp down on so called 'business Churches' allegedly registered to secure tax benefits and state subsidies. Based on the pretext that the previous law was not tight enough to effectively regulate the registration of Churches, the Government argued that Hungary was too small to host over 300 Churches.

In 2012, several Churches in Hungary were deregistered and given the option to register as civic associations. Deregistration and downgrading Churches to civic associations did not only violate rights of religious freedom, but also resulted in: the government imposing an administrative structure on associations that excludes clergy; introduction of public membership with democratic rights; accounting procedures that required documenting individual Church donations in a service; denying the organization the right to own land; forfeiture of tax exemptions and the right to run schools or hospitals. If for any reason a deregistered Church's application for civic association status is unsuccessful, the organization is liquidated, and its assets are seized by the state.

There are other examples of Government strategies to undermine Christian values. Firstly, there has been a campaign by the Chinese Government to remove crosses from Church buildings on the pretext that they violated building rules. Secondly, Russia passed a legislation against sharing the gospel in public and converting people to Christianity. Thirdly, the UK passed legislation regarding how lesbian, gay, bisexual, and transgender (LGBTQ2) people are treated in

Churches. These and several other strategies are efforts to suppress Christianity and promote other faiths. These government activities reduce the prominence of Christianity and magnify other faiths.

The 21st century has seen a proliferation of national laws to separate the state from the Church, promote multiple faiths, and to impose restrictions on Christian practices, which deprive the Church of independent champions of Christianity. Traditionally, a nation that exalts God depends on three offices - king (government), priest and prophet.

In a society with competing faiths, people are presented with several choices, and the onus is on each religious group to prove that it is the best explanation of reality. This implies that the Church must fully live out, symbolise, and conserve her belief system in a way that presents her as the best explanation of reality.

Christians must view themselves as a complete embodiment and expression of all Christian truth claims in a culture that looks at Christianity as any other worldview. Postmodernists argue that Christianity is just like any other religion unless it can prove its worth. The marginalised Church needs to reposition itself as the sole carrier and disseminator of her beliefs, values, and practices.

Mainstreaming postmodern values in Christianity has also generated internal disputes and divisions within the body of Christ. The Church is split based on varied responses to postmodernism: conservatives resist the integration of principles and values of diversity, tolerance and inclusiveness that contradict Christian truth claims; Christians who believe that such principles are wrong, but the Church should not interfere with private lives of her congregants; and liberals believe that the Church should embrace diversity, tolerance and inclusiveness, which they argue is based on correct interpretation of the Word of God.

Differences within the Church have generated philosophical, theological, and denominational debates, which are shaping the views of society and its response to the gospel. This poses a big challenge to Christians who are trapped in an environment that seems to trash Christian principles and values, which have largely been incontestable for ages. This toxic environment labels a conservative Christian as a fundamentalist, exclusivist, and intolerant species that should have no place in our postmodern culture. Are we not witnessing marginalisation and persecution of true believers? What impact does this have on those exploring Christian discipleship?

The Devil is trying to make people believe that all religions are the same and none of them can claim to preach the truth. There is also a notion that Christianity has been unduly favoured at the expense of other faiths, an anomaly that society must correct. This has involved revisiting government incentives and subsidies, allocation of airtime on national television and radio, support for Christian programmes, and Christian practices in public.

Christian life has become even more complex given the increasing hostility against Christianity. The Church is experiencing excessive pressure as society strives to remove Christianity from the centre of the public life. Marginalization of Christianity has serious implications for its adherents. What does this mean for a potential follower of Jesus Christ? There is a spotlight on life of a Christian, which is scrutinized for compliance with national legislation, policies, and rules and procedures, which contradict the Christian doctrine, principles, and practices. In many countries, this has legalized persecution of the Church. Will a potential follower of Jesus Christ brave the tide and decide to follow Him despite fierce persecution of the Church?

The 21st century is credited with phenomenal scientific breakthroughs, which have been high jacked by atheists and other sceptics who dismiss Christianity as a credible explanation of reality. Postmodern universities are generating information, publishing articles, engaged in scholarly debates, and established societies that critique, question and even disqualify Christianity as an intellectually sound worldview worth embracing. The impact on students, especially those with a Christian background, is devastating especially in a society, which William Craig describes as intellectually neutral. He contends that students at all levels, Christians, clergy, and an average member of our society are intellectually disengaged, leaving them exposed to knowledge, ideas and philosophies that contest Christian truth claims.

Deficiencies in Christian scholarship mean that we cannot stand up to scientific and theological scholarship that contradicts our Christian values. Considering that universities breed world leaders who shape worldviews, the Church cannot afford not to contribute to shaping the views of our next generation through engaging the academia to ensure students are provided with intellectual evidence that justifies Christianity as the best worldview. The university environment that is hostile to Christianity might have a very significant influence on the decision an individual makes in response to the call to Christian discipleship.

The Church in the 21st century is experiencing an unprecedented degree of acculturation and commercialization of the gospel. Desacralization of the Church and secularization of our society are two of the most virulent enemies of Church in this age. I watched a BBC TV documentary entitled 'The hunter becomes the hunted', which shows a reversal of positions where the prey hunts the predator, the hunted animal pursues the hunter, or the attacker becomes the victim. I watched a video in which a lion attacked a giraffe but was itself killed.

When the lion launched itself on the hind of the Giraffe, it was determined to bring the victim down. But as fate would have it, the giraffe shook off its predator, which dropped to the ground right behind its long hind legs and the victim unleashed its deadliest kick that sent the lion sprawling to the ground. The giraffe repeatedly kicked the helpless lion until it was dead. The Safari camera crew that filmed the incident could not just believe what they saw – the hunter became the hunted. This is how some commentators view the current relationship between the Church and society. In an ideal situation, the Church should evangelize the world, but commentators argue that society is evangelizing the Church, desacralizing its truth claims. The world is invading the Church, and in several cases, believers are accepting foreign doctrines and teachings.

Opportunists are using the Church as a milk cow to satisfy their own desires. Douglass Webster observes that the market-driven evangelical Church embracing a highly psychologized gospel conditioned by self-centred consumer-oriented, media-induced felt needs seek popularity. These Churches seek to carve out a niche and their evangelism is driven primarily by the need to increase the number of congregants and the financial benefits. As such they are aggressively coercing people to their programmes at any cost, including watering down the gospel of Christ.

As Jesus Christ watches how the Church is abused for self-appeasement while sinners needing help are escorted to hell, His heart bleeds. This century is witnessing a different scale of commercialization of the gospel. Desacralization of the Church and secularization of society imply that the Church lacks cultural authority and social power to be the light and salt of the earth. Douglass Webster argues that the acculturated mainline denominations and market-driven evangelical Churches need evangelization starting with the biblical theology of sin. How do these Churches impact would-be followers of Jesus Christ?

While previous Church ages have faced diverse challenges, the 21st century is experiencing a social, cultural, philosophical, theological disposition that is conditioning the way Christians practise their faith. The impact of these conditioners on the Church, individual Christians, and society varies in space, time, and intensity. The medium in which these impacts manifest assumes a continuum from communities, countries, or regions which have outlawed Christianity to the other extreme where it is embedded in the national constitution as the only recognized faith group in a nation. The unique features of the 21st century and the catalogue of challenges define the human factor and the environment in which Christianity is practiced. Any potential disciple of Jesus Christ must confront these issues. The god of this world, and particularly this century, has ramped up his activities to kill, steal and destroy people destined for God's Kingdom.

What is the impact of postmodern culture on Christian living?

Since 2007, many banks in the United Kingdom have paid out huge sums of money to compensate their customers for mis-sold payment protection insurance (PPI) for loans, mortgages, credit cards, and other financial agreements. The banks didn't follow guidelines for selling PPI, which covers clients in case they were unable to repay their debts. Mis-selling of PPI resulted in thousands of clients buying insurance they didn't want, need, or even know about. The underlying problem in this case was that the client did not have adequate information to make an informed decision about the product.

A variant of this problem occurs in Christendom where would-be followers of Jesus Christ are not provided with adequate information to enable them to reach an informed decision to become Christ's disciples. As a consequence, there are many disgruntled Christians whose expectations have not been met. Such Christians have either struggled to accommodate the unexpected or given up their faith. Of course, there are circumstances that may not allow the evangelist to fully explain the terms of discipleship. That is fine if you quickly follow up the convert to teach them the terms of discipleship.

How many spiritual children have we given birth to and then dumped? The unique conditions of this century and the challenges facing would-be disciples of Christ underline the fact that no one should blindly decide to become a disciple but should consider terms of discipleship and knowingly consent to them. This section summarises some of the key considerations in making a wise decision regarding discipleship.

a) Have I carefully considered the terms of discipleship?

Jesus Christ categorically stated that following Him demands sacrifice and He did not hide the cost of discipleship. His teachings on discipleship were hard and uncompromising. Nicodemus, a Pharisee and member of the Jewish ruling council, was troubled by what he heard the Master teaching the multitudes and His disciples about His kingdom.

Nicodemus was a custodian of the Law and prophecies, but he observed the ministry of Jesus Christ and realised that Pharisees did not comprehend the things that the young Rabbi taught. Despite his senior position in the Jewish society, he decided to have a private discussion with Jesus to sort out his own theology, belief system and relationship with God. Jesus Christ gave His senior student, Nicodemus, conditions for citizenship of the kingdom of God (John 3:1-7, NKJV).

Nicodemus, a Jewish ruler, a senior custodian and teacher of Jewish Law and prophecies, did not understand the process of entering and experiencing the Kingdom of God. Jesus taught him that he needed to be born again to *see* the Kingdom of God and to be born of the water and Spirit to *enter* it. The questions he asked Jesus Christ show that Nicodemus did not know, and let alone understand, the conditions for seeing and entering God's kingdom. This raises a major question. If Nicodemus did not understand this kingdom principle, what did he teach the people?

It is not surprising that Jesus criticised the Pharisees for blocking the people who strove to enter the Kingdom of God and even they could not access it. One may be tempted to condemn the Pharisees for misleading people through their ignorance and arrogance, but most of them were genuinely convinced they were doing the right thing. They might not have realised that their religion was denying them, and the people access to the Kingdom of God. Today, there are many 'Christians' who do not fully understand the teachings of Jesus Christ and are misleading people of God.

When Jesus Christ called a person to become His disciple the life of that individual drastically changed. The followers had to abandon whatever they had or were doing to take on a new vocation of fishing men. These were not easy decisions as evidenced by cases of people who just gave up the idea of following Jesus because they could not obey His instruction. The rich young man who desired to follow Jesus (Matthew 19:20-22, NKJV) abandoned his mission when the Lord instructed him to sell his possessions and give to the poor.

Jesus asked the man to apply a basic principle of the Kingdom of God – the principle of commonwealth. Jesus asked him to surrender ownership of personal wealth for use in the Kingdom of God. The young rich man was assured that he would accrue treasure in heaven. This condition for following Jesus touched what the rich young man valued most, and he could not let go of it. This is a basic requirement for becoming a follower of Jesus. The man went away in sorrow, and we don't hear about him again.

If the rich young man found it difficult to follow Jesus because he could not sell all that he had to give the proceeds to the poor, Dr Luke provides an even more complex set of criteria for following Jesus Christ (Luke 14:26-33, KJV). Many Christians would have preferred that Jesus said, "If any man comes to me, and becomes my disciple, he shall have wealth and honour in abundance." I am afraid; the Lord veered in the opposite direction and gave five tough terms of discipleship.

First, a disciple of Christ must *forsake* or *hate* all relations. Every normal man loves his wife, children, father and mother, and brother and sister. Does this condition mean that I must literally detest or hate my relations to the extent that I could harm or even kill them? Doesn't the Word of God teach us to love our wives, honour our parents, and love our neighbours as ourselves? I would suggest that 'hate' or 'forsake' in this context means make them of 'lower priority' or 'love them less' than Jesus. Your 100% love for your relations should still be less than that lavished to Jesus. The Lord demands that our loyalty and love for Him be greater than any other attachment. Did He not demonstrate this attitude Himself?

Jesus Christ left the fellowship of Father and the Holy Spirit to come to the earth and redeem humanity. While on earth He forsook, Joseph, Mary, and His brothers and sisters to do the assignment the Father gave Him. He said, *My food is to do the will of Him who sent Me and to finish His work* (John 4:34, NKJV). The Master requires that those that choose to walk with Him must have the same attitude to prioritise God's work above all other.

A disciple of Jesus Christ said, *Lord, first let me go and bury my father.* His response was, *Follow Me, and let the dead bury their own dead* (Matt. 8:21, NIV). When duty to our relatives competes with our obligation to God, we must give God preference. Some people would say this is unthinkable in our culture, but the Kingdom of God to which a Christian belongs has a different culture.

Second, anyone who decides to follow Jesus Christ must hate his own life. Any normal human being loves himself and desires quality life. Our tendency is to focus primarily on preserving and sustaining our lives. As such, people aspire to have the best in every sphere of life. But Jesus bids His disciples to love Him more than they love themselves. A disciple of Jesus Christ must be concerned above everything else with the Kingdom of God and what is required of him. Then, the Lord will preserve his life and provide him with everything he needs for life and godliness (Matt. 6:33, KJV).

A disciple must be willing to give up his life, if need be, for the cause of Christ. To become a follower of Christ is to surrender control over one's life to the Lord. This reverses the process of human rebellion against God that started in the Garden of Eden when man sought independence from God. Hating your life is to say, Lord Jesus Christ, I accept you as my creator, maker, redeemer, author and finisher of my faith, and You have called me by my name, and I am yours.

Third, a disciple of Christ is someone who bears his own cross and follows Christ. In our society, this is one of the most abused verses of the Bible. Many people refer to certain responsibilities, such as looking after their elderly parents, disabled or sick relatives, orphans, widows, or wayward children, as their crosses. What they really mean is carrying the burden(s). Is this what Jesus meant when he asked his disciples to bear their crosses? Not quite.

In the first century, a cross meant death by the most painful and humiliating means that humans could develop. A criminal convicted of death by crucifixion by the Roman justice system was forced to carry his own cross to the place of crucifixion. Bearing the cross meant a convict carrying his own crucifixion device while facing ridicule along the way to death. As a disciple of Jesus Christ, the world will unjustly judge, condemn, persecute, ridicule, and laugh at for the sake of Christ. Disciples of Jesus Christ were scorned, arrested, flogged, imprisoned, beheaded, hacksawed, crucified for the sake of Christ.

Bearing the cross means willingness to die to follow Jesus Christ, dying to self, a call to absolute surrender, or putting down your own ideas, plans, and desires in exchange for Jesus' own. Didn't Jesus Christ experience this for the sake of fulfilling the will of the father? The cross, consisting of an intersection of linear objects also depicts the intersection of the way of life of humanity and God's way of life, a point where self-will and God's will collide with the latter overriding the former.

In the Garden of Eden Jesus asked His Father to take away the cup, but the Father wanted Jesus to take His cup. When Jesus' will collided with the Father's will, Jesus submitted to the will of the Father. While his flesh sought to avoid the cup, yet He chose that the will of the Father be done. His will died to allow for full expression of His Father's will.

A key question every believer must ask himself or herself is, 'Am I willing to take up my cross daily and to give up my hopes, dreams, possessions, and even life, if need be, for the sake of Christ? One of the greatest concerns about our Christian practice is that this question is rarely asked, and many preachers seem to avoid this hard teaching for fear they may lose members. Jesus expects every disciple to bear his or her own cross.

Every would-be disciple of Jesus Christ must sit down first and count the cost to ensure he/she has adequate resources to comply with terms of discipleship. Before a builder can decide whether to construct a building, there must be an assurance that the project can be done within a stipulated budget. The builder normally engages a Quantity Surveyor to prepare a bill of quantities, which is an itemized list of materials, parts, and labour (with their costs) required to construct a specific structure.

Any king who considers going to war with another king must assess his capabilities to ensure he has what it takes to win the war. Failure to count the cost may be catastrophic. For buildings or other physical structures, this could lead to an unfinished structure or task, substandard structure, structural failure, reputational damage, litigation, and tying resources in a structure that is not fit for purpose. For a king, it could result in losing a war, territory, subjects and their property, kingdom's treasure, resources, or imprisonment or even death.

Jesus Christ requires that every potential disciple sits down first to itemize specific requirements of discipleship and to cost them. Discipleship may involve giving up relationships, possessions, a job, dreams, plans, and even life. This does not mean that a disciple must reject all these, but that all he/she has is placed at Christ's service and under His guidance. Depending on the circumstances, Christ determines how they are used. You literally cease to own and control your life and possessions. You relinquish ownership and become a custodian of God's property.

Can a man or woman have every resource to meet the terms of discipleship? Fortunately, Jesus does not expect us to have all the resources. After counting the cost, He expects you to commit what you have to Him, and he provides the rest. Jesus expects you to know the full cost of discipleship and understand your deficiency. This drives you to fully depend on Him, understand the process and commit to do your part. After counting the cost, are you ready to follow Jesus?

Jesus demands that anyone who considers becoming His disciple must forsake *all*. This a very difficult condition because human nature wants to own, control, and manage people and things. If there are believers who have understood this term of discipleship, Paul is an excellent example. He testified to the Philippian Church when he wrote that, *But what things were gain to me, I counted loss for Christ. Yet indeed I also count all things loss for the excellence of the knowledge of Christ Jesus my Lord, for whom I have suffered the loss of all things, and count them as rubbish, that I may gain Christ and be found in Him* (Philip. 3:7-9, NKJV). Paul examined his life and identified all his qualities, possessions, and accomplishments that defined his elite religious status and considered them as valueless as dung. If we knew how valuable these things were in Paul's era, we would understand better the gravity of Paul's decision.

Listen to him as he describes what he lost: *If anyone else thinks he may have confidence in the flesh, I more so: circumcised on the eighth day, of the stock of Israel; of the tribe of Benjamin, a Hebrew of Hebrews; concerning the law, Pharisee; concerning zeal, persecuting the Church; concerning the righteousness which is in the law, blameless"* (Philip. 3:4-6, NIV). These qualities were core to Paul's elitist identity, which many envied in his society, but he considered them a distraction to his bid to know Christ. He literally stripped himself of everything that defined his identity. This involved giving up a high profile and honourable status in society to become a slave or servant of Jesus Christ.

Very few people genuinely give up their worldly status to serve our Master. The common occurrences include rich and honourable people either rejecting the call or accepting the call, while marinating their worldly identity. Genuine discipleship requires forsaking our all.

b) Do you believe God exists?

You may be wondering why some people consider this to be an absurd question. Is it not obvious that God exists? It is this assumption, which might cause problems because a potential disciple of Christ does not fully understand. When we introduce Jesus Christ as the Son of God to an unbeliever, we usually assume the person believes that God exists.

In trying to make Christianity as easily accessible as possible, we tend to either omit or dilute the Word of God ending up with immature Christians who easily succumb to trials. Being fully convinced that God exists is one the key requirements of true discipleship. Do you realise that questioning the existence of God is a tactical move of the enemy to destroy the foundation of our Christian belief system?

If someone can doubt the existence of God, the identity of Jesus as the Son of God and the testimony of Christ's death and resurrection fall apart. Unless you believe God exists, the legitimacy of the written Word, the living Word, the Word in our hearts, the Book of nature, and the Holy Spirit become questionable. The Son of God presupposes that there is God the Father who begot the Son. The phrases 'Y son of X' and 'X begat Y' are common in Biblical genealogies. A father is a vital link in one's lineage.

The earlier a believer is assured of God's existence the more secure will be his or her faith in Christ. When faith is based on inadequate knowledge of God, there is a higher probability that a conversion is driven by emotions rather than deep conviction of the finished work of Christ. Such believers may not make much progress in their spiritual life because they lack depth of conviction or a firm foundation for their faith. They must know the God they are choosing to believe in. Worldviews offer millions of gods, but disciples of Christ must seek God the Father of Jesus Christ, the creator of the universe and everything in it.

c) Do I believe in the story of Christ?

Understanding the identity of Jesus Christ is fundamental in one's decision to walk with Him. Many potential disciples of Jesus Christ approach the gospel with enormous baggage, which may include beliefs and values that do not recognize Jesus Christ as the Son of God, creator, maker, redeemer, sustainer, part of Trinity, or as God. They may not believe in the death, burial, and resurrection of Jesus Christ because of other belief systems before hearing the gospel. Knowledge of the identity of Christ is the bedrock of the gospel.

When Thomas asked Jesus to show His disciples the way to God the Father, Jesus said to him, *I am the way, the truth, and the life. No one comes to the Father except through Me* (John 14:6, NIV). Jesus Christ makes a fundamental statement about His identity and how it benefits a believer. First, Jesus declares Himself as the only way to His Father. Navigating a distorted world system with numerous worldviews is a complex task. What makes the task even more challenging is that the world offers a variety of 'ways' to God.

Acknowledging the existence of many false alternative ways to access God that the world offers, Jesus presents Himself as the only way to the Father. What is a way? A way may refer to a method, style, manner of doing something or a road, track, or path for travelling along to a defined destination. Jesus helps His disciples to understand that He is the complete or self-sufficient method, style, and process of accessing God the Father. Wrapped in Jesus are resources and processes that enable a disciple to live a Christ-like life that leads him or her into the presence of God. No other worldview (Islam, Judaism, Buddhism, Shintoism, atheism, scientism) leads to God, except Christianity, which recognizes Jesus Christ as the only way.

Jesus Christ declared himself as the truth. There are many definitions of the word 'truth, but John MacArthur uses the Bible to define truth as that which is consistent with the mind, will, character, glory, and being of God. Truth is the self-expression of God. God the Father is truth just as Jesus is the Truth. Paul affirms that Christ is the visible image of God (John 18:38). Since the definition of truth flows from God, truth is theological. In our society, scientism, and other worldviews either dispute God as the truth, believe in other truths, or dismiss the Christian perspective of truth as one of several others.

Despite all the opposition, Jesus Christ is the truth and every potential disciple must recognize Him as such. Jesus also told the disciples that He was the life. He came to earth in the likeness of flesh and was sacrificed to put an end to the control of flesh. The Spirit of life in Christ defeated the spirit of sin and death liberating man from sinful nature.

Faith in Christ includes death, burial, and resurrection of believers in union with Christ symbolized by baptism in Him. This is the authentic and distinctive feature of Christianity, which makes Christianity the only true worldview of reality. Thus, Jesus as the way, the truth and the life symbolizes the totality of life lived in Christ, for Christ and with Christ in God. This is a commitment not to be entered into lightly.

As a follower of Christ, one must know and believe in Jesus Christ, and understand what living in union with Christ entails. One must be convinced that He fulfilled several dozens of prophecies made hundreds of years before His birth, he lived a sinless and miracle-filled life, and He died and rose triumphantly and bodily from the grave. Also important is our Christian truth that Jesus is both man and God. Jesus Christ is God incarnate and whatever He teaches is true.

Jesus is the full and final revelation of God. Anyone who desires to follow Jesus must recognize His deity. Do you believe that Jesus is the Son of God? Do you believe in the actual birth, life, teachings, death, burial, and resurrection of Jesus Christ? Do you believe that His death and resurrection are still as potent now as they were over two thousand years ago?

d) Do I believe in the inspiration and authority of the Bible?

Christianity has historically stood on four great revelations of God: the personal revelation of God in Christ, the propositional revelation of God in scriptures, personal revelation of God through nature, and personal revelation through the law written in hearts and minds of men. In our society, people are exposed to various worldviews, which seek to discredit or even deny Bible as the authoritative Word of God.

I have heard some people dismiss the Bible as a collection of fairy tales or a historical document with little or no relevance to our lives. However, the Bible is God's personal communication to humanity, written by men who were inspired by the Holy Spirit. The written Word is the authoritative Word of God.

In the New Testament Jesus Christ confidently declares that He is God incarnate and proves this by fulfilling messianic prophecy, living a sinless and miraculous life, predicting, and accomplishing His death and resurrection. He taught that the Old Testament was the Written Word of God and promised that His disciples would write the New Testament. Fulfilment of prophecies demonstrates that the Bible is the authoritative word of God.

The Bible and the Bible alone contains all doctrinal and ethical truth that has been revealed to mankind, and it is the only canon or norm of all truth. This does not suggest that there are no extrabiblical writings (e.g. and other religious books) that contain truth. There are several writings outside the Bible including Greek poetry, the Apocrypha, and the records of Assyrians, Romans, and Babylonians that verify the historical accuracy of different places, persons, and events. These writings contain truth that has helped to corroborate the existence of people in the Bible.

The British Philosopher Bertrand Russell (1872-1970) argued in his famous essay '*Why I am not a Christian?*' that 'Historically, it is quite doubtful that Christ ever existed at all and if he did, we do not know anything about him.' But researchers found more than 30 extrabiblical writings within 150 years of His life, including those of Josephus, which verified that Jesus was He who the Bible described as the Son of God. The Bible alone embodies God's infallible Word. A Christian must bring all other alleged truth to the bar of the Holy Scriptures to be tested. Christians believe that the Bible is the inspired and authoritative Word of God in the 21st century.

e) Has God's agenda for me changed?

As I reflect on 21st century culture, it is important to assess my ability to follow Jesus in view of God's agenda for humanity on earth. From the beginning, God created the earth which man would govern to display His glory (Isa. 43:7, NKJV). The requirement for good governance is summarized in Ecclesiastes 13: 12, (NIV), *Let us hear the conclusion of the whole matter: Fear God, and keep his commandments: for this is the whole duty of mankind.* Unfortunately, man disobeyed God and abdicated his position as ruler of the earth to the Devil. Humans decided to unilaterally attain a higher position than provided for in the hierarchy of the Kingdom of God. Did God change His agenda for humanity and the earth? Not at all!

God foresaw how humanity would abuse his authority over the earth and pre-emptively prepared a redemption plan to ensure the aim of an earth ruled by humanity to His glory was not decimated. As a true, loving, faithful and just Father, God disciplined Adam, but He did not destroy him, and Adam did not commit suicide.

We know that God sent His Son to reconcile humans to Himself and to restore them as rulers over the earth. Jesus Christ has completed his assignment of redeeming human and non-human creation, and the redeemed of the Lord are spreading the gospel and harvesting souls in God's vineyard. God designed the earth and planned for the four key acts of Bible (creation, fall, redemption, and consummation) to fully restore humans in their position as rulers of the earth.

While the Lord is redeeming souls, the saved souls are sealed with the Holy Spirit as a guarantee of the promises to come. Both humans and other creatures are waiting for the completion of salvation when the promises will be fulfilled - consummation of salvation to the glory of Lord. Paul reminded that Church at Rome that, *For the creation waits in eager expectation for the children of God to be revealed* (Rom. 8:19, NIV). Both man and the rest of creation have not yet attained God's desired position.

We have the Holy Spirit as a deposit for the promise, but we are waiting for Him to complete the process of making us His own sons or daughters when our bodies are made free. Then creation will be freed from corruption to have the same freedom and glory that belong to sons of God. When this is achieved, humans will fully regain their position as rulers of the earth. Are the 21st century challenges weighing you down? God's agenda for His creation has not changed.

f) Have circumstances made it impossible for me to retrace my way back to God?

Society makes us believe that in the 21st century people are more enlightened, and they understand their rights and privileges better than the older generation. This literate society is less receptive to the gospel of Jesus Christ. Commentators claim that circumstances have changed, and it is more difficult to win people to

Christ now than in the past. Some societies, especially in western countries, believe that following Jesus Christ is more difficult now than it has ever been before. Are the circumstances in the 21st century that place humans beyond the redemptive hand of God?

In the early years of my career in Zambia, thieves broke into my house a couple of times and went away with several items. As I reflected on these events, I learned several valuable lessons about their strategies and manoeuvres. While I don't fully understand them, I still learned that they were good planners, high-risk takers, up to date with information about me, very brave and determined to get what they wanted at any cost. They were also good security analysts who easily identified weak points in my security system, were up to speed on any condition that could jeopardize their plan, and they easily adapted to the fast-changing conditions.

Whatever the circumstances, they were able to adapt and carry out their plans to accomplish their purpose. Within their operational environment they hatched plans and implemented them. What impresses me most is that no matter how clever they may seem, the security system still tracked them down. What this means is that both thieves and security experts are always finding new ways of doing things to adapt to changing conditions. If this is happening based on plans of created beings, anyone who lives in this century is capable of following Jesus Christ regardless of the circumstances. As far as God is concerned nothing in this century is too difficult to deal with as long as we follow His instructions.

Paul assured the saints in Rome that in everything they were more than conquerors through Christ who strengthened them (Rom. 6:38-39). God's everlasting love delivered Jesus Christ to be sacrificed for our redemption and He still intercedes for us day and night before His Father. Everyone who abides in Jesus Christ is guaranteed victory through Him. Paul has listed everything within the created world, which could ever affect us and yet he declares that none of them can ever separate us from the love of God. No matter how unique the conditions appear to be if they are created or derived from created beings or creatures they can never separate us from the love of God. *What shall we say to these things? If God is for us, who can be against us?* (Rom. 8:31, KJV). Regardless of the time, place, or circumstances, what God has willed for our lives will surely come to pass.

g) Has God's perception of my value changed?

As we pass through waters, we are tempted to doubt God's everlasting love for us. We usually create our virtual reality in which God looks at us as worthless human beings because of the things we have done or are doing. It is as if you are no longer precious in God's sight. Something tells you; God loves and values those that are obedient. This is a complex situation that we create for ourselves, and we ruthlessly judge ourselves using our standards or our limited interpretation of God's love and attachment to us.

What is so extraordinary about your life in the 21st century that could force God to devalue you? Can we for a moment step back and look at God's approach to man? First, *The earth is the Lord's, and all its fullness, The world and those who dwell therein* (Psa. 24:1, NKJV). Every human being is a creature of God. God loves and values everything He has created. The Psalmist said of the Lord (Psa. 145:16, KJV), *You open Your hand and satisfy the desire of every living thing.* Why would God waste resources on something or someone He does not value?

Look at what Jesus Christ (Matt. 5:44-46, KJV) taught: *But I tell you, love your enemies and pray for those who persecute you, that you may be sons of your Father in heaven. He causes His sun to rise on the evil and the good, and sends rain on the righteous and the unrighteous. If you love those who love you, what reward will you get?* Jesus Christ, the visible image of the Father teaches His followers the secret behind sustaining a rebellious human being. Our natural wisdom is to hate our enemies and to ensure that they also feel the pain they afflicted on us. That is not the route Jesus Christ takes. He teaches His followers to love their enemies and pray for them. That is difficult.

Are you saying, I should love and pray for my enemy: after killing my only child; cheating on me; unlawfully dismissing me from my job; abandoning me with my children; and wrecking my career and marriage? Yes! Jesus demonstrated the love and value He had for His enemies on the cross when He prayed for us, *Father, forgive them for they do not know what they are doing* (Luke 23:34, NIV).

Is it not amazing that Jesus taught His followers that loving our enemies and praying for them are virtues of the sons of our heavenly father. These are traits we inherit from our heavenly Father. Earthly wisdom can justify why God caused the sun to rise upon the good and the rain to fall on the fields of the righteous. But what would make God to cause sun to rise upon the evil and the rain to fall on the fields of the unrighteous? This teaches us that there is no state of human depravity that is beyond reach of God's love. There is no condition that is irredeemable.

God values you and me not because of who we are, what we have done or what we can do for Him, but because He created us and chose to love and value us. God loved us and reached out for us when we were deeply entrenched in sin and relishing evil. Look at how God offered a rebellious house of Israel in Babylon an opportunity to return to Him when He said, *Come now, and let us reason together,"* … *"Though your sins are like scarlet, they shall be as white as snow; Though they are like crimson, They shall be as wool* (Isa. 1:18, NKJV).

God invites the children of Israel to discuss their plight or cause of captivity (sin) with Him and offers to cleanse it. He uses scarlet and crimson to describe the shades of sin, which He can wash away leaving them as white as snow. God can forgive any sin.

Jesus Christ also demonstrated the value of a lost soul using the parable of the lost sheep. He said, *What do you think? If a man owns a hundred sheep, and one of them wanders away, will he not leave the ninety-nine on the hills and go to look for the one that wandered off?* (Matt. 18:12, NIV). On face value, this is a risky approach. How does a farmer abandon 99 sheep to look for one that is lost? Wouldn't leaving 99% of his wealth without oversight expose them to predators resulting in an even bigger loss? But this is what reveals the value of an individual lost sheep in the sight of a shepherd. Jesus teaches us that every stray soul is as valuable as those in the fold and God will do everything to bring it back to the fold.

God values every human being He has created in His image regardless of his state, place, or time of existence. The value He places on individual does not and will never change. His desire is for all to be saved and be with him every day. As a (potential) disciple of Jesus Christ, do you fully understand how much God loves and values you?

h) Am I ready to give up my worldly citizenship for that of the Kingdom of God?

Walking with Jesus Christ involves giving up your citizenship of the kingdom of Satan for the citizenship of the Kingdom of Heaven. In His discussion with Nicodemus, Jesus Christ said, *Most assuredly, I say to you, unless one is born again, he cannot see the Kingdom of God. Nicodemus said to Him, "How can a man be born when he is old? Can he enter a second time into his mother's womb and be born? Jesus answered, "Most assuredly, I say to you, unless one is born of water and the Spirit, he cannot enter the kingdom of God* (John 3:3-5, NKJV). Anyone intending to migrate to a new country must find out what the entry requirements are and the conditions for obtaining citizenship.

When Nicodemus realised that his theology and practice suggested that he was wrong, he was troubled and decided to visit Jesus Christ to enquire about the Kingdom of God. For a man of his status, the questions he asked revealed his naivety about the Kingdom of God, but that did not bother him if his relationship with God would be restored.

Until Jesus Christ came on the scene, Nicodemus, like any other member of the Jewish council, must have assumed that he was a citizen of the Kingdom of God. However, after listening to the teachings of Jesus Christ, he realised that there was a possibility he was not a citizen of the Kingdom of God and he needed to resolve the matter immediately.

Jesus Christ told Nicodemus the conditions for becoming a citizen of the Kingdom of God. At this stage, Nicodemus struggled with the process of becoming a citizen of that Kingdom. Jesus helped the Jewish leader to understand that heavenly citizenship would require him to be born of water and the Spirit. This story of Nicodemus has taught me that there are people who believe to be citizens of the Kingdom of God and yet they are not. Can we like Nicodemus examine our Christian beliefs and practices to find out whether we are truly citizens of the Kingdom?

There are two types of people this case study will appeal to. First, Christians who need to review their understanding of the Kingdom of Heaven. Pride can easily hinder us from seeking help when we are unsure about our kingdom status. We need to ask Jesus to help us understand how to attain full citizenship of His Kingdom. Second, there are Christians who believe that their citizenship is a struggle because of the pressures of the 21st century. You may be asking yourself, "Can I meet the conditions for the citizenship of the Kingdom?" Yes, you can but you cannot do it on your own. Jesus Christ can help you.

There is no situation we cannot handle with Christ. Paul wrote, *I can do all things through Christ who strengthens me* (Philip. 4:13, NKJV). Considering how the Lord had walked him through times of plenty and lack, and through times of hardships and peace, he had all the confidence that he was able to do all things because the ever-present Christ gave him the strength.

I find Paul's testimony of life in the Kingdom of God amazing. He claimed he could do all things through Christ who strengthened him, yet he was imprisoned and experienced times of lack and abundance. Is this something a disciple of Jesus Christ should be experiencing? In the Kingdom of God, you are guaranteed victory and prosperity, but not as the world defines it.

Success in the Kingdom of God means fulfilling the will and purpose of God for your life. How this translates in everyday life depends on the Lord who determines your path. Success may mean: the Lord averts trouble; the Lord walks with you in trouble; or the Lord delivers you from trouble. The common denominator of the three scenarios is that the Lord is with us and He lightens our burden. This is a glimpse of Kingdom life.

It is true that the 21st century brings its own brand of troubles, but the Lord's presence and power are as effective today as they were when they manifested in lives of believers in the past. Are you a citizen of the Kingdom of God and do you observe its constitution (the Bible)?

Can I walk with the Lord in the 21st Century?

I understand that Christians in the 21st century are facing conditions that are unique because things are always evolving and the culture in which Christianity is practiced is constantly changing. Does this imply that we cannot walk with the Lord in this century?

How does the God factor contribute to whether we can walk with God? We need to acknowledge the fact that God is the creator of the universe and everything that is in it and He alone owns and determines the ultimate outcome of the earth project. God created a good earth in Genesis 1 & 2 and ends with a new earth and New Jerusalem city (Rev. 21), while everything in between is a process of corruption and restoration of creation. God's plan for planet earth was established before its foundation and it has never changed. Can we trust Him? Does He have a track record of delivering what He has promised?

God said, *I am God, and there is none like me. Declaring the end from the beginning, and from ancient times the things that are not yet done, saying, My counsel shall stand, and I will do all my pleasure* (Acts 46:9-10, NKJV). The sovereign Lord makes known things to happen at the end of His work at the beginning of His assignment. Whatever happens between the beginning and the end is part of a process that must ultimately feed into a predetermined outcome.

At any point in time, humans and non-human creation are part of a bigger process that will eventually lead to God's desired outcome. Whatever God has willed for your life no one can prevent it from happening. As His workmanship God prepared good works for you before the beginning of time that you may walk in them (Eph. 2:10) and no one stand in the way. Our role is to ask God to open our eyes to see what these good works are and to ask God to give us His grace and a measure to faith to do them. Unfortunately, our faith at times wavers and we are terrified by the storm like Peter who began to sink, when he took his eyes off Jesus. God works through the process with us to bring us to His desired end of the earthly project.

Humans are witnessing events that are unnerving and create uncertainties. Average surface temperature increases have broken records, natural disasters have become more frequent and severe, and world systems have tumbled and become unpredictable, to say the least. Despite all these uncertainties, God's systems are forever stable and no one can disturb or stop them. Gamaliel, a Pharisee understood this when told his colleagues that, *if it is from God, you will not overthrow them. You may even find yourselves fighting against God* (Acts 5:39, NKJV).

What God has set in motion, none of His creation can stop. This assures us that whatever He has decided to do in your life nothing can obstruct it except your unbelief. Isaiah said, *The Lord of hosts has sworn, saying, "Surely, as I have thought, so it shall come to pass, And as I have purposed, so it shall stand* (Isa. 14:24, NKJV). If we understand that whatever God thinks is as good as done and everything he has purposed has to happen, the secret to our success is unlocked. Seek the will of God for your life and you will be guaranteed of success.

Anyone who decides to walk with Him will confidently finish the race regardless of what life throws at him/her. God revealed His will when He said, *He who overcomes shall inherit all things, and I will be his God and he shall be My son* (Rev. 21:7, NKJV). He expects us to overcome obstacles and is looking forward to the day when He will become our God and we will become His children.

In the thickets of philosophical and theological debates that claim that God has become powerless and unreachable, allegations that Christianity has lost its relevance, skepticism that attempts to disprove Christian doctrines, persecution of saints, and cases of secularization of society and desacralization of the Church, God provides for people to know and serve Him. He created us in His image to be His children and whatever mills we are going through, He is still expecting to have children at the end of the age. God's plan for humanity has never changed.

We need to consider the Church factor. The stiff opposition the Church faces from academia, the marketplace or public sphere and from her own members has been interpreted as weakness, irrelevance, inconsistency, or intolerance. Marginalization and persecution of the Church has become a common feature of the century. Some scholars suggest that the Church is losing ground to other faiths, especially Islam.

On the academic front, some scientists, philosophers, and theologians have put across theories to suggest that Christianity does not sufficiently explain reality. Has she lost her potency and purpose? Some commentators have reported a drop in numbers of Christians attending Church in some countries and denominations, and probably concluded that the Church is seriously in trouble. Is it?

While secularization is on the increase and the Church is bleeding in the West, the global trends show that the population of Christians is still growing. The Center for the Study of Global Christianity Report published by Gordon Conwell Theological Seminary in 2023 stated that there would be over 2.6 billion Christians worldwide by the middle of 2023 and around 3.3 billion by 2050, relative to 2.2 billion in 2010. Africa has recorded the highest growth rate (2.77%). In addition, there were fewer atheists around the world in 2022 (147 million) than in 1970 (165 million) (The Status of Global Christianity, 2022).

Church growth is unstoppable because Jesus Christ is the Head of the body of Christ. Did He not assure His disciples that the Church would grow regardless of the forces working against it? When Peter recognized Jesus as Christ the Son of the living God, the Lord said, *And I tell you, you are Peter, and on this rock I will build my Church, and the gates of hell shall not prevail against it* (Matt. 16:18, NKJV). If the gates of hell are the worst barriers to becoming a disciple of Jesus Christ, He has disarmed them and there is nothing to hold us back if we decide to walk with Him. The Church has great potential for growth because Jesus has provided everything needed to sustain God's children.

On the cross, Jesus Christ paid for our sins to satisfy the requirement for righteousness. He died for humanity, was buried, and resurrected once, but the efficacy of His redemption is eternal. Paul wrote, *Who is he that condemns? It is Christ that died, yes rather, that is risen again, who is even at the right hand of God, who also makes intercession for us* (Rom. 8:34, NKJV). As we hide in Christ, He consistently intercedes for us before His Father declaring our righteousness through His blood. Christ guarantees His followers salvation and protection. If we commit to walk with Him, there is every provision to sustain us.

The human factor considers the status of the individual Christian or would-be disciple of Jesus Christ. What is the probability of overcoming the pressures of life to follow Him in the 21st century? Christians are facing enormous pressure in their families, at places of work, in colleges and universities, and in communities. Living a Christian life is like being a leper in some communities. Depending on the location, persecution of believers is evident almost all the time.

In many countries Christians are killed for their faith. If we must follow Jesus Christ, where is the protection against these atrocities? The bad news is that Jesus never guaranteed His followers a trouble-free life. In fact, he assured us that trouble would be our cup of tea. He told His followers that: *In the world you will have tribulation. But take courage; I have overcome the world* (John 16:33, NKJV).

Apart from predicting His arrest, crucifixion, and burial, Jesus told His disciples that they would scatter in the face of trouble. He also warned them that if they lived in this world they would face tribulation. This is true of any disciple of Christ. When everyone disserted the Lord, the Father was with Him.

The good news is that when we face tribulation, Jesus Christ is always with us provided we believe in Him. When Meshack, Shadreck and Abednego were cast in a fiery furnace, their tormentors including Nebuchadnezzar saw four men unbound, walking around in the fire unharmed, with the fourth one looking like a god (Dan. 3:22-25, KJV). God, who was with the three Hebrew men went with them in the blazing furnace where He revealed Himself to let all people present know that the God of Israel was there to defend the Hebrew men.

God assured Jacob of His presence in times of trouble (Isa. 43:2, KJV). Tribulation (deep waters, rivers of difficulty, fire, and flames) will surely come, but the good news is that you will pass or go through them; you will not die or get stuck in them. Jesus Christ will be with you as you pass through tribulations, and you will not be destroyed. The Hebrew men and Jacob defied the instruments of torment, fire and water.

Why will God invest so much in you? He has given a very strong justification for His action – the LORD created you, He formed you, He ransomed you, and He called you by name. Holding you firmly to His chest, He boldly declares for all to hear that you are His. What an investment God has made in us. Anyone who comes to God is assured of this expression of love and protection.

Jesus Christ calmed His disciples because He overcame all the troubles in the past, present and future. What I like most is the fact that Jesus Christ did not name specific tribulations, but everything that can answer to that name. He did not set a time limit to the period His conquest would remain effective. It doesn't matter whether the tribulation occurs in the 3rd, 10th, 20th, or 30th century, Jesus will always empower His followers to conquer their troubles.

The socio-cultural factor is major a player in defining the life of a disciple of

Jesus Christ, providing a medium in which Christianity is expressed. The governments, media, business community, and other sectors of society influence the perception of, and response to, Christianity. The laws, policies, procedures, publications, and other sociocultural systems appear to restrict the practice of Christianity in public and in some private places. Can these apparatuses cage Christianity?

The Word of God cannot be caged. If Jesus Christ just preached to people who were free to practice religion, may be one could entertain the thought of restricting the worship God. But after resurrection, He also went and preached to imprisoned spirits in the lower parts of the earth. What we would normally consider as very difficult places to take the gospel to, are accessible to the Lord.

As I reflected on the tenacity of Christianity, the names of three Christian Sunday School teachers (Pastor Dr Rebekka Zakaria, Ratna Pangun and Eti Pangesti) in Indonesia came to my mind. These disciples of Christ were accused of breaching the Child Protection Law by attempting to convert Muslim children to Christianity in a Muslim country. Although they never committed a crime, the pressure exerted by Indonesian Clerics Council and Islamic extremists on the judicial system resulted in a three-year jail term. What impressed me most was the sheer determination of these three women to share their Christian faith in an Islamic jail, which resulted in salvation of souls.

According to the CEO of Open Doors, these three ladies remained powerful witnesses for their Christian faith throughout their two-year imprisonment. They transformed the prison through their voluntary acts of charity including cleaning washrooms and toilets, scrubbing cells, working in the garden, and even painting the walls of the rooms they used as Church meetings. Their calming influence reduced quarreling in the women section to the extent that the guards overruled prison protocol and allowed each of these women to have a knife and spoon in their cells.

Who could have imagined that the Muslim prison service could allow

Church meetings and conversions to Christianity in this environment? Dr Rebekka referred to the jail as the University of Trust. In our ministry, ministering to spirits in captivity is not something we would consider doing, but Christ has never deprived anyone of the opportunity to know Him or to be saved. No condition, place, person, or circumstance can resist the workings of God.

Jesus Christ died for all creation and His redemption covers everything affected by the fall of humanity. What marvels me is the degree to which institutions are deploying different instruments to suppress the body of Christ. They are trying to push against a rock that could easily crush them. Local and international bodies are working together to try and halt or reduce the growth of the Church. Does this bother God? No, it doesn't.

The Lord questions human strategies to suppress His work: *Why do the nations rage, And the people plot a vain thing? The kings of the earth set themselves, And the rulers take counsel together, Against the Lord and against His Anointed, saying, "Let us break Their bonds in pieces And cast away Their cords from us." He who sits in the heavens shall laugh; The Lord shall hold them in derision"* (Psa. 2:1-4), NKJV. Unsettled by the advancement of the Kingdom of God raging rulers conspire against the LORD and His anointed to derail God's plan and purpose for His creation.

The desire to free ourselves from what we wrongly term as slavery to God is a dangerous plot. How do you detach yourself from your source of life? But when God who rules in heaven looks at the futility of human plans, He laughs. How does God react to vain plans of humanity? *He is before all things, and in him all things hold together. (Col. 1:17, NIV); and who being the brightness of His glory and the express image of His person and upholding all things by the word of His power* (Heb. 1:3, NKJV). God holds the entire universe together and causes all its parts to function according to His purpose. How can rulers or kings who are just tiny parts of God's system plot to restructure the system when they have no control over it and the Word of God's power? What does this mean for God's predetermined goal?

When rulers act in rebellion against God, He scoffs at them and rebukes them in anger. They soon realize the vanity of their plans and the sheer fierce fury of God terrifies them. The schemes of man against God cannot succeed. Whatever social and cultural posturing society engages in to prevent God's work turns out to be a disaster waiting to happen. Socio-cultural factors cannot restrain a person who decides to become a disciple of Christ.

God's goal is for humans, created in His image, to rule with Him and His plan has not changed. Whatever He thinks happens. His truth holds regardless of place, time, and circumstances. Can we walk with God in the 21st Century? The answer is: yes, we can walk with God in the 21st century if we totally depend on Jesus Christ.

CHAPTER 13

How can I walk with God in the 21st Century?

God has made an open invitation to everyone to come to Him. There is nothing that can stop anyone, at anytime and anywhere from becoming a disciple of Jesus Christ if the individual fully understands and accepts His terms of discipleship. Walking with God requires complying with the principles, practices, and rules of His Kingdom. God's invitation to His Kingdom is extended to everyone on earth, but only those who voluntarily and willingly accept the terms and conditions of the Kingdom can become disciples of Jesus Christ. There are established Kingdom principles and practices which followers of Christ need to observe as they walk with Him. This section briefly explores how disciples of Christ start and maintain their walk with the Lord.

As we consider a potential relationship with Christ, we are sometimes lured into believing that our decision to follow Christ starts with somebody sharing the gospel of Jesus Christ with us. This belief presupposes that God appears on the scene when we choose to hear the Word of God. But God's work in our lives started as soon as He thought of creating the earth and its inhabitants.

God, who knows the end from the beginning, visualized your existence in pre-creation, created, fallen, redeemed, and consummated states and has never abandoned you since then. Because our entire lifespan, if Jesus tallies, is embedded in the period before the final salvation, we tend to think narrowly about our redemption within the context our current environment. The process of winning a soul over to Christ started long before God created the earth.

Salvation is a scheduled event in God's grand operational will, purpose and plan for His universe and your life. Our perception of discipleship needs to be placed within the broader context of God's will and purpose for the universe. As we ask ourselves whether God has made any provision for us to walk with Him in the 21st Century, we need to consider events within God's eternal plan, purpose, and provisions for us. Are disciples of Jesus Christ adequately resourced to walk with God in this century. Yes, God has adequately resourced us to walk with Him anytime. But how can we do it?

Embrace the Kingdom of God as a model of Christian life

God relates with humanity based on His Kingdom principles. We are created in God's image to extend His heavenly concept of the Kingdom to the earth. Although we live in nations and kingdoms modeled after His Kingdom, we struggle to apply kingdom principles in our lives. Jesus Christ frequently used the phrase, the Kingdom of God, in the first three Gospels of the New Testament. But what does it mean?

Biblical and extrabiblical literature provide several definitions of the Kingdom of God. The "Kingdom of God" (Hebrew *Malkuthey Shamaim*; Greek *Basileia*; Aramaic *Malkut* and their cognates) is concerned with the activity of the King himself, his exercise of sovereign power. Timoth R. Wilson asserts that the Hebrew equivalent and virtually all biblical scholars define these terms as the "kingly rule, reign, sovereign authority" of God. It refers to the rule of the eternal, sovereign God over the entire universe; the authority to rule; the sovereignty of the King; the rank, authority and sovereignty exercised by the King; sovereignty of the King over all the earth; a spiritual rule over the hearts and lives of those who willingly submit to God's authority.

The Kingdom refers to that which God does which depicts God as the King. Timothy R. Wilson defines the 'Kingdom of God' as His sovereign reign and rule over a people He has called out, set apart, and sent forth to carry out His mission in the world. The gospel of the Kingdom of God emphasizes the rule of God in the lives of people and brought out by the "now and not yet" elements of Christian hope. This Kingdom is both a present reality and a future hope. It exists already, but it is not yet fully realized.

The supreme and sovereign reign of Christ has been established through His sinless life, sacrificial death, and bodily resurrection. But the Kingdom of God also includes the eschatological literal rule of Christ on the earth during the millennium - the future consummation of power. Jesus victoriously inaugurated His reign, and it will be finally consummated when He returns at the end of this age.

The Kingdom of God is universal. It is not a territory, place or community ruled by God. Neither is it an abstract idea of kingship of God. Timothy Wilson emphasizes that the Kingdom of God is not defined in geographical, spatial, physical, temporal, or territorial terms. It is a condition of the heart, mind and will where God is Lord of all. William Barclay describes the Kingdom of God as "the dominion of God" and not "a domain". Jesus is the Kingdom of God.

God initiated the original concept of the kingdom, which stands alone as the perfect prototype of government built on righteous judgment. God reigns as King and absolute Sovereign over all things in both the spiritual and physical realms. The Kingdom of God is a real government established by Jehovah. The Psalmist acknowledges that, *The LORD has established his throne in heaven, and his kingdom rules over all* (Psa.103:19, NKJV), while King Nebuchadnezzar declared that "His Kingdom is an eternal Kingdom" (Dan. 4:3, NKJV).

God is the Sovereign King in both space and time. Heaven is the palace of the King of the Universe and decrees and laws governing the universe flow from there. At the same time, His reign is eternal. It follows that the Kingdom predates creation and incorporates everything that is. God has established every authority that exists in the universe (Rom. 13:1, KJV). For the Jew, the Kingdom of God is everlasting: God always was, and always will be King, and the activity wherein He manifests Himself as such is to be everlastingly experienced.

God created the universe and ruled over it before He created man. *The God who made the world and everything in it is the Lord of heaven and earth and does not live in temples made by human hands* (Acts 17:24, NIV). God declared that He is the creator of the universe and the Lord (owner and ruler). After creating the earth and everything in it, God made man and installed him as king over the earth and all other creatures.

Moses documents the decision of the Council of God the Father, God the Son, and God the Holy Spirit to create man to rule over the earth and everything in it (Gen. 1:26, KJV). He made humans in His image and likeness with traits of a king to rule over the earth and all the creatures it hosts. While God rules the heavens, He installed man as His representative king on earth (Psa. 8:4-8, KJV). God has made man to govern or manage His earthly creatures. God seeded the kingdom concept in the heart of man as the purpose for which he was created.

Man is a potential ruler, governor, leader, and manager, capable of ruling the earth. After planting the Garden of Eden, God installed man as king to rule over it as an extension of the reign of the sovereign from heaven, the throne of God. Unfortunately, the earthly king (Adam) rebelled against God in heaven and compromised the mandate to rule the earth.

Adam abdicated his throne to Satan who became the king of this world. When he abdicated his throne in the Garden of Eden, the Kingdom of God became the kingdom of Satan, which he refers to as the kingdoms of the world. The authority to rule over kingdoms of the world was not inborn but delivered to him. The ability of man to rule the earth is built within human nature, but Satan's authority is externally sourced. Nonetheless he has acquired authority from man to rule the earth and he boasts about his freedom to give this authority to whomever he chooses to bless. He offered to give it to Jesus on condition that He worshipped him. The irony is that the Devil still depends on man to rule his kingdoms.

The fall of humanity created an internal conflict between the image and nature of God and the acquired nature of Satan. Disobedience meant that human allegiance to the Sovereign King in heaven was severely compromised. The once authoritative king in the Garden of Eden was so disillusioned that he could not face the Sovereign God.

Abdicating his throne came at a price of ruining his relationship with God and the rest of earthly creation originally under care of humanity. In its place, the devil established the kingdom of darkness, which rules over rebellious humans and other earthly creatures. The devil established counterfeit earthly kingdoms and installed his kings. The Old Testament documents many kingdoms including the Babylonian, Persian, Greek, and Roman empires. However, these models of governance were at variance with God's original model.

When God chose the nation of Israel to be His vessel for blessing the nations of the world, Jehovah was the sole King of the Jewish nation (1 Sam. 8:7; Isa. 33:22). The Israelites reasoned with Samuel, the Prophet, to have earthly kings like heathen nations and God gave them Saul, David and Solomon before the nation broke up into Israel and Judah. Among these kings, David was an imperfect but true representative of the ideal covenantal king.

David, a "man after God's own heart" (1 Sam. 13:14; Acts 13:22), provided the standard by which the reigns of subsequent kings were assessed. The failure of the kings of both Israel and Judah to live up to the covenantal ideal provided a suitable platform for Israel's prophets to speak of a future king who would be a worthy occupant of the throne of David. The Law and the Prophets all pointed to the coming of Jesus Christ to sit on David's throne (Deut. 18:15). Isaiah prophesied about a Messiah who would reign on David's throne and over his kingdom, establishing and upholding it with justice and righteousness from that time on and forever (Isa. 9:6-7). David's throne was the earthly similitude of the Kingdom to come, but it would uphold justice and righteousness forever.

The Christian characterization of the relationship between God and humanity inherently involves the notion of kingship of God. God relates to humans based on terms and conditions of His Kingdom. God expects us to live our lives based on the principles and rules of His Kingdom. The problem is that very few Christians approach their lives from a kingdom perspective. Although we sing, talk, pray, and recite verses about the kingdom of God, we do not have a coherent mental picture or life in the Kingdom.

God has hinged the mandate for humanity to rule over the earth on the Kingdom of God. While God is King over his people in a special sense, by virtue of his covenantal relationship to them, his kingship is at the same time universal, extending to all nations and peoples and even the natural environment. The passion and priority of Jesus Christ was the Kingdom of God: *Jesus came to Galilee, preaching the gospel of the kingdom of God, and saying, 'The time is fulfilled, and the kingdom of God is at hand. Repent, and believe in the gospel* (Mark 1:14, NKJV). Jesus consistently preached the gospel of the Kingdom throughout His ministry.

Jesus taught about the Kingdom of God using parables of the farmer scattering seed, wheat and weeds, the mustard seed, yeast; treasure that a man found hidden in a field, merchant searching for choice pearls, a fishing net that caught fish of every kind, the ten virgins, and of a wedding feast, among others. Through these parables Jesus taught key features of the Kingdom of God, the nature and attributes of the King, what we must do to enter the Kingdom, what to expect in His Kingdom, the keys of the Kingdom, diversity of Kingdom citizens, the priceless value of the Kingdom, Kingdom practices, the moral code of the Kingdom, and how to inherit the Kingdom of God.

Jesus stressed that those who seek to enter and live in the Kingdom must deny everything for its sake (Luke 18:29-30). Only those who receive Christ like children are fit for the Kingdom. Jesus reveals the Kingdom to those that accept His Lordship. He spoke in parables to fulfill what God had spoken through the prophet: *I will speak to you in parables, I will explain things hidden since the creation of the world* (Matt. 13:35, NIV).

The Lord Jesus Christ used parables to reveal the mysteries of the Kingdom to His followers. When the disciples asked Him why He spoke in parables, He told them that they were permitted to understand the secrets of the Kingdom of Heaven, but others were not (Matt.13:11). As believers, we have access to God's mysteries, which are hidden to unbelievers.

Considering the importance of the Kingdom of God, Jesus trained His 12 disciples and sent them out *to preach the kingdom of God and to heal the sick* (Luke 9:2, NKJV). Likewise, Paul described his ministry as preaching "the Kingdom of God" (Acts 14:22) and referred to his fellow ministers as "workers for the Kingdom of God" (Col. 4:11). The Old Testament prophets also wrote about the Kingdom.

The Kingdom of God is indispensable to all Christians as its citizens and co-workers. We now know that the Godhead and believers are key players in the Kingdom of God. For many Christians, the concept of the kingdom is not clearly understood as evidenced by diverse views of what it means. The history of humans is punctuated by several varieties of kingdoms, but the common thread running through them all is the model of governance. The salient features of God's model of governance of His Kingdom are briefly outlined.

(i) The *King* as the Sovereign ruler is the embodiment of the Kingdom of God, expressing His glory and nature. He exercises authority and the Word of the King is supreme. From His throne in heaven, the King rules the universe. God is the Great King and Ruler of the universe. His children will by nature become kings and priests, ruling under Christ.

(ii) The *Territory* is the domain over which the king exercises total authority. As the sovereign and rightful owner of everything (territory and its resources, and people) in the domain, the king is lord overall. The title 'Lord' is only given to a sovereign owner. Moses acknowledged this when he said, "B*ehold, to the* L*ord* *your God belong heaven and the highest heavens, the earth and all that is in it*" (Deut. 10:14, NIV). David also declared that, *The earth is the Lord's and the fullness thereof; the world, and they that dwell therein* (Ps. 24: 1 KJV). The Lord owns the universe and we are His subjects.

(iii) The *Constitution* is a set of fundamental principles or rules according to which a king rules his territory. Myles Munroe defines it as the covenant of a king with his subjects and expresses the mind and will of the king for his citizens and the kingdom. The constitution constitutes the intent of the sovereign for his people and contains the benefits and privileges of the kingdom. The constitution, which consists of documented words of the king, is basically the law of the kingdom. The Bible is the constitution of the Kingdom of God which details his will, purpose, and plan for his citizens. It guides Christians to live their lives on God's terms.

(iv) The *rights and privileges* of a Kingdom are only accessible to the citizens. Citizenship and the favour of the king are privileges in the kingdom. A citizen has rights to life, protection, and welfare. In God's Kingdom, Christians have rights to God's name, live in union with Christ, inherit "all that the Father has" (Rom 8:17; Gal 4:7; Jam. 2:5, KJV), serve in the Church, to marry within the faith or a fellow citizen of the kingdom (2 Cor 6:14; 1Pt 3:7, KJV), be absolved from payment for sins. God has anointed us to exercise our delegated power to pray and fast, to study the Word of God, to fellowship with God and fellow citizens, share meals and the holy communion, to share things with those in need, to preach the gospel to the poor, heal the sick, and to raise the dead, among other things.

(v) The King lavishes benefits on his faithful citizens. In a kingdom, people always desire citizenship because the king is personally responsible for his subjects and all their needs. The Lord can give to any citizen any or all desired wealth because he owns everything in his kingdom. The Psalmist said, *You open your hand; You satisfy the desire of every living thing* (Psa. 145:16, NIV).

(vi) A *Code of ethics* is the acceptable conduct of the citizens in the kingdom and their representation of the kingdom. This code includes moral standards, social relationships, personal conduct, attitude, attire, and manner of life. It is a community's way of life. According to IVP New Testament commentaries, followers of Christ must be meek, must not retaliate, "must go beyond the letter's law to its spirit, must do what is right when only God is looking, must depend on God for their needs and pursue His interests rather than their own, and must leave spiritual measurements of others' hearts to God."

(vii) The *security* of the Kingdom is the responsibility of a king. God has the most sophisticated security system. We need to know that: the LORD is a warrior (Exod. 15:3) and has an army (Josh. 5:14, NLT); He fights for citizens of the Kingdom (Exod. 14:14-15, 25; Josh. 10:14) and assigns angels to guard them in all their ways (Psa. 91:11); the Lord builds a hedge around his citizens and their houses and everything they own (Josh. 1:10); every citizen has access to the whole armor of God to stand against the schemes of the enemy (Eph. 6:11); the Lord watches over the way of the righteous; the blood of the lamb and word of the testimony of the citizens guarantees the citizens victory over their enemies (Rev. 12:10-11); and the citizens have access to the power of God that raised Jesus from the dead and placed Him at the right hand of God (Eph. 1:19-20).

(viii) The Lord has an obligation to protect citizens of the Kingdom and to secure the territory. In God's Kingdom, the army of the Lord is an enlistment of angels and citizens who fight along with God as the commander. Christians are soldiers (2 Cor. 10:3). Since God is a warrior, everyone born of the Spirit is a warrior.

(ix) The *social culture* of the Kingdom of God represents a common way of life, which is embedded in institutions shaped by moral standards, principles, and values. It reflects a way of life of the king and his citizens. In the Kingdom of God, the word or decree of our king is law and it defines our way of life as subjects. The citizens depend on the word of the king to develop a dominant inner conviction that manifests the nature of the king through their lifestyle. Jesus taught his disciples the kingdom principles and rules that should shape the life of citizens through the beatitudes (Matt. 5:3-11, KJV). The common social culture should be evident in our daily activities and our association with fellow citizens of the Kingdom.

(x) The *Citizenry* of the kingdom consists of people who live under the rule of a king. The *Immigration system* of the kingdom sets the conditions for becoming a citizen, which are stringent, costly, and non-negotiable. This kingdom is unusual because its citizens are redeemed descendants of the original earthly monarch, which rebelled against the Sovereign ruler of the heaven and earth and abdicated the throne. You and I are citizens of the Kingdom of God.

(xi) The Sovereign King could not restore earthly citizenship to the subjects who rebelled against Him. However, driven by his love for the world, God sent His Son to earth to bear the punishment of death on behalf of the disobedient human race and whoever believes in the death and resurrection of the King is restored as a citizen of the Kingdom. But those that accept the king's invitation to become citizens of the Kingdom must be converted, changed, and reconciled to Him before they are given such authority to rule the earth.

(xii) Jesus Christ defined the condition for admission to the Kingdom of God when He addressed Nicodemus (John 3:3-5, NKJV). Being born again is the sole condition for entering His Kingdom. All citizens are clothed with the righteousness of God before they can become citizens of the Kingdom. The death and resurrection of Christ inaugurated the Kingdom of God, which will be consummated when Christ returns. Our current status of citizenship is a precondition for entry into the future realm of the Kingdom.

(xiii) The *Law* of the Kingdom is a set of rules the king makes and enforces to protect the life, liberty, and property of his subjects, and everything else within His Kingdom. It refers to standards and principles established by the King, which underpin the kingdom functions and administration. The law of the kingdom is legally binding on all the citizens and other people within its jurisdiction. Jesus stressed this point when He said, *Man shall not live by bread alone, but by every word that proceeds from the mouth of God* (Matt. 4:4, NKJV). Every word that flows from the mouth of the King must be obeyed to the letter. God writes His law in the minds and on hearts of people (Matt. 22:37-40; Rom. 13:9-10, NKJV). The law of the Kingdom, which steers us to His desired state, cannot be amended or revoked by anyone, any group or institution, except the King Himself.

(xiv) The law is not subject to democratic processes, such as citizen referendum or debate. King David acknowledged this when he said, *I will bow down toward Your holy temple and will praise your name For your love and Your faithfulness, for You have exalted above all things your name and Your Word* (Psa. 138:2-3, NKJV). Observing the law guarantees citizens access to provisions of the king and the kingdom, but disobedience attracts the wrath of the King. King Solomon concludes that the whole duty of man is to fear God and obey His commandments (Eccles. 12:13). God's law rests on two pillars: love for God and love for fellow man.

(xv) The Kingdom of God is resourced through the commonwealth of its citizens. A *Commonwealth* is the kingdom's economic model, which ensures that all citizens have equal access to the resources of the kingdom. Contrary to worldly economic systems that encourage competition, self-centered pursuit and accumulation of wealth, the commonwealth model engenders the king's desire that all his citizens share and benefit from the wealth of the kingdom. Describing the fellowship of believers in the early Church, Dr Luke recorded that, *All the believers were together and had everything in common. They sold property and possessions to give to anyone who had need* (Acts 2:44-45, NIV). This kind of fellowship guaranteed social security for everyone in the Kingdom. The principle of commonwealth prompted Ananias and Sapphira to sell their property and put the money at the apostles' feet (Acts 5:1), although this charitable act went horribly wrong when they decided to withhold part of the money. Some countries practice variants of the commonwealth concept through their national social welfare schemes.

Salient features of the Kingdom of God set it apart from earthly governments that we are familiar with. There are other accessories that enable the kingdoms to function as a system. The administration in the Kingdom of God involves leading, managing, organizing citizens, resources and other creatures using Kingdom principles. The administrative system consists of the king's governance or executive structure to ensure that his will, purpose, and plan are accomplished in the kingdom. In Israel, Samuel wrote down the rights and duties of kings of Israel and deposited them before the Lord (1 Sam. 10:25, KJV).

The Kingdom of God needs citizens who are diligent in administration. The officers in the king's court included the recorder (2 Sam. 8:16; 1 Kings 4:3, KJV); the scribe (2 Sam. 8:17; 20:25, KJV); the house officer, the chief steward (Isa. 22:15, KJV); the king's friend or a confidant (1 Kings 4:5, KJV); the keeper of the wardrobe (2 Kings 22:14, KJV); captain of the bodyguards (2 Sam. 20:23, NIV); officers over the king's treasures (1 Chron. 27:25-31, KJV); commander-in-chief of the army (1 Chron. 27:34, KJV); the royal counselor (1 Chron. 27:32; 2 Sam. 16:20-23, KJV). The Holy Spirit gifts citizens and gives them faith and grace to serve in the Kingdom as administrators.

The Kingdom of God has a provision for its citizenry to relate to the world around it. The department of foreign affairs and diplomatic corps are concepts borrowed from the kingdom. Once an individual becomes a citizen of the Kingdom of God, he or she automatically renounces his/her citizenship of the kingdom of Satan. However, God does not remove his children or citizens from the earth. Jesus confirms this in His prayer for His disciples when He said, *I do not pray that You should take them out of the world, but that You should keep them from the evil one. They are not of the world, just as I am not of the world* (John 17:15-16, NKJV).

Citizens of the Kingdom are mosaics or islands surrounded by the world. Jesus Christ prayed to the Father to protect citizens from the world of evil while they live with it, but their status changes to diplomats. In qualifying this, Paul described citizens of the Kingdom as ambassadors of Christ (2 Cor. 5:19-20). We are permanent representatives of the Kingdom of God accredited to the earth.

The Church consists of *ambassadors* and witnesses of His Kingdom on earth. The Body of Christ, the continuation of His incarnational presence in the world, has the duty to reflect the character and priorities of Christ and His Kingly rule. We represent the reign of God in the same way an Ambassador or High Commissioner represents the President or Sovereign in a foreign country.

The judicial system in the Kingdom of God is founded on pillars of righteousness, justice, truth, holiness, loving-kindness, equity, faithfulness, compassion, integrity, honesty, wisdom, knowledge, understanding, perfection, and transparency. Moses and the psalmists capture these features of kingdom justice in their declarations: *Righteous are You, O LORD, And upright are Your judgments"* (Psa. 119:137, NKJV*); The Rock! His work is perfect, For all His ways are just; A God of faithfulness and without injustice, Righteous and upright is He* (Deut. 32:4, NKJV); *Righteousness and justice are the foundation of His throne* (Psa. 97:2, NIV). The king executes judgment for people based on his flawless law. This model of justice and penal code delivers judgment that is upright, just, and perfect.

The health service in the Kingdom of God ensures that citizens have access to quality health care regardless of their status. The royal service is holistic in nature, meeting diverse needs of citizens to ensure quality human health. The King's desire is for his citizens to prosper and to be in good health just as their souls prosper. He, who owns everything, provides an unrivalled health services for his subjects.

In the Kingdom of God, there are principles of health care that distinguish its health care service from any other. The Chief Physician: is the creator and maker of every human being and other living things; created every part of a human being and knitted them together, and hence knows the accurate and precise structure and functions of every part of the body; created everything on earth and knows how they can cause, prevent or cure human diseases; has the ability to command beings and objects to either afflict or remove diseases; has inert ability to diagnose, treat, and heal any disease at any time; can be consulted by any citizen at any time without making an appointment; owns and dispenses the greatest diversity of medicines; has inbuilt power to heal every disease, which he gives to citizens to exercise on His behalf; and He is a self-contained health practitioner with all health care specialties – a doctor without boundaries.

In the Kingdom of God, the health care service is established on several distinctive pillars: (i) the crucifixion of the Son of the King, which destroyed the power of sin and root of every disease; (ii) the covenant and Abrahamic blessings to all descendants of Abraham or all nations; (iii) faith in God; (iii) the intrinsic creative and healing power of the Word of God; (iv) the anointing of the Holy Spirit that breaks every yoke to disease and infirmity; (v) power and authority of the King; God's love for His people; (vi) observance of the commandments of God; (vii) employs supernatural power; (viii) prayer and fasting; and ability to make a human being and his parts. These royal health care services ensure a superior health care delivery that surpasses any worldly service.

In the Kingdom, health care takes different forms. First, the King protects citizens against diseases. We are assured that: God does not put diseases on his citizens (Exod. 15:26; Deut. 7:15; Psa. 91:9-10, NLT); the Word of God is health to all our flesh (Prov. 4:20-23); God blesses our bread and our water so that they do not cause disease in the body; Christ redeemed us from the curse of the law when He became a curse for us (Gal. 3:13) and protects us from diseases associated with the curse; God confers resistance or immunity on His citizens so that they will pick up serpents; drink any deadly thing and it shall not harm them (Mark 16:18); our Shepherd provides us with good food and water when

He makes us to lie down in green pastures and leads me to quiet waters (Psa. 23:2); maintaining sound mind and emotions using a sense of beauty as Moses records that God made every tree that is pleasant to the sight and good for food to grow out of the ground (Gen 2:9, KJV). The Lord who saves also gives us everything we need to live godly and fulfilled lives.

The King is committed to restoring good health to citizens that are sick, ill or infirm (Jer. 30:17). He diagnoses and cures diseases and infirmities. The King aims at taking sickness away from the midst of His people or citizens (Exod. 23:25-26: Deut. 7:15, NIV). As the Chief Physician, the King can heal all the diseases (Psa. 103:3; Matt. 15:30-31) whether physical, mental, emotional, or spiritual. Jesus is the greatest medical expert, who heals every disease and infirmity presented to Him. The Spirit of the Lord anointed Him to diagnose and cure all diseases and infirmities. We can exercise our delegated authority to heal all diseases, if we seek and do His will.

For citizens to access the health care benefits, the King has provided them with a health care toolkit of the His Word (Psa. 107:20), faith in God, prayer of faith (Jam. 5:13-16), His delegated power and authority over demons and to cure diseases (Luke 9:1-2); intercession by the Holy Spirit (Rom. 8:26-27); the union with Christ (Eph. 1:1-18), His divine power that has given them everything they need for a godly life (2 Pet. 1:3); access to the healing hand of God (Acts 4:29-30); access to elders who can lay their hands on the sick and anoint them with oil (Mark 16:18); and the anointing to heal the sick.

Citizens of the Kingdom are assured of divine health through the death and resurrection of Jesus Christ. This is exemplified by Isaiah's prophecy when he said, *he was wounded for our transgressions, he was bruised for our iniquities: the chastisement of our peace was upon him; and with his stripes we are healed* (Isa. 53:5, NIV). Apart from spiritual liberation, bruises and wounds inflicted on Jesus Christ constitute the penalty He paid for every transgression and iniquity humanity ever committed or will commit until we are translated into glorious bodies when the king returns.

Physical, emotional, psychological, and spiritual distress that accompanies transgressions and inequities, and their effects, including diseases, rob humans of their peace. But Jesus was chastised so that peace can be restored to us. Accused of committing sin, transgression and iniquities, the stripes that reaped His flesh causing diseases brought healing on diseased citizens of the Kingdom. As descendants of Abraham, citizens of the Kingdom of God can also access Abrahamic blessings, which include good health.

The Kingdom of God has a *communication* system that ensures that all components are coordinated and enabled to function according to the King's will, purpose, and plan. The Holy Spirit encodes and transmits messages between subjects and the King. He also decodes the King's messages to the citizens. The Spirit of the Lord ensures that citizens communicate with each other effectively through diverse spiritual gifts. The Kingdom also employs angels to serve the citizens.

Central to understanding and execution of the King's will and plan is a functional educational system that ensures citizens know the King and His desire for them and His territory. The Spirit, who inspired the writing of the Word of God, has given the gift of teaching to some citizens, which they must utilize according to the grace and measure of faith given to them (Rom. 12:6-7; 1 Cor. 12:27). In the Kingdom of God, the educational system caters for children and adults through individuals, families, House Church, Sunday School Bible studies and other teaching opportunities.

The Kingdom of God has an *economy*, which is an arrangement or operating system for producing, dispensing, trading and consumption of products and services. *God's economy is His plan to dispense Himself into His chosen and redeemed people as their life, their life supply, and their everything in order to gain a corporate expression of Himself, consummating for eternity in the New Jerusalem* (Anonymous). God is like an immensely wealthy householder who desires to dispense His unsearchable riches (Eph. 3:8) to all of His people. To accomplish this task, He needs a plan, an arrangement, and an economy.

God has a business in the universe and His creatures constitute the capital and wealth. The economy is based on principles of giving and receiving, seedtime and harvest time, and stewardship. In God's economy, the King owns resources and citizens transact on His behalf and He directs them on how to utilize them.

Ultimate salvation will culminate in change from mortal flesh and blood to an immortal being at Christ's return (1 Cor. 15:50-53), and we will become kings and priests serving in God's Kingdom on earth (Rev. 1:6; 5:10, NIV). As citizens, we are progressively being transformed into the original and intended shape of life in Jesus Christ. God lives and breathes in us through the Holy Spirit.

Understanding and applying the concept and principles of the Kingdom allows Christians to become responsible citizens whose lifestyles please and honor their king. We cannot claim to be disciples of Christ if we are not citizens of the Kingdom of God. Citizenship of the Kingdom is the normal status of any subject. It is the only desirable and designated place for humanity. Living outside the Kingdom of God is like keeping fish outside its normal aquatic environment, asking humans to live in water, or expecting an ostrich to fly like an eagle.

By design, humans are meant to live in the Kingdom of God. Apart from enjoying the incarnational presence of God, citizens of the kingdom enjoy the king's provisions. Humans must submit to Christ to regain their position in the Kingdom to which they rightfully belong. Like the father of the prodigal son, the king has provided every necessary resource to facilitate the homecoming trip of His wayward people. The Kingdom expects disciples to walk with God in this century.

God as the architect of discipleship from precreation times

As we examine precreation times, the right place to start from is God's will, purpose, and plan for humanity before the creation of the earth. Paul summarizes this in his letter to the Church at Ephesus: *Praise be to the God and Father of our Lord Jesus Christ, ... For he chose us in him before the creation of the world to be holy and blameless in his sight. In love he predestined us for adoption to sonship through*

Jesus Christ, in accordance with his pleasure and will (Eph. 1:3-5, NIV). God prepared a redemption plan for humanity and other creatures before creating the earth. He gave us the potential, resources and the ability to be redeemed and to live in Christ according to His will and pleasure.

God predestined to become His children. Paul stressed that, *In Him we were also chosen as God's own, having been predestined according to the plan of Him who works out everything by the counsel of His will,* (Eph. 1:11, NKJV). Someone approached you with the gospel of the Kingdom because God chose you and predestined you for adoption as His son or daughter. God worked out everything according to the counsel of His will. Every believer is a citizen of God's Kingdom by design regardless of his status in the world.

Before we received the Gospel, God still watched over us in our dark alleys while we walked in rebellion against Him. Has he not said He makes rain to fall, and the sun to shine, upon the unrighteous? Does He not open His hand to feed every living thing He has created? Does He not keep our hearts pumping even in our disobedience?

God loved me even as a sinner. It doesn't matter where, when, or how you received the gospel, it was all planned before creation of the world with prior knowledge of all our failures. If you have not yet surrendered your life to Christ, be assured that God has already invested in your salvation. All you need to do is to accept His invitation to become His child.

God foreknew how every human being would respond to His call to salvation before laying the foundation of the earth (Rom. 8:29). He has been, and is still, committed to transform such people to the image of Christ and to adopt them as His sons. Everyone the omniscient God identified to have a potentially receptive heart was predestined to be conformed to the image of His Son that He might be the firstborn among God's children. Whatever God did before creation, is doing now, and will do in future, has one aim, to adopt anyone with a receptive heart as His son or daughter.

Redemption is not a sporadic act, but a well planned and executed act. That is not to suggest that people just easily give their lives to God or surrender their will to God. There are several cases in the Bible of people who have struggled, run away from God, and resisted the call of God. But God foreknew those who would posture as defiant sinners, while their hearts had potential for accepting the gospel. This is where God's foreknowledge of our condition kicks-in His patience as He works with us to eventually adopt us as His sons.

During His acts of creation, God built within His creation resources to assist people to retrace their path to the Kingdom of God. First, God wrote His law on the hearts and minds of humans with indelible ink. When humanity disobeyed God, the law was not erased but suppressed (Rom. 2:14-15). The gentiles did not have access to the Torah, and yet their conduct was compliant with the requirements of the written Law. The work of the Law written on their hearts guided their consciences and their thoughts to act as though they read the written Law given to the Jews. Everyone has a God-consciousness that is still active even in a fallen state. Although suppressed, it is still sensitive to the call of God regardless of the circumstances, place, or time.

God's book of creation embodies the voice of God. The vegetation, animals, humans, galaxies, oceans, sky, sun, moon, soil, minerals, days, and seasons carry the fingerprint of God. The nature and creative power of God are revealed in creation. Reading the book of creation gives humanity an opportunity to understand the attributes of God. He has disclosed His invisible attributes, eternal power, and divine nature through creation (Rom. 1:20). Frances Bacon said, *God has laid before us two books or volumes to study, if we will be free from error: first the scriptures revealing the will of God and then the creatures revealing His power.*

Andrew Halestrap, a Professor of Biochemistry also said, *If exploring God's truth in Scriptures is the realm of the theologian, exploring God's truth in creation is the realm of a scientist, and both are noble vocations that increase our knowledge of God's power and majesty.* A major deficiency of 21st century lifestyles is their disconnect with nature. Our built up environments, busy work schedules, entertainments, and failure of the Church to care for creation, have created a superficial environment that has distanced humanity from creation.

Through the Bible, God has revealed His divine nature, will, purpose, and plan for His creation. It reveals the mind of God behind creation, the fall, redemption, and ultimate salvation. It also provides the terms of reference for humanity's life on earth. We need the Word to walk with God.

Every human being is a display of the image of God although it may be distorted in fallen man. All citizens of the Kingdom of God are meant to be a mobile temples and domiciles of the Godhead through the Holy Spirit. God lives and breathes through His children who should be His visible image, just as Christ is the visible image of the invisible God. This qualifies us as disciples of Christ or citizens of the Kingdom, Ambassadors of Christ, and the light and salt of the earth. God expects from His children nothing less than being His representatives in the world. God designed us to be His representatives before the creation of the world.

God has made provision for redeeming humanity and restoring citizenship in the Kingdom of God

God foresaw the fall of humanity before creation and developed a redemptive plan for the regeneration and restoration of his position as the image of God and a citizen of the Kingdom of God. Embedded in His love, the redemption plan involved a sacrifice (John 3:16). God hates sin so much that any sinner must die. Since He is a just and faithful God, the sinful man was condemned to death, but Jesus Christ paid the penalty for our freedom from sin through shedding of His blood. Through His death and resurrection, the disobedient humanity has been reconciled to God and restored as citizens and rulers in the Kingdom of God.

The precreation redemption plan was God's initiative and He knew all the people who would accept or reject it (Rom. 8:29-30, MSG). God, who knows the end from the beginning, predestined those who would accept His call to become His Children to be transformed to the image of Christ. For these people, God calls, justifies, and glorifies. No one can go to Christ unless the Father who sent Him draws him (John 6:44) or allows it. While God takes the initiative of drawing a sinner to Christ, the sinner must accept the invitation because God does not impose His will on people. *Behold, I stand at the door and knock; if anyone hears My voice and opens the door, I will come in to him and will dine with him, and he with Me* (Rev. 3:20). Jesus' desire is to sup with a sinner the Father introduces to Him. But He does not forcibly enter an individual's heart. He wants us to exercise our freedom to either let Him in or keep Him out. If the sinner opens the door, Jesus Christ enters the home and dines with the person. Such a person who receives Christ as the personal savior becomes a child of God.

God's redemption places greater responsibilities on the Godhead, who has no preferences for time, place, or circumstances. God is the same yesterday, today and forever, and hence His power to save and sustain life knows no limit. Considering that God conceived the redemption plan before creation, it accounts for all conditions from eternity past, eternity future and the bridge of time. No theological, philosophical, scientific, socio-cultural, political, technological, psychological, or mental challenge you face at any time or place in your life has power to change your destiny unless you reject God's invitation to save and guide you.

God has more than sufficient resources to sustain citizens in His Kingdom

Citizens of the Kingdom of God have a pool of resources at their disposal to sustain them and ensure they fulfil their purpose in alignment with the will and purpose of God. What are these resources?

A: The Holy Spirit as the helper of a citizen of the Kingdom of God

The citizens of the Kingdom of God are *sealed* with the Holy Spirit for two reasons. First, the Holy Spirit is a seal of approval that one is a child of God and citizen in His Kingdom – He authenticates the transactions of salvation and sanctification. The Spirit is God's mark of ownership. Whenever the Devil and his cohorts see the Holy Spirit, they know that such a person is a legal citizen of the Kingdom of God and belongs to the Lord. The Holy Spirit leads the sons and daughters of God (Rom. 8:14). He is an assurance from God of a secure future. The Spirit indwelling believers guides them in the way of the Lord to show that they belong to the Lord: "*The Spirit Himself testifies with our spirit that we are God's children*" (Rom. 8:16, NKJV). The Spirit is proof that we are citizens of the Kingdom of God.

Second, believers are sealed with the Holy Spirit as a guarantee of the promises to come. The Spirit is like a deposit or down payment for promises that God is yet to fulfil. God will consummate redemption when Jesus Christ comes. God intimates that *the earnest expectation of the creation waits for the manifestation of the sons of God* (Rom. 8:19, NKJV). Although we are saved, creation is eagerly waiting for a time when our redemption will be consummated and the full glory of the sons of God will be revealed when Jesus returns. For then will creation also be fully liberated from the bondage that humanity brought upon it. God has also promised that those that are dead in Christ will be resurrected, and that believers will receive an inheritance as joint-heirs with Christ.

Believers are *filled* with the Holy Spirit to empower them to live a life that honours and glorifies God. The infilling of the Holy Spirit happens as soon as a sinner accepts Christ as his saviour. However, a child of God loses the infilling of the Holy Spirit when he/she is out of fellowship with God. Restoration of the fellowship with God and infilling of the Holy Spirit occurs again if the child of God repents of his sin (1 Peter 1:9, KJV).

All citizens of the Kingdom need to be consistently filled with the Holy Spirit as they walk in light. Being filled with the Holy Spirit takes four forms: filling the *deficiency* with the Holy Spirit, who anoints the believer to learn and apply the Word of God to live a godly life; being fully possessed (controlled) by the Holy Spirit to do great acts of faith; the infilling of the Holy Spirit releases the power, which influences every sphere of life; and the infilling of the Holy Spirit instils a sense of quality in a believer's life.

The difference between living in sin and living a holy and blameless life is the power of God that comes with Jesus Christ and the Holy Spirit. Have you ever wondered why each time God decided to carry out an assignment in the Old Testament, the Spirit of the Lord came upon that individual? For example, the Spirit of the Lord came powerfully upon Samson, and he killed thirty men in the town of Ashkelon and took away their belongings (Judges 14:19, KJV).

In Exodus 35:31, the Sovereign Lord filled Bezalel with His Spirit, giving him great wisdom, ability, and expertise in all kinds of craftsmanship to build the sanctuary of God. Similarly, the Spirit of Lord came upon Jesus Christ to carry out His earthly ministry (Isa. 61; Mark 1:10). Examination of different events in the Bible establishes a trend, which shows that God's creatures cannot function effectively and efficiently without depending on the Holy Spirit.

In the Old Testament, some patriarchs (including Noah, Joseph, and Job) led holy and blameless lives and overcame the power of sin in their bodies. The Word of God testifies that people in their generation faced challenges and buckled under the weight of sin, but these men of God still walked before God and were blameless.

Jesus Christ, born as a Child inherited a body that had the capacity to sin, but He never sinned. However, if Jesus Christ was born with a flesh that was pure and never capable of sin, then humanity has no capacity to live a holy life because Jesus cannot identify with humanity. The common denominator between Jesus and other heroes of faith is that the flesh desired to sin, but the power of God enabled them to resist the urge to sin. Jesus Christ, in the Garden of Gethsemane, expressed His human nature by asking if His Father could take away the cup of suffering. However, He was quick to ask the father to do His will.

The ability to override the desires of the flesh comes into effect the moment we choose to apply the power of God. Since Jesus Christ and our patriarchs were able to live holy and blameless lives, we can also be assured that if we abide in Christ, He will give us victory over the law of sin and death in our flesh. A citizen in the Kingdom of God is *baptised* with the Holy Spirit when He receives Jesus Christ as his personal Lord and saviour. When a believer is united with Christ, he is submerged in Christ. Thus, the Spirit is essential to a believer's achievement of his purpose and plan for life on earth. He enables believers to fully express what God has deposited in them.

In the Church, the Holy Spirit gifts believers to serve each other and God. He distributes diverse spiritual gifts and talents to individual believers including the word of wisdom, the word of knowledge, faith, the gift of healing, the gift of performing miracles, prophecy, distinguishing spirits, tongues, administration, ministry of helps and interpretation of tongues. All citizens of the Kingdom of God exercise their unique gifts according to the grace and measure of faith God gives them to do what He has assigned him.

Paul reminded the saints in Ephesus that, *we are His workmanship, created in Christ Jesus for good works, which God prepared beforehand that we should walk in them"* (Eph. 2:10, NKJV). The Holy Spirit gives a believer a gift to do good works God prepared for him/her beforehand. Spiritual gifts are foundational to growth and development of the body of Christ and individual Christians.

Paul underlines the significance of diverse, and the operation of, spiritual gifts in the Church (Eph, 4:11-13). This Scripture presupposes that citizens in the Kingdom of God have knowledge and skill gaps that limit their abilities to exercise their gifts of ministry. While Christians grow and develop their gifts, they still have rugged edges in their faith, which aren't quite fitly knitted together to express unity of faith.

The citizens of the Kingdom are imperfect, immature, and are a blurred image of Christ, susceptible to false doctrine and spiritual fraud. But God foresaw these vulnerabilities and prepared a perfect plan and strategy beforehand for the body of Christ to be processed into a perfect image of Christ. Jesus Christ gave five spiritual gifts and offices (apostles, prophets, evangelists, pastors, and teachers) to the body of Christ to equip the saints for works of service.

The five foundational gifts respond to key deficiencies of believers that limit the expression of their spiritual gifts. They equip believers with knowledge, wisdom, skills, and other godly resources for works of service. Believers depend on other gifts in the body of Christ to develop and exercise their gifts to serve others and to bear the fruit of the Spirit. Foundational gifts also assist believers grafted on the true vine, Jesus Christ, to produce fruits in abundance.

As believers are equipped in works of service, they grow and develop in their faith and works, they provide quality services to the body of Christ, and they glorify, honor and please God. When believers exercise their gifts, God adds to their numbers, resulting in the extension of the Kingdom of God. This organic and spiritual growth of individual believers and the Church must continue until their desired states are attained.

The five-fold ministry must continue to equip the saints and facilitate the building of the body of Christ until seven outcomes are achieved in the Church. First, there must be unity of faith. The ministry should build and refine the faiths of individual believers until they are able to express unity of faith – until all their Christian beliefs are aligned. This entails harmonizing the faiths of individual believers to achieve unity through the Holy Spirit.

Second, the ministry must produce unity of knowledge of Jesus Christ. The Lord quizzed the disciples about His identity. On their way to the villages around Caesarea Philippi, Jesus *questioned His disciples: "Who do people say I am? They answered, Some say John the Baptist; others say Elijah; and still others say You are one of the prophets. But who do you say I am?" He asked. Peter answered, "You are the Christ* (Mark 8:27-29, NIV). Just as the knowledge of unbelievers about the Lord differs from one person to the other, believers also have varied knowledge of Jesus Christ. But the five-fold ministry must continue to build the body of Christ until all believers have the same knowledge of Christ.

Third, foundational gifts will eventually produce mature Christians who are efficient and graceful in response to Christ. These are individuals who allow the Godhead to live and breathe through them to the extent that living life on God's terms becomes an involuntary act. Fourth, the gifts must build a believer into a Christ-like being, expressing a stature, which depicts the fullness of Christ. This is achieved when believers become visible images of the invisible Jesus Christ just as He was the visible image of the invisible God the Father.

Fifth, the five-fold ministry and services of other believers should confer immunity or resistance to deceitful doctrines and theological fraud or trickery. The effect of spiritual gifts should stabilize our faith in Christ just as the ballast water in a ship stabilizes it as it ploughs through violent waves and current. Despite the craftiness in the body of Christ, citizens of the Kingdom of God should be able to stand their ground in Christ.

As spiritual gifts equip the body of Christ, believers are expected to bear spiritual fruit in abundance. In admonishing the Philippian Church, this was Paul's conclusion, *Therefore, my beloved, just as you have always obeyed, not only in my presence, but now even more in my absence, continue to work out your salvation with fear and trembling. For it is God who works in you to will and to act on behalf of His good pleasure* (Philip. 2:12-13, NKJV). Salvation is a free gift, but a believer is responsible for nurturing and developing it with fear and trembling to produce spiritual growth. Understanding our weakness, God has provided for us to will and act according to His good pleasure as long as we voluntarily and willingly submit to His authority and power.

God has given us the Holy Spirit to empower us to live a life that honors and pleases Him. As citizens of the Kingdom of God we can walk with God through the Holy Spirit. The work of the Spirit in the Church age is not limited by time, place or circumstances. What determines whether Holy Spirit works in our lives is our freedom of choice. We can choose to accept the invitation of Christ and subject ourselves to Kingdom principles, rules and practices through the Holy Spirit or reject the invitation and deny ourselves the services of the Holy Spirit.

B: Live a life in union with Christ in the Kingdom of God

Paul asked a rhetorical question seeking to address how a person trapped by the law of sin could possibly be rescued through Jesus Christ our Lord (Rom. 7:24-25). Paul breathes a sigh of relief because he discovers the guaranteed way out of this predicament through Jesus Christ, the way, the truth, and the life (John 14:6). When anyone surrenders his life to the Lord Jesus Christ, he is sealed with the Holy Spirit (Eph. 1:13-14) and his/her life is hidden with Christ in God (Col. 3:3).

The secret of overcoming the law of sin lies in living our lives in union with Christ. When a sinner believes the gospel of the Kingdom of God, the convert and Jesus Christ are united through the Holy Spirit. The believer is grafted on the body of Christ – he and Christ become one. This union is symbolised by the vine-branch relationship (John 15:5, KJV). The branch will bear much fruit if it remains organically connected and alive on the vine. The branch depends on the stem and root for nutrition, health, water supply, projection in the atmosphere, gaseous exchange, and other life-sustaining processes. Jesus stresses that believers must abide in Christ and Christ in them if they are to function optimally.

Believers have exclusive access to benefits of the Kingdom of God when they live in union with Christ. They include access to every spiritual blessing in heavenly places (Eph. 1:3); being chosen before the foundation of the world to be holy and blameless in Christ (Eph. 1:4); predestination to adoption as sons of God (Eph. 1:5); redemption through His blood of Jesus and forgiveness of our sins according to riches of His grace (Eph. 1:7); revelation of the mystery of God's will (Eph. 1:9); obtaining an inheritance (Eph. 1:11); trusting in the gospel of salvation when the word of truth was preached (Eph. 1:13); sealing with the Holy Spirit of promise after believing the gospel (Eph. 1:13); receiving the spirit of wisdom in knowledge of Christ (Eph. 1:17); enlightening the eyes of understanding (Eph. 11:8); knowing the hope of His calling (Eph. 1:18); knowing the riches of glory of His inheritance (Eph. 1:18); and the infilling with Jesus Christ (Eph. 1:22-23). Christians united with Jesus Christ have access to the same irresistible power, which raised Jesus Christ from the dead (Eph. 1:20). This power operates in us and guarantees us victory over sin and the flesh.

Jesus Christ has changed the principle of life governing the behaviour of believers. The rule, law, belief, or chain of reasoning governing the behaviour of Christians who genuinely desire to observe God's law guarantees more than adequate power to translate their desires to do what is right into actions. Different spheres of your life (marriage, family, ministry, career, education, or business) will go as far as Jesus Christ and the Holy Spirit take you.

The exclusive union between Christ and a believer is fundamental and indispensable in living a Christ-like life. These benefits demonstrate the providential care of God for citizens of His Kingdom and are not accessible to outsiders. They also underline that God makes all these things to happen and believers can access these benefits anywhere, anytime and in any environment. Exclusion of Jesus Christ and the Spirit of God spells death. Study any life that has genuinely succeeded, it is one that had access to the power of God through the Holy Spirit.

C: Embrace God as the good Shepherd

In the Kingdom of God, the LORD is the good Shepherd of every citizen or believer. The Psalmist summarized the key duties of the Shepherd: He makes the sheep to lie down in green (fresh, succulent, and nutritious) pastures and leads them beside still waters (Psa. 23:2); He restores the souls of His children and guides them in paths of righteousness for His name's sake (Psa. 23:3). The Shepherd accompanies, strengthens, comforts, and protects His sheep as they pass through the shadow of death. He prepares a table for believers amid their enemies, anoints their heads with oil, and causes their cups to run over. When they dwell in His presence, His goodness and mercy follow them all the days of their lives and He settles them in His house forever. Jesus Christ is the good Shepherd and the door to the Kingdom. He gave His life for His sheep. He knows them and they know Him. God knows you personally and searches for you when you stray from the Kingdom. The Shepherd of the Kingdom of God is responsible for provision, protection, and welfare of citizens.

The good Shepherd ensures that the sheep under His custody survive and produce abundantly. If they are brought under His care, no predator can attack them. In our 21st century, every citizen of the Kingdom of God is guaranteed security if he submits to the power and authority of the King. No circumstance or condition can remove a believer from the hand of the Shepherd.

D: Observe the discipline of a disciple of Christ

Every disciple of Jesus Christ is guided by love for God and love for his neighbour, which must be lived out daily. The primary priority of life is to seek God's kingdom first and His righteousness so that every other thing comes as an addition (Matt. 6:33). A believer must cultivate a lifestyle that embodies these principles and values through right choices and application of accessories in His toolkit.

Fellowship: Believers grow and develop their spiritual lives through consistent fellowship with the body of Christ in the house Church and local Church. These groups consist of believers with gifts of the Spirit that equip the saints for works of service, edify the body of Christ, and assist to meet the physical and spiritual needs of believers, to ensure holistic development of saints.

The author of Hebrews encouraged saints to continue gathering with other believers (Heb. 10:25). Church is not optional, but an integral component of believer's life. Being part of a local Church ensures that believers maintain their union with the body of Christ, exercise their gifts to serve others, feel part of the broader Church, and are strengthened and sharpened by spiritual gifts of others.

Studying the Word of God: Believers must steadfastly study the word of God through regular Bible studies at the local Church, in house Churches and family Bible studies, and through personal devotion. Apart from sermons, Church group Bible studies, topical Bible expositions, and Christian publications, are useful in studying the Word of God. It must be emphasized that personal studies are very useful in spiritual growth.

Prayer and fasting: Every disciple of Jesus Christ must learn to pray and fast regularly. The Lord Jesus Christ started and ended the day with prayer. Apart from instantaneous prayers when we suddenly encounter trials or happy moments, Christians walking with Christ must cultivate a prayerful life.

While serving as a means of communicating with God, prayer also activates promises. It is such an integral part of a Christian's life that we are always encouraged to pray. We are taught to pray without ceasing. This involves living in continual God-consciousness, where everything you see and experience becomes a kind of prayer, lived in deep awareness of God and in total surrender to Him.

Christians are also encouraged to pray and fast, especially in unusual circumstances that require a believer to dig deeper in faith. When making major decisions or seeking God's direction regarding any sphere of life, prayer and fasting are an indispensable spiritual act. Jesus Christ prayed and fasted before He started His ministry on earth.

Sharing meals and breaking bread: As children of God breaking bread in remembrance of the death of Jesus Christ is an important practice. Saint Luke documents a practice of the early Church: *So continuing daily with one accord in the temple, and breaking bread from house to house, they ate their food with gladness and simplicity of heart, praising God and having favour with all the people* (Acts 2:46-47, NKJV). These fellowship meals unite the believers in their faith and enable them to interact and serve as a constant reminder of the death of Christ. When believers share meals, they forge deep relationships that cement their friendships.

Sharing faith and experience with others: Every child of God has experienced the saving grace of our Lord Jesus Christ and miracles He has performed in their lives. The Lord has baptized believers with the Holy Spirit and empowered them to be His voice to the nations. Christians are commissioned to make disciples of all nations through the work of the Holy Spirit (Acts 1:8). They are privileged to share their experience in Christ. As Ambassadors of the Kingdom of God, they are accredited to the world to tell them what Jesus Christ has done in their lives and what He is able to do in every other human being.

Sharing everything: The early Church understood the principle of sharing everything and ensured that no human being lacked basic needs of life. Dr Luke records that *"Now all who believed were together, and had all things in common, and sold their possessions and goods, and divided them among all, as anyone had need"* (Acts 3:44-45, NKJV). Governments that provide necessities for the poor in society practice this biblical principle. Christians are challenged to share things with their brethren to cover the nakedness of the poor. Rich nations ought to support poor nations. God has created the earth with abundant resources for every human being. Unless an individual chooses not to work, everyone should have access to basic needs of life. Are you able to share what you have with those who are genuinely in need?

Custodian of God's creation: God's original assignment to humanity was to take care of His garden (creation). God planted the Garden of Eden and put man in it to tend and keep it (Gen. 2:15). After abdicating our kingship over the earth to Satan, God is restoring our rule over the earth through the incarnated Jesus Christ. Although believers have not actively engaged in caring for creation, we have a duty to do so.

We must understand that science is a tool God has placed in the hands of humanity to understand and manage creation. When the Church cares for creation, she also cares for people who depend on it for their livelihood. The Church needs to engage with major issues facing humanity – poverty, biodiversity loss, climate change, pollution, disease epidemics, wars, and politics. A holistic gospel of the Kingdom of God encompasses salvation of souls and the rest of earthly creatures that depend on humanity for expression of their potential.

The Christian principles and values described above are foundational to the life of a citizen of the Kingdom of God. In any age, place or situation, living a life that honours, glorifies, and pleases God requires application of these principles and practices. The Godhead resides and breathes through us. The mind of Christ, the nature and power of God, and the gifts of the Holy Spirit should enable us to live our lives on God's terms. A citizen of the Kingdom of God has every resource needed to live a godly life. Peter wrote that, *as His divine power has given to us all things that pertain to life and godliness, through the knowledge of Him who called us by glory and virtue, by which have been given to us exceedingly great and precious promises, that through these you may be partakers of the divine nature, having escaped the corruption that is in the world through lust* (2 Pet. 1:3, NKJV). This Scripture reveals the secret of walking with God in any environment. In the 21st century, God expects believers to draw on these resources to be able to live a Christ-like life.

CONCLUSION

The 21st century Church faces unprecedented challenges in a rapidly changing world. In this world where basic tenets of Christianity are openly contested and often perceived as intolerant, archaic and retrogressive, can a Christian realistically walk with God?

Despite the fierce opposition to Christianity in this century, every child of God has the power and resources to walk with God. God's original design of humanity had an inbuilt capacity to walk with Him. The only condition for living a God-centred life in any environment is abiding in Christ, living a life in union with Christ. A life that recognises Christ as the source of power and life-sustaining support fulfils His will and purpose.

We can do all things through Christ who strengthens us if we abide in Him and He abides in us. *Neither death nor life, neither angels nor demons, neither the present nor the future, nor any powers, neither height nor depth, nor anything else in creation will be able to separate us from the love of God that is in Christ Jesus our Lord* (Rom. 8:37-39, NIV). When we yield to the call of God, He redeems our souls and places us in the custody of Christ. No matter how difficult your situation is, you have what it takes to walk with God. His divine power has given you everything you need to sail through this life and for eternity. God has resourced us to do good works which He prepared in advance for us to do.

Just as Noah and Enoch walked with God although their generations were wicked and violent, Christians can also walk with God in the 21st century if they totally depend on Him. Nothing can stop us from living a life that is fully dedicated to God. The God of Enoch and Noah is still as powerful today as He was when they lived on earth, and He will preserve us in these turbulent times.

Walking with God does not guarantee a trouble-free life. We will face fierce opposition to our Christian faith and practice. The fact that a typical Christian life is based on beliefs, values, principles, and practices that are different from those of non-Christians means opposition is inevitable. But God has equipped us to surmount all obstacles. If we stumble, He will help us to rise again. For a righteous man may fall seven times and rise again.

In this world, we will have tribulation, but we must be cheerful because we have overcome the world through the finished work of Jesus Christ. There is nothing in God's calendar of events, which happens outside God's power and authority. The creation, corruption, reconciliation, and consummation of salvation of the human and non-human creation are minute but essential episodes in God's eternal plan. But we must fear God and obey His commandments.

Only children of God can walk with Him. If you have never accepted Jesus Christ as your Lord and Saviour, or if you walked away from Him, you could invite the Lord into your life now by saying a short prayer from your heart. "Lord Jesus, thank you for dying for me on the cross. I know that I am a sinner. I confess and repent of any sin I have committed. I believe that you died for me on the cross, you shed your blood for the remission of my sins. I believe you rose from the dead. I invite you to come in my life. Be my Lord and Saviour. Let your blood wash away my sins. I believe I am born again. Thank you for accepting to be my Lord. AMEN!"

ABOUT THE AUTHOR

Dr Martin Kaonga is a pastor, theologian, and a scientist. He has a PhD in Christian Apologetics (science and religion) and another in Earth Sciences (Carbon Biogeochemistry). With over 26 years of pastoral ministry in Africa and the United Kingdom, the author has a strong teaching ministry. His strong background in theology and science enables him to help Christians and unbelievers to understand how science and faith complement each other to enhance a holistic understanding of the physical and metaphysical world. His ministry is enriched by several years of university teaching, environmental stewardship, and a career in the private sector. He is very passionate about creation care.

References

Baigent, M., Leigh, R., Lincoln, H. 2006. *The Holy Blood and the Holy Grail.* Jonathan Cape, 461.

Baron, D. 2015. Who defines marriage? https://blogs.illinois.edu/view/25/195030

Buber, M. 1951. *Two types of faith.* London, Routledge & Kegan Paul.

Craig, W.L. 2007. An in intellectual neutral. In: P. Copan, W.L. Craig, *Passion Conviction: Contemporary Discourses on Christian Apologetics.* Academic, Nashville, Tenesee, p.2-18

Downes, G. 2013. The Bible and Homosexuality: Part Two. Accessed April 8, 2018. https://en.wikipedia.org/wiki/The_Bible_and_homosexuality

Draine, G.G. 2016. Living in the Son. LifeRich Publishing. Encyclopaedia Britannica, s.v. "marriage". Accessed April 8, 2018, https://en.wikisource/wiki/1911 Encyclop%C3%A6dia Britannica/Marriage

Fournier, K. 2011. Shop baptism gifts today! 20% OFF Sale.

Catholic Church, 2018. Conjugal love and charitable disagreement. Accessed April 8, 2018, https://www.catholic.org/news/national/story.php?id=39997

Gove, M. 2013. Michael, Daily Mail, November 23, 2013:16-17.

Halestrap, E.A. 2016. Science as a Christian vocation. Accessed on April 8, 2018, https://www.cis.org.org.uk/wp-content/uploads/2016/02/23802-Thinking-about-Science-as-a-Christian-Vocation-AW-ir.pdf

Hoebel, E.A. 1958. Man in the Primitive World: Introduction to Anthropology. In: Umanah, A.C.A., Eds., *The History of Offot Ukwa and the Influence of Colonialism*, MEF Nigeria Ltd., Uyo, 99-100.

Manion, J. 2014. *Satisfied. Discovering contentment in a world of consumption.* Zondervan.

Marinchick, J. 2014. The definition of marriage. Accessed April, 2018, https:www.linkedin.com/pulse/definition-marriage-modern-justin-marinchick

Mallon, J. 2006. *The Primacy of Jesus, the Primacy of Love.* ISSN 1068-8579,

Miller, J.R. ____ The Story of Enoch (Genesis 5). Accessed April 8, 2018. http://gracegems.org/Miller/story enoch.htm

Misaras, S. 2015. **The Goal of God's Eternal Economy is the reality of the Organic Body of Christ.** https://agodman.com/blog/the-goal-of-gods-eternal-economy-is-the-reality-of-the organic-body-of-christ/

Otto, R. 1923. *The Idea of the Holy.* Oxford University Press. P7. ISBN0-19-500210-5. Accessed October 19, 2016. https://en.oxforddictionaries .com/definition/wisdom

Piper, J. 2012. 15 days in the Word with John Piper – 6 aspects of humility. Accessed April 8, 2018, https://www.christlikeminkstriesnwa.com/2012/08/23/15/days-in-the-word-with-john-piper-6-aspects-of-humility/

Sampson, R. 2005. *The Heart of Wisdom Teaching Approach: the Bible-based Homeschooling.* **Heart of Wisdom Publishing Inc.**

Stanford Encyclopaedia of Philosophy s.v. "Pleasure", Accessed April 8, 2018, https://plato.stanford.edu/entries/pleasure/

Stanton, EC.1898. The Woman's Bible.

Stewart, D. How has God revealed Himself through nature, Accessed April 8, 2018, https://www.blueletterbible.org/faq/don_stewart_377_.cfm

Taylor, R. 2013. School children as young as 8 told they would be labelled as racists for missing school trip. Dail Mail, November 22, 2013. Accessed April 8, 2013, https://www.dailymail.co.uk/news/article-2511841/Children-8-racist-miss-Islam-trip-Schools-threatening-letter-parents-met-outrage.html

The Free Dictionary s.v. https://legal-dictionary.thefreedictionary.com/marriage

The Institute of Basic life Principles. 2014. What is the fear of God. Accessed April, 2018, https://iblp.org/questions/what-fear-lord

Webster, D.D. 1992. *Selling Jesus. What's wrong with selling the Church*. Downers Grove, IL, InterVarsity Press.

Wikipedia, s.v. "Greed", Accessed April 8, 2018, https://en.wikipedia.org/wiki/Greed

Zimmer, H. 1993. *The King and the Corpse*. New Jersey: Princeton University Press.

www.ingramcontent.com/pod-product-compliance
Lightning Source LLC
Chambersburg PA
CBHW011306150426
43191CB00017B/2354